I0094672

Reflections on Identity in Four African Cities

Edited by
Simon Bekker & Anne Leildé

Lomé
Libreville
Johannesburg
Cape Town

AFRICAN
MINDS

First published in 2006 by African Minds.
www.africanminds.co.za

© 2006 Simon Bekker & Anne Leildé

ISBN: 1-920051-40-6

Edited, designed and typeset by Compress-DSL
www.compressdsl.com

Contents

Preface and acknowledgements

This book arose out of an international three-year collaborative programme launched in 2001 and funded by South Africa's National Research Foundation (NRF) and France's Centre National de la Recherche Scientifique (CNRS). The research programme was coordinated in South Africa within the Department of Sociology and Social Anthropology at the University of Stellenbosch and in France within the Centre d'Etudes d'Afrique Noire (CEAN) at the University of Bordeaux IV. Fieldwork on local government issues and on the construction of urban identities in selected African cities was conducted by researchers from France, from South Africa, and from a number of other African countries. The programme culminated in a conference organised in Stellenbosch during the first half of 2004, which was attended by researchers from France, Gabon, South Africa, and Togo. Eighteen papers were presented, five by graduate students.

The editors of this book selected a number of these papers and authors were requested to finalise these for publication. The editors also approached one author who had not attended the conference to contribute a chapter. Other conference papers were selected for a book currently being published, which is edited by Laurent Fourchard of CEAN and entitled *Des Villes sans Gouvernement? Etat, Gouvernement Local et Acteurs privés en Afrique au Sud du Sahara* (Karthala, coll. Afrique Politique, Paris). This work addresses local government themes in a number of African cities.

In a collaborative international research programme of this nature, credit and thanks need to be given to many. Research was carried out in Johannesburg, in Libreville, and in Lomé as well as in Cape Town. Workshops were organised for researchers and graduate students in Stellenbosch and in Bordeaux. Draft research papers were presented at a number of conferences. In deeply appreciating the support and assistance from the many people involved in these activities, I would like to single out for personal thanks four participants who enabled the programme to undertake work and exchanges beyond South Africa: Tamasse

Danioue from the University of Lomé in Togo, Anaclé Bissielo and Fidele Nze Nguema from Omar Bongo University in Gabon, and Dominique Darbon from CEAN in Bordeaux, France.

The editors would like to express their gratitude to both the NRF and the CNRS for financial backing without which this publication would not have been possible. Thanks are also due to the University of Stellenbosch for contributing additional funds to enable relevant research to be completed. Opinions expressed by authors are not necessarily shared by these funding bodies.

Simon Bekker
Stellenbosch
August 2006

CHAPTER 1

Introduction

Simon Bekker

The Office of the South African Presidency was recently tasked to assess how well South Africa as 'a nation in the making' was doing in moving from its apartheid past 'towards non-racialism, equity and unity in diversity'. The method they used was to gather and interpret information and trends in four life domains: material conditions, social mobility, primary organisations (such as family and household), and collective identities. It is significant that the fourth domain – collective identities – has been included with the three others - domains that have become traditional if not classical themes in establishing the 'health' of a nation. It would appear that the career of identity politics and of identity studies has turned out to be a success, at least in terms of state recognition of their importance. The discussion document that has been produced within this fourth life domain, *A Nation in the Making*, drew the following conclusions:

> South Africans evince a strong sense of national identity ... However ... diversity ... in terms of race, class and nationality/language [remains] ... strong. While race and nationality/language seem to be receding as primary forms of self-definition, class identity seems to be on the ascendance. (Republic of South Africa, 2006: 97)

These generalisations offer an appropriate way to introduce the chapters of this book. Analyses within these chapters in fact may even be used to test the extent to which such claims ring true, in what everyone knows is a much more complex and shifting terrain of shared meanings than can ever be captured by such generalisations.

Before such an appraisal, why have identity studies and the politics of identity become so popular? And what is the relevance of locating them within an African urban context? Sometime around 1989 the world changed. The Soviet Union dissolved, an event which spawned an array of new states in its former empire. A host of newly-elected governments professing to Western democratic constitutional principles became established in that and other parts of the globe, creating – at least within constitutional theory – new rights and freedoms for millions of new citizens. Market-friendly rules came to hold sway over the global economy, binding governments, economic institutions, and individuals into an increasingly complex, though deeply unequal, web of interdependence.

Swelling migration streams across national borders are but one visible consequence of these changes. Intimately related to this shift, at roughly the same time, fundamental changes in local politics also emerged. Whereas policies of modernisation, whether Marxist or liberal in conception, had held local communities captive in the iron grids of class and homogenising national ideologies embedded as they were within the three world blocs of West, East, and Third World, this geopolitical shift offered opportunities to new and old citizens alike publicly to declare identities they considered they shared with others. Belonging to a democratic nation-state, in their view, no longer implied having to supplant sub-national identities with a dominant national identity. Accordingly, most national governments across the globe, both new and old, were faced with an increasing number of claims from sub-national groups for recognition and for equity – for treatment of their group identity as different from those of the rest of the nation. The more frequent such claims became, the more visible opportunities for cultural mobilisation became in the global community and to those within that community who aspired or planned to mobilise along similar lines. Global mass communications fuelled this demonstration effect, both in its benign form of peaceful cultural pluralism in democratic settings and in its destructive guise of threats and acts of violence intended to force the hands of national governments or of supra-national authorities. In short, democratic governments in the early twenty-first century, while facing the perennial problems within their societies of poverty and growth, welfare and order, are confronted with two new challenges: the increasing loss of sovereignty to new regional and global authorities and the politics of identity, which require reconciling the building and elaboration of a nation with acquiescence to different citizens' demands for recognition of communal identity – in Crawford Young's words, the reconciling of democratic governance with cultural pluralism (Young, 1993: 19).

This viewpoint suggests that the focus of identity studies in the developing world ought to be on the national question, on the extent to which governments succeed in their quest for reconciliation and the extent to which those in civil society acquiesce to, or resist, nation-building strategies. A scan of recent studies related to collective identities in South Africa is instructive in this regard (Leildé, 2006). Before the early 1990s, under the shadow of apartheid, studies focused on race and class issues, with structural analyses predominating. Once a new democratic government began to emerge, interest in identity studies grew. The questions underlying this interest derived from the ghosts of South Africa's past and the dreams of its future. Does race continue to carry deep meaning? Have South Africans developed a new national identity? The implication appeared to be that South Africans are able to make one choice only: to belong together to a new nation, or to remain divided by offensive cleavages inherited from an unjust past. The two choices stand in an inverse relationship to one another, it was said. If older racial and ethnic identities persist, a national identity cannot emerge and, conversely, if and when the former identities dissolve, pride in and identification with the South African nation will flourish. Accordingly, after about a decade of research and debate on this national question, it became apparent to many in South Africa that this perspective obstructed the examination of new sub-national and supra-national identities that may be emerging. Such an examination has become the new research agenda on collective identities – a particularly appropriate one in the post 9/11 world – and is considered to be of increasing importance within government circles, a point introduced in the opening paragraph above. This, too, is the agenda that guided the authors of chapters in this book.

Societies at the beginning of the twenty-first century are experiencing a second challenge. For the first time in human history, the majority of the world's population lives in cities. In the developed world, the era of rapid urbanisation has already been and gone. In sharp contrast, however, the proportion of urban dwellers in the developing world at the turn of the century was about 40 per cent. Here, the process of urbanisation is rapid and enduring. Within this developing region moreover, Africa is the latecomer to the process of urbanisation. The continent has the least urban tradition of long historical duration and most Africans accordingly have the most recent experience of city life. A strikingly large proportion of Africa's urban residents in fact are rural born. In 1980, only some 27 per cent of Africans lived in cities. This jumped to 38 per cent in 2000 and is expected to reach 50 per cent in the year 2020 (Hall & Pfeiffer, 2000: 3). Simultaneously, given its recent colonial past, local government practice in African cities led to the systematic segregation of urban spaces, to differential access both to entry into the city and to formal housing and service delivery within the city, as well as, in the South Africa case, to strict residential segregation on a racial basis. In reaction to these policies and practices, urban residents have at various levels (neighbourhood, suburb, and city) constructed collective identities that seek forms of solidarity and of survival strategies different from those offered or imposed by city government.

If the value of studying collective identities has been established and the relevance of tackling this task in an African urban context justified, how ought this study to be done? The theme of a transforming world at the beginning of this century is again pertinent. It is not only global geo-politics and rural–urban migration streams themselves but the ways they are conceptualised and interpreted that have changed. Our knowledge of the world is reflexive and incomplete, is based on particular and selected events, and is deeply influenced by our own cultures and our own histories. In a repeated dialectic chain, empirical change and conceptual analysis inform and clarify one another. Accordingly, particularly in the domain of identity studies, postmodern analysis has come of age and has succeeded in posing challenges for researchers that are both theoretical and methodological in nature. It is fitting therefore that this book opens with these issues specifically addressed in chapter 2.

The four African cities that were studied by authors of chapters in this book are Cape Town and Johannesburg in South Africa, Libreville in Gabon, which is located in Central Africa, and Lomé in Togo, located in West Africa. In part 2 of the book, chapters 3 and 4 present succinct overviews of these four cities, overviews that comprise demographic and socio-economic profiles relevant to later chapters as well as certain key urban development features. These chapters also introduce each city with a brief historical sketch of its development. Since identity research in the Francophone African cities of Libreville and Lomé proved difficult to accomplish in what were unfamiliar settings for most researchers, and because challenges of language diminished the number of researchers capable of field work, most of the work completed by authors took place in Cape Town and Johannesburg. There are a number of chapters that offer explicit comparisons between Cape Town and Johannesburg, whereas only one compares Libreville with Lomé (chapter 11). In addition, in chapter 12 of the book, urban residents' perceptions of the African continent and of South Africa have been compared on the basis of research conducted in all four of these cities. Concisely, therefore, the primary value of comparisons drawn here accrues to knowledge about the South African cities, since there is more information about, and interpretation of, these cities than for the other two. Simultaneously, particularly for younger South African scholars, research experience in other countries and cities on their continent has not only been valuable but also the beginning of a process of discovery.

Two of the three chapters in part 3 are written by geographers, the third by an anthropologist. Chapter 5 explicitly raises the question of the way in which space informs identity, of the shared meanings that urban residents project onto the places they live and work in. The aim of the chapter is to introduce the notion of a territorial identity and to illustrate its importance by way of South African urban examples. These examples draw on memories of the imposition of apartheid territorial identities (at various spatial scales, such as that of group area and of homeland) and of identity responses by urban dwellers to these impositions. They also draw on individual life histories of black urban residents in Johannesburg to highlight the ways in which individual and collective identities intersect in places known and places imagined. Race, class, and culture may well be the most studied identities, the author argues, but it is impossible to understand contemporary South Africa without introducing the idea of a sense of place. When constructing both individual and collective identities, in fact, South Africans' narratives are replete with territorial identity references.

The next chapter (chapter 6) tackles the issue of domestic workers in Cape Town and in Johannesburg. This form of work, which used to be regulated in a highly paternalist and publicly well-nigh invisible manner by white employers, has become more flexible and more visible since 1994. Attempts to professionalise the sector are also apparent. On the basis of their fieldwork in these two cities, the authors argue that a social-group consciousness (a possible precursor of a shared class consciousness) is developing among many domestic workers as a result of legislative development and NGO action in civil society. Emergent work identities, accordingly, appear to offer more self-esteem to women employed in this sector. The authors also argue, with regard to identities in this sector, that 'place matters'. These workers are aware of the spatial locational advantages they share with others working in a suburb, and they construct from this not only social but also spatial capital to cultivate the networks they create among themselves.

The challenge of facing up to and improving the lot of households living in sprawling informal settlements in and around South African cities is the subject of chapter 7. The author is deeply critical of utopian elements in the thinking of city planners who propose, for informal settlements, a new socio-spatial order that all too often fails to conform to the realities of their residents. Drawing from a case study of an informal settlement upgrade in Cape Town, he argues that modernist planning typically makes the mistake of assuming that poor people will plan and routinise their lives in a new built environment as the middle classes often have done in the past. The mistake is found in a misreading of the nature of attempts by the poor to sort out their everyday problems of shelter and livelihoods. Rather than linear policies from above, where problems are addressed in a rational and sequential fashion, solutions from below are needed to take into consideration actually existing social conditions.

The four chapters in Part 4 are written by sociologists and anthropologists. As the title of this section reflects, these studies consider the relative importance urban residents give to belonging to class, race, and speech communities. Each chapter employs recently gathered evidence drawn from a series of interviews or a series of non-directive focus groups, or both. Chapter 8 investigates white middle-class views of the changing nature of South African society. Interviewees were Johannesburg residents and their views were explored by asking them to reflect on changes that have taken place recently in their city's middle-class suburbs, inner-city areas, and informal settlements. Though a number of scholars have argued that class is replacing race as a dominant identity in South Africa,

SIMON BEKKER

the author believes, on the basis of his interview material, that this is principally a popular and strategically wise stance in public conversations. A social taboo regarding racist expressions has emerged recently in the country, and interviewees are keenly aware of it. Accordingly, caution surrounds expressions regarding race even though, implicitly at least, race consciousness remains pervasive among this group of interviewees.

The first question posed in chapter 9 is whether Cape Town and Johannesburg are developing the attributes of a dual or of a divided city – a city characterised by social and spatial separation between a cohesive middle-class core and a fragmented peripheral 'underclass', or a city in which the real divisions are ethnic, racial, and religious though socio-economic differences do exist. The second question is to consider in which ways Cape Town and Johannesburg differ from one another in respect of this categorisation. Conclusions inferred from residents' focus-group narratives suggest that both cities share attributes of the dual city and that their respective 'underclasses' experience frustration over exclusion and anger at stigmatisation. Simultaneously, Cape Town appears to have significantly stronger attributes of a divided city than Johannesburg. Middle-class Capetonians perceive themselves to be culturally diverse at both neighbourhood and city levels, while 'underclass' Capetonians experience access to shelter and livelihoods as racialised – thereby adding race as a significant dimension to their 'underclass' identity. Johannesburg, on the other hand, is experienced at least in comparison with Cape Town as a city divided by class.

The next two chapters investigate the relative importance that urban residents give to belonging to a speech community in a multilingual city. Using personal observation and experience, as well as focus group techniques, the author of chapter 10 argues that there is a significant difference among black residents between belonging to one of the various African speech communities in Johannesburg and being an isiXhosa speaker in Cape Town. Though English, as the international language of both cities, is generally accepted, the *lingua franca* of Afrikaans in Cape Town is experienced by these residents as a symbol of exclusion of those who are not able to speak it. Black residents of Johannesburg, in contradistinction, use their multilingual situation to celebrate a unique form of urban Africanness. In chapter 11, the same question is posed in the Francophone African cities of Lomé and Libreville. Though both cities have national language policies requiring that indigenous languages are recognised in public, French is in practice both the international and vehicular language. As in the case of South African cities, this does not appear to be resented by urban residents. In the case of Lomé, Ewe-Mina as *lingua franca* does not appear to be rejected by residents within minority speech communities. In Libreville, on the other hand, narratives from Fang-speaking focus groups identified significant shared sentiments of exclusion among members of this speech community by the Gabonese state. Accordingly, the cases of isiXhosa speakers in Cape Town and Fang speakers in Libreville suggest that language identities are rarely solely about language. It is when they are linked to ethnic identities and when they are experienced as stigmas that they may become salient.

The last chapter of the book, chapter 12, asks the simple question: What is an African? Information drawn from focus-group discussions in all four cities under scrutiny suggests that there are various responses to the question. In Cape Town and Johannesburg, responses are deeply coloured by a belief in South African exceptionalism – the belief that South Africa is different and better. Africa is in fact perceived by these respondents not as a black continent but as a continent in disarray. Respondents had no knowledge whatsoever about Francophone Africa. For urban respondents in Gabon and in Togo, the continent is divided into a Francophone Africa and an Anglophone Africa, implying that the idea of Africa should be located in a European or at least in an Afro-European context. Regarding South Africa, these respondents perceive it to be a potential motor for development on the continent. It is this African mentor role rather than an economic exploitative role that emerged from these narratives. These images of South Africa are sometimes racialised when, for example, it is South Africa's black brothers and sisters who are called upon to offer protection further north. In the totality of narratives collected, there are a variety of ways of being African. The divides are both between Francophone and Anglophone Africa and between a poor and a rich Africa. South African respondents strengthen their identification with their country and the rights derived from its citizenship from their belief in its exceptionalism on the continent. For Francophone African respondents, South Africa's membership on the continent is sometimes called into question as a result of its highly visible white minority.

How ought these chapters to influence the generalisations proposed in the South African Presidency's discussion document, *A Nation in the Making*? Let us first repeat the two most prominent of their claims:

- South Africans evince strong national identity, and
- while race and nationality/language recede, class identity is becoming the primary form of self-definition.

The outcomes of research reported on in this book signal that these generalisations need careful and constant qualification.

It is generally accepted that race as an identity remains in the consciousness of most South Africans. What is at issue is the question of the conditions under which it becomes salient. Chapter 8 suggests that race consciousness among the white middle class, though often strategically camouflaged, often persists as a primary identity. Chapters 9 and 10 suggest that race emerges as primary where racial boundaries are perceived to coincide with boundaries excluding residents from access to urban resources. Similarly, as argued in chapters 10 and 11, it appears that language and ethnicity (or nationality) emerge as salient identities when membership of a speech community promotes ethnic mobilisation as a result of shared perceptions of discrimination. The geographers' plea in Part 3 of this book is that territorial identities ought to be given as much attention as identities relating to race, ethnicity, and class. Recent turmoil in South Africa relating to resistance from urban communities to their relocation across South African provincial borders is a pertinent example of the importance of such territorial identities. This leads to the related issue of dangers in terms of crafting and applying linear policy – tackling issues in a rational and sequential fashion – rather than constantly investigating existing conditions on the ground. Finally, do South Africans evince strong national identity? Chapter 5 suggests that a South African identity is fashioned to a significant extent from shared sentiments of South African exceptionalism – from the belief that South Africans are different and better than their African counterparts. Otherwise, national loyalties have not figured strongly in the research reported on here. This reveals that collective identities need always to be investigated as situational, as shared meanings of people in a specific place and at a given time. Though some identities may persist across places and over time, all are constructed and accordingly may change. The journey from an apartheid past 'towards non-racialism, equity and unity in diversity', in the words of this discussion document, is not linear and appears to be pioneering various pathways that lead to various destinations.

PART 1: SOCIAL IDENTITY: CONSTRUCTION, RESEARCH AND ANALYSIS

CHAPTER 2

Identity studies in Africa
Notes on theory and method

Charles Puttergill & Anne Leildé

2.1 Introduction

Most societies at the beginning of the new millennium are caught up in seemingly never-ending processes of social transformation. One consequence for members of these societies seems to be increasing insecurity about 'fitting in' and belonging. Debate and collective action on these issues have moved to the centre of politics, and it is accordingly unsurprising to observe that identity has become a key concern within the social sciences and humanities. Identity has become, in fact, 'the watchword of the times' (Shotter, 1993b: 188).

Various disciplines have addressed issues of identity in various ways and have produced a substantial, albeit disparate, body of theory and research. It appears in fact that the flexibility of this notion has enabled researchers to use it to frame questions that are of particular interest to them. This has led Goldberg and Solomos to argue that the question of identity has 'taken on so many different connotations that sometimes it is obvious that people are not talking about the same phenomena' (Goldberg & Solomos, 2001: 5). Furthermore, alongside conceptual debates on identity, empirical research has drawn on diverse methodologies. It is therefore appropriate to introduce this book with a number of conceptual and methodological tools commonly used by its various contributors in their studies of identities in urban Africa.

2.2 Exploring the notion of identity

Conceptions of identity have changed dramatically over time. Identity in pre-modern (traditional) societies was perceived as undifferentiated, socially derived, fixed to a position, and unproblematic. Change then took place, from the absolute certitude of traditional or feudal forms of social and economic organisation, culture, and thought, to notions of autonomy, openness, and questioning. Contemporary theorists concede that a stable and coherent cultural context no longer serves as a base for a stable identity and acknowledge the role played by contingency and uncertainty in collective and individual representations. In the words of Bauman,

> [P]ostmodernity is the point at which modern untying (dis-embedding, disencumbering) of tied (embedded, situated) identities reaches its completion: it is now all too easy to choose identity, but no longer possible to hold it ... Postmodernity is the condition of contingency ... nothing seems impossible, let alone unimaginable. Everything that 'is', is until further notice. (Bauman, 1996: 50–51)

Identity formation in 'late modernity' is indeed influenced by a multiplicity of factors, as Driessen and Otto point out: '[g]lobalising markets and media, the flow of people, ideas and values, ethnic revival and the redrawing of political frontiers, all contribute to identity questions ... at all levels of socio-political integration and differentiation' (Driesen & Otto, 2000: 12).

In opposition to former notions of all-encompassing and essential identities, postmodern formulations of identity emphasise the notion of subjectivity and reject 'grand theories that attempt to incorporate the totality of social experience' (Prinsloo & De la Rey, 1999: 72). Gilroy describes a postmodern attribute of identity as follows:

> [Identity] offers far more than an obvious common-sense way of talking about individuality, community, and solidarity and has provided a means to understand the interplay between subjective experiences of the world and the cultural and historical settings in which those fragile, meaningful subjectivities are formed. (Gilroy, 2000: 98)

With the notion of subjectivity, individual agency in identity construction is recognised. As Giddens points out, loosening social ties, fluidity of social relations, increasing individualisation, narcissism, emphasis on the self and reflexivity in modernity facilitate the opportunity to choose between lifestyles (Giddens, 1991).

Simultaneously, it is now widely acknowledged that individuals draw meaning from belonging to more than one group. They construct and maintain multiple identities that emerge under different circumstances in their daily lives. According to Agger (1998: 53) 'people are seen as dispersed into a wide variety of subject positions from which they speak polyvocally about their experiences and meanings ... and multiple subject positions'. Although identities can overlap, the significance and nature of each possible identity varies over time and not all identities are equivalent or interchangeable. It is in their social relations that individuals manage their identities according to their significance and nature.

Identity is therefore 'socially bestowed, socially sustained and socially transformed' (Berger, 1963: 116). It is neither essential nor immutable but a social construction open to change as circumstances, strategies and interactions fluctuate. Since identities do not transcend space and time, they need to be situated historically and relationally. Accordingly, identity is best viewed as a process rather than a property. Viewing identity as a process problematises the notion of an already existing fixed identity. Indeed, as a process, identity is emergent, never complete, finalised, or fixed, but rather always in the making (Castells 1997; Shotter, 1993b). It is something we 'do' rather than something we 'are'.

The notions of agency, subjectivity, and multiplicity in identity formation remain contested within the African scholarship. They are at the heart of a debate between 'a younger generation of "postmodern" scholars and Africanist intellectuals claiming loyalty to the anti-colonial and nationalist struggles' (Robins, 2004: 18). While Western media continue to portray the African continent and its people according to a framework of ontological difference (Pottier, 2003; Nyamnjoh, 2000), the struggle against colonialism and continued economic imperialism has produced a legitimate discourse on African identity, based on the unity of African people, the commonality of the experience of subjugation and the authenticity of African culture. However, according to postmodern scholars, the Pan-Africanist ideal constitutes the substitution of one hegemonic discourse by another and fails to take into account 'the enormous differences within Africa and amongst Africans that inhabit the continent; differences that express themselves along the lines of gender, sexuality, class, ethnicity, religion, language, region, nationality, and so on' (Robins, 2004: 24). Mbembe, in particular, argues that

> Marxism and nationalism as practiced in Africa throughout the twentieth century gave rise to two narratives on African identity and experience: *nativism* and *Afro-radicalism*. .... When analyzed closely, these two orthodoxies are revealed to be faked philosophies (*philosophies du travestissement*). (Mbembe, 2002b: 629, original emphasis)

While the former (re)asserts the uniqueness and authenticity of African culture and calls for the establishment of 'an African interpretation of things', the latter stems from a 'reified vision of history' whereby 'the present destiny of the continent is supposed to proceed not from free and autonomous choices but from the legacy of a history imposed upon the Africans – burned into their flesh by rape, brutality and all sorts of economic conditionalities' (Mbembe, 2002a: 243). Postmodern scholars call for a re-evaluation of such historical, economic, and cultural determinism. They draw attention to the fact that 'postcolonies are radically unalike' and to the need to study 'the disparate identity strategies emerging in everyday life' (Werbner, 1996: 2). Criticisms of African postmodern scholarship, on the other hand, contend that postmodern theories are Eurocentric and 'insist upon the need for theory to continue to draw attention to the material consequences of imperialist and colonial legacies in contemporary Africa' (Robins, 2004: 22).

2.3 Constructing identity: Discourses and social representations

In researching identity, researchers implicitly and explicitly pose questions on the nature of social reality and open debates on epistemology. According to Hughes and Sharrock, 'the emphasis on meaning as the distinctive characteristic of human life brought language very much to the fore in social science concerns' (Hughes & Sharrock, 1997: 161). A key premise is that social reality is knowable through discourse. This does not imply that social reality is discourse; it is an epistemological, not an ontological claim. Identities are closely related to social representations and, as representations, they are not neutral independent reports on a pre-given reality. They are shaped by an exchange and interaction process (Moscovici, 1988). Since alternative accounts are possible, representations are always partial. Discourse therefore actively constitutes reality, drawing on cultural constructions. If discourses work to produce rather than merely to reflect 'reality', they need to be considered against the conditions forming the backdrop for their enunciation. Two interrelated levels – the socio-cultural level, which structures everyday discourse, and the interactional level, at which meanings are negotiated in everyday communication – are acknowledged in an attempt to navigate between the Scylla of a determining discourse (culture) and the Charybdis of a constructing discourse (agency). This prevents falling into the trap of either relativising or reifying the discourse. Therefore, discourses can be read and understood in terms of both the interactional and the social context in which they occur. Striking a balance between the two prevents extreme positions – characterising the subject as a product of the social structure or overemphasising variability (Harré, 1998; Shotter, 1993a).

The linguistic turn led to a shift in research practice from collecting accounts of objects or things in an objective detached manner towards acknowledging an involvement in a social context of both researcher and respondent. The notion that lived experience can be reported independently by a subject and directly captured in research has been problematised by researchers influenced by this methodological assumption. In these debates, the unparalleled powers of a knowledgeable subject providing authentic access to a pre-existing static reality, and a neutral researcher detached from the context in which this information is dispensed, are questioned. However, the linguistic turn, with its emphasis on the constructed nature of knowledge and on the notion of reflexivity, potentially holds the danger of a retreat to abstract theoretical discourse and debates in which researchers become trapped within a hermeneutic circle.

Contextualising the narrator

The assumption that interviewees are knowing subjects benefiting from full insight into their experiences and that they passively reveal this privileged access they have to researchers has been questioned by Becker, who argues that research subjects are not simply 'carriers of the conventional world's thoughts', serving as a source of information (Becker, 1998: 8). Accordingly, Hall (1996) argues that, in addressing questions of identity, what is needed is a theory of discursive practice rather than one of a knowing subject. Through a focus on discursive practice, subjects are not treated as simple repositories from whom information can be extracted. Subjects are seen as being reflective, since their accounts respond to an active intervention by a researcher and are constructed within an interactional context. Through their interaction, a researcher and subject create and shape their understandings of the world. Accounts therefore construct rather than merely describe social reality, and knowledge is situated and open to contestation and revision (May, 2002; Parker, 2002; Seidman, 1998; Silverman, 1993). Subjects are therefore active participants in the research process, in which they express and articulate positions, contributing to the complexity of studying reality.

Narratives cannot be treated in a simple referential way with subjects unproblematically knowing, remembering, and telling. Memory is not a passive store of facts, and discourse does not provide a simple description of experiences in an unmediated fashion. Changing contexts may lead to a reinterpretation of the past. Accounts provide indeed a hearable description of experience, revealing what a narrator is willing to share with others. It is a social practice in which accepted and familiar modes of telling are appropriated from a cultural repertoire and moulded into personal stories. According to Sacks (cited in Lepper, 2000: 110), accounts are 'worked up for the occasion' and may be told differently to different persons and on different occasions. This variability of accounts does not imply that they are untrue. Poststructuralism has played a key role in establishing an awareness of the constructed nature of knowledge claims and notions of what counts as truth. This results in a contextualist, rather than absolutist, seeking of knowledge. Truth is not seen as a foundation or ultimate definition of reality, but rather as a product of language games and power (Parker, 2002; Riessman, 1993).

Discourses that in the past were considered legitimate and normal are now considered unacceptable. Subjects may be careful in the way they express themselves, as social change brings about new norms about what is deemed acceptable practice. Such influences function within the public domain, and may reflect what is permissible and impermissible discourse, what is politically correct, and what is not. Discourses are ultimately self-representations, and attempt to project a positive image. Accounts are constructed retrospectively and contain justifications to make them credible, especially with interview-based research where they are displayed for public consumption. As Michael (1996: 22) points out, there is always the concern to appear as 'good accountable persons whose actions are warrantable'. This demonstrates how identities are publicly occasioned and socially negotiated, in interaction, albeit in a specific context. The fluidity and incompleteness of accounts do not imply distortion of a 'true' identity. People live in changing contexts, and the narratives they develop about their lives provide structure and meaning for these changing contexts. Lives are restored within a particular context, taking both past experiences and future orientations into consideration.

Contextualising the researcher

The notion of the researcher as a neutral observer has also been questioned. Researchers need to be reflexive about the impact they have on their research. Being reflexive implies probing the relationship between the researcher and the subject, and, in particular, sensitivity to the multiplicity of identities and the relationships associated with them, as well as to the way in which data are generated and analysed (Fine, 1994; Smyth & Shacklock, 1998). The researcher influences the research process both during field research and during the analysing process.

During field research, subjects categorise the researcher as belonging to particular groups in society and embedded in collective social relations. Sharing some characteristics with subjects may facilitate initial access. However, in spite of establishing a relationship, full access is seldom attained as the self is carefully guarded within the public realm (Kram, 1988). Punch (1994) argues that a researcher's category inscriptions both open up (enhance) and close down (intrude on) particular lines of inquiry. There is fluidity to insiderness and outsiderness, with each position holding benefits and costs as far as research is concerned. While the latter can cause feelings of cultural and social alienation from the subject, raising the possibility that a researcher may be misled by a subject, strangeness may be an advantage, in the sense that subjects may be more willing to discuss matters with researchers they are not likely to meet again.

When discussing sensitive topics, one of the difficult decisions confronting a researcher concerns the degree of self-disclosure, participation and distance maintained. Since the researcher expects openness from the subject, some reciprocity is expected in return. Letting the balance of power shift by allowing subjects to ask questions may be a beneficial strategy. Answering questions of the research subject may facilitate frank exchange, although there is some debate on the extent that it does. Weber and Carter (1998) argue that disclosure implies reciprocity. However, this reciprocity does not necessarily require a counter-disclosure. Weiss (1994) warns that extensive disclosure by a researcher shifts attention away from the subject.

Denzin and Lincoln (1994) argue that each researcher is historically, socially, and academically located and therefore speaks from within a distinct interpretative community. The perspective of the researcher therefore guides the research process. Researchers do not only describe, they interpret the social world through theoretical frameworks available to them. They construct representations of social life, by engaging in a dialogue between theory and evidence. Besides hearing subjects, the researcher frames these responses within an interpretative context in order to get a grasp on social phenomena. The challenge, then, is to place the discourse in a context – historically and socially – while retaining the integrity of the accounts (Denzin, 1989; Fine & Weiss, 1998; Ragin, 1994).

Contextualising the topic

Research, as a public activity, is not conducted independently of a political context. A researcher needs to attend to questions about whose interests are served by conducting the research and how its data can be used. The openness and flexibility of qualitative research makes it impossible to anticipate research outcomes fully. Researching sensitive topics often requires some ambiguity about the purpose of the study in order to gain access. The guidelines of informed consent and confidentiality assist researchers in negotiating dilemmas that are posed by research as an intrusive activity. Managing risk and avoiding harm are crucial where research intersects with alignments and/or tensions in society. A key concern is how to deal with what Fine and Weis (1998: 20) term 'treacherous data': discourses that do not flatter either the research subjects or those 'othered' by the data. Such data potentially solidify stereotypical perceptions. In this regard, the politically charged context in which research is conducted and the way in which findings may be used should be taken into account.

Contextualising research in Africa

Identity studies in Africa pose specific challenges in terms of research contextualisation. Cross-cultural research is difficult in societies marked by deep class, racial, or ethnic cleavages, since the researcher will be categorised as a member of a specific group. The ability to conduct comparative studies across different communities is therefore limited.

In societies under authoritarian regimes, talking about sensitive issues (research on social conflict for instance) carries risks for both the research participant and the researcher. Fears of retaliation may influence the level of dissent expressed and therefore the truthfulness of responses. Self-censorship may also be necessary on the part of the researcher.

In a context of extreme inequality and injustice, it is difficult for the researcher to maintain a neutral stance. Partisanship may in fact become essential to establish trust. It was certainly the case during apartheid in South Africa, as Schutte aptly argues: 'during the heydays of apartheid ... under conditions of oppression the fieldworker, more than in any other situation faces the question: "On whose side are you?"' (Schutte, 1991: 127). This, to a large extent remains true today. The challenge here is to find a balance between 'action' research and political activism.

The issue of partisanship reaches beyond the interaction between respondent and researcher. In South Africa, and at the continental level, it conditions to a large extent the theoretical and interpretative framework of identity studies. As was mentioned before, the struggle against colonialism and neo-colonialism produced a legitimate discourse on African identity, leading postmodern scholars to argue that the study of identity in the African context confuses 'what is' and 'what should be' the dominant identity of Africans. Accordingly, 'the urgency today is to restore a separation on an intellectual level between the desire *to know and to think* and *the urge to act*. The two moments are both legitimate, but there needs to be a line of autonomy between them' (Mbembe, 2002b: 636, original emphasis). This position, however, remains contested by scholars such as Zeleza, whose contention is as follows:

> African scholars, surrounded by material poverty and political tyranny, by underdevelopment, to use a once popular term, are [more] preoccupied with questions of development and democracy than about gazing at sexuality that seems to titillate the intellectual imaginations of some of our colleagues in 'postmodern' societies. (Zeleza, forthcoming, quoted in Murunga, 2004: 29)

In the context of South Africa, social research during apartheid was intrinsically ideological: In broad terms, it was used either to provide scientific legitimation for government policy or to denounce it (Schutte, 1991). Although political democratisation lifted those boundaries within social inquiry, there is still a resistance among certain academics against studying ethnic identities or any identity that might distract from what they perceive as a progressive agenda.

2.4 Qualitative research methodology

How is discourse accessed operationally? Selecting a method requires careful reflection on the purpose of research and type of analysis envisaged. There are numerous research techniques that can be used to study identities. McAllister has been particularly harsh in his critique of survey-type interview research, arguing that questionnaires have a descriptive rather than an explanative value, and that they 'disguise ... the assumptions and presuppositions of those who design them' (McAllister, 1999: 181), hence 'we can never learn anything totally new from questionnaire studies' (1999: 182). A significant proportion of social science research is based either fully or partially on data generated by individual or collective interviews. Interviews are often chosen for pragmatic reasons by researchers such as 'ease of access' to data. Such an orientation may undermine the 'investment' in time and effort required by an adequately conducted interview-based study.

Sampling and representivity

Sampling decisions draw boundaries for research. At the most basic level, the location or setting is decided. Within such a setting, research subjects serve as sampleable units. The immense amount of data generated in qualitative research places a restriction on sample size. Such qualitative studies do not conceptualise representivity in an empirical or statistical sense. Bauer and Aarts (2000) suggest a selection for diversity as an attempt to typify unknown attributes. They compare this strategy to random sampling, which depends on selecting from known attributes. In a qualitative study, a matrix of characteristics can guide the selection of subjects to ensure diversity. This strategy is termed maximum variety sampling, and allows for the exploration of commonalities and differences. The selection of sampleable units is based upon a relevant range of characteristics linked to the population without representing the population directly in a statistical sense. Weiss (1994) recommends using a matrix to guide the selection of sampleable units purposively when drawing small samples. The dimensions of such a matrix reflect potentially different social locations, resources, and experiences. The characteristics used purely as criteria for determining selection ensure access to subjects who have diverse experiences.

Interviewing

Methods are not self-validating (Hughes & Sharrock, 1997). Interrogating the relationship between a method used and the data generated by it reveals both contributions and limitations. In line with the arguments made for a social constructionist perspective, a qualitative approach relying on account-centred methods provides an appropriate way to study processes of identity construction. Social constructionism leads to a concern with charting the way in which the meaningfulness of the social world is constructed. Interviews provide opportunity for recording conversations between the researcher and subject and between subjects themselves, where more than one is involved. Such an approach enables a researcher to pay close attention to what is said in social interaction and to ways in which meanings are constructed.

In-depth interviews provide an opportunity for subjects to describe their lives. Such accounts are based on recollections as well as statements about their feelings and perspectives. However, researchers should be mindful of an exchange developing where the researcher does all the asking and the subject all the answering. In-depth interviews are social events where researchers consciously facilitate a conversational style, to create a more 'natural' and less intrusive context. The assumption underlying such a strategy is that subjects talk more freely about their perceptions and feelings in such an atmosphere. The data generated in this way cannot be separated from the social interaction that produced them (Denzin, 1989; Fielding, 1993).

Focus group interviews generate collective accounts that emerge from interaction between subjects within a social context. To facilitate communication, participants need to become acquainted with one another and should be selected, to a degree, on criteria of homogeneity. Focus-group interviews provide the researcher with an opportunity to observe interaction between subjects sharing, negotiating, and socially constructing their viewpoints within a group context. They provide subjects with an opportunity to draw comparisons, reflect on what others say, and re-evaluate their own understanding of their specific experiences. While this deflects attention from the researcher, it introduces other dynamics. The researcher needs to take the impact of the group processes into consideration when analysing these data. Although group influences lead to collectively shared discourses, these are not more or less authentic. They provide insights that would otherwise not have been accessible (Gaskell, 2000; Morgan, 1997; Macun & Posel, 1998). In particular, since by its very nature focus-group research is open ended and cannot be predetermined, it is often able to provide exploratory insight (Gibbs, 1997).

2.5 Conclusion

This chapter has argued against the notion that interview data reflect an external reality, unproblematically. The term data generation is more appropriate than data collection, since it captures the broader range of relationships between researcher, social world, and data. The researcher and subject are recognised as active rather than passive, and as parties with particular interests rather than being detached (Denzin & Lincoln, 1994). Subjects have certain preconceptions about what researchers do, what their expectations are, and what role to play ('identity' to take on), and this affects their responses. In this respect, an interview, as a social encounter in its own right, becomes an object of study. The exchange between the researcher and subject is a conscious social performance, with each one aware of the other's presence and intentionality, mutually orientating to one another (Cicourel, 1964). In this respect, 'interviewers must hear not only *what* the subjects say, but also *how* they say it.' (Berg, 1995: 49, original emphasis). Ten Have (1999), citing Alasuutari, argues that interviews are part of the reality studied rather than a means of obtaining statements about, or reflections on, reality. The purpose of social inquiry into discourse is to uncover the meaningfulness of interaction. In this regard, interpretative procedures or conversational practices occurring within an interview should be taken into consideration as the knower becomes part of what is known. Simultaneously, overemphasising the interview's interactional context reduces everything to that and sets a hermeneutic trap. Balance is required to avoid being ensnared within constructions at the expense of what is communicated about social reality (Chase, 1995; Collins, 1998; Fontana & Frey, 1994; Silverman, 1993).

PART 2: PROFILES OF FOUR CITIES

CHAPTER 3

Demographic profiles of Cape Town and Johannesburg

Izak van der Merwe & Arlene Davids

3.1 Introduction

A city is not simply one great homogeneous mass of people, but consists of diverse groupings of individuals. Each city has its own characteristics, derived from the unique demographic profiles of its inhabitants. The social structure of a city is not stable over time, but is in a continuous state of flux as a result of historical, economic, political, cultural, and environmental influences.

> [I]t is impossible to tell the story of any individual city without understanding its connections to elsewhere. Cities are essentially open; they are meeting places, the focus of the geography of social relations. (Massey, Allen, & Pile, 1999: 2)

This chapter discusses some urban development features and the demographic and socio-economic profiles of the Cape Town and Johannesburg metropolitan areas during the decade of establishment of democracy in South Africa. In the past, South Africa's apartheid-structured cities developed a unique demographic character, as a result of explicit segregation-driven policies. At present, the country's post-apartheid cities are in a dynamic restructuring process of loosening and opening up. A conspicuous component of this development is changing urban demographic profiles – the most obvious driving forces in the process being adjustments to lifestyles in desegregated urban communities and extended global networks. One can expect a more diversified profile for certain demographic indicators in the present post-apartheid city, as against a more compressed or concentrated profile in other cases.

Therefore, the authors of the present study will interpret their empirical research findings within the framework of post-apartheid urban structures and concomitant globalisation effects. The question is to what extent these phenomena can already be observed in Cape Town and Johannesburg – South Africa's two most prominent post-apartheid global cities (Van der Merwe, 2004). The specific aims are to find answers to the following research questions:

- To what extent did the historical development and local government structures prevalent in the twentieth century influence the development of the demographic identity of Cape Town and Johannesburg?
- Do the demographic and socio-economic profiles of Cape Town and Johannesburg differ substantially when their 2001 census results are compared with the national norm?
- To what extent do post-apartheid lifestyles and globalisation explain their observed demographic profiles?

3.2 City development in the twentieth century

The internal structure of a South African city displays politico-economic, functional-morphological, spatial, and managerial dimensions, with clear resemblances to city structures in other countries. The cities have, however, also responded to local conditions and to some extent acquired a distinctive identity. Although the international traits of a first-world Western city are to some extent present, the overall impression of a South African city is predominantly that of a changing colonial third-world city, which has generally developed historically through four different phases (Van der Merwe, 1993):

- The *colonial beginnings* of urban settlement originated during the seventeenth century in Cape Town and its hinterland.
- The *segregated city* developed nationally after 1910, with the South African government filling the role of the colonial power in urban development.
- The *apartheid city* became consolidated due to the *Group Areas Act* of 1950, which, for the first time, produced legally enforced segregation in South African settlements, with definite effects on urban demographic profiles.
- The *post-apartheid city* emerged towards the end of the 1980s. Influx control measures were abandoned in 1986, followed by the scrapping of various other apartheid laws, including the *Group Areas Act*, in 1991. The abandonment of the discriminatory legislation finally opened up South African cities to all races. While high levels of segregation were recorded in most cities during the apartheid era, these trends began to show a downward turn in the post-apartheid city, with white

segregation indices decreasing between 1991 and 2001 from 89 to 83 in Johannesburg and from 96 to 92 in Cape Town. The coloured population experienced a significant break with the apartheid past, with its index declining from 95 to 85 in Cape Town and from 91 to 77 in Johannesburg over the same years (Christopher, 2004). However, the tendency does not, as yet, reflect a dramatic movement away from the 100 per cent level indicative of full segregation. In spatial terms, the South African city is still highly segregated and still in the process of recovering from the effects of socio-culturally and economically imposed apartheid structures. It seems unlikely that the cities will experience a rapid transformation.

According to the South African Cities Network, South African cities are currently facing many challenges, including issues relating to their changing demography, economic challenges, social-cultural restructuring, and changes in both the built and natural environment, as well as problems related to the governing of the emerging urban structures (South African Cities Network, 2004). South African cities still have specific population issues regarding their demographics that were grossly distorted by apartheid policies. Apartheid left its mark on the urban population by regulating where people lived, as a large part of the population was allowed to work, but not to live, in the urban centres, and had to migrate from rural to urban areas to make a living. Cities have tended to grow much faster than has the national population, as the average urban growth rate was approximately 4.4 per cent from 1991 to 2001. The accelerated growth rate of cities in South Africa is a direct result of the abolition of apartheid policies that had placed restrictions on the movement of people. Currently, migration to the cities accounts for most of the urban growth trends.

The demographic profile of a city is closely related to the success of a city's economy. Large cities support wealth-creating activities, but also lead to population increases above the natural growth rate, as migrants are attracted to the greater economic opportunities present in urban settings. Apartheid left many cities with a weak economic base, as the system was based on the existence of a rich racial minority driving the demand for goods and services, as well as on the maintenance of a large labour force to ensure industrial development. While the primary and secondary industries of South Africa have declined over time, the tertiary and service sectors have become more important.

The social development of a city goes hand in hand with its economic development. Cities do not only have the responsibility to provide remunerated work opportunities, they also have to ensure that their residents have the opportunities to enjoy the benefits of an urban lifestyle. In the past, many of South Africa's population were excluded from these benefits, as black residents were concentrated in areas on the urban outskirts. The main aim of city government after apartheid was to instate social equality for all. However, an increasing number of people have been taking up residence in informal settlements, which are usually situated far from the opportunities that cities have to offer. These residents are far from their workplaces, and, consequently, have to make use of inefficient public transport, or have to walk to work. Social crises, such as the HIV/Aids pandemic, unemployment and poor education levels, are other areas of concern. Many cities are addressing these problems by implementing poverty-relief and development strategies. Factors that impact on the urban built environment are population growth, economic development, technological developments, the policy framework, and the social aspirations of city dwellers. Urban economic prosperity and the quality of life in the city also impact on the above-mentioned factors. A city is sustainable only if the built environment and population do not overburden the available natural resources. The apartheid system created an urban form that was not resource-efficient. Apartheid cities were designed in such a way that they had a disproportionately high negative impact on the urban environment, including poorly serviced township areas, poor waste and sewage management systems, excessive energy use, and time inefficiency resulting from travel on urban road networks (South African Cities Network, 2004).

The challenge that encompasses all these other factors is the state of city governance. A city where the political and institutional context is stable and dynamic enough to provide all residents with a secure framework, allowing for the expression and accommodation of varied interests, is a 'well-governed city'. Apartheid left South Africa with very specific governance problems, such as relatively weak institutions of local government, conflicting relations between communities and municipalities, poor public participation, discord between and within communities, and high levels of crime and violence. Currently, South Africa's cities are recovering well as they lay the foundations for stable local democracies. Cape Town and Johannesburg should also exhibit these general trends.

The City of Cape Town has undergone three-and-a-half centuries of urban development, and in 2001 had a culturally and socio-economically diverse population of about three million inhabitants. The Cape was originally a small settlement founded in 1652 by the Dutch East India Company, specifically to serve East India shipping. By 1850, it had developed into a town whose ethnically diverse population had grown to almost 17 000. By 1865, the population of the Cape Town municipal area had reached 28 400 (Wilkinson, 2000).

The Act of Union in 1910 designated Cape Town as South Africa's legislative capital and Pretoria as South Africa's administrative capital. Although Johannesburg became the largest city during the 1920s and the Witwatersrand established itself as the core of South Africa's developing industrial economy, Cape Town consolidated itself as an important administrative, cultural, and service centre. Manufacturing, particularly in the clothing, textile, paper and printing, food and beverage, and light engineering sectors, emerged as a significant part of the local economy. This resulted in the influx of growing numbers of people from the rural areas, and the population of Cape Town rapidly grew to 307 000 in 1921. Official segregation of the city's African population was initiated in 1901, and was later extended through the establishment of a 'model Native village' at Langa in 1927. Physically, the city expanded relatively slowly during the inter-war period, with growth occurring primarily along the southern suburbs railway line and into the Cape Flats, as can be seen in figure 3.1 (see appendix B). By 1950, the city's population had grown to 742 400. In Cape Town, the implementation of Group Areas legislation had a devastating impact, leading to the dislocation of well-established communities and the forced removal of an estimated 150 000 people to new public housing estates or townships on the Cape Flats (Wilkinson, 2000).

Currently, Cape Town's administrative area occupies roughly 2 200 km², whereas the built-up portion of the Cape Metropolitan Area (CMA) occupies about 774 km², with expansion mainly on the Cape Flats, along the northern coastal plain, and towards the agricultural landscape in the north-east. There has been significant suburbanisation and decentralisation of office, retail, manufacturing, and services, especially in the northern suburbs. The residential densities range from as low as two to four units per hectare in the wealthiest suburbs to about 90 to 100 units per hectare in the inner city areas, with their large proportion of apartment buildings. As expected, the population densities are highest in the informal settlement areas on the Cape Flats, where densities between 350 to 450 people per hectare exist (Wilkinson, 2000). Figure 3.1 illustrates the widespread development of Cape Town during the twentieth century.

After the discovery of the Witwatersrand gold reef in 1886, the city of Johannesburg, within a relatively short period of time, became the financial and commercial hub of Southern Africa. It maintained this position throughout the earlier half of the twentieth century. By the late 1980s, however, the restructuring of the global economy and increasing political pressure had resulted in a city of which the economic base was declining and of which the social and economic base was no longer sustainable. This resulted in successive attempts by the urban authorities to reinvent a city that could claim a position in the mainstream global economy and become a city of which all its citizens could feel part.

Within the first ten years of its existence, banks, finance houses, and mining company headquarters lined Johannesburg's streets. From its inception, the city was constructed to conform to Western standards of modernity. By 1936, at the time of the British Empire Exhibition, Johannesburg was described as the largest and most densely populated European city in Africa (Chipkin, 1993). This image, however, due to growing opposition to apartheid in the 1970s, quickly gave way to that of a city characterised by racial segregation and political divisions (Rogerson, 1996). During this period, there was a gradual movement of people from the black townships into the inner city. This resulted in rapid physical decline and the racial stereotyping of its new residents (Morris, 1996). The economy of the city also suffered during the 1980s. In 1951, just over one in three of the Witwatersrand labour force were employed by the mining industry. By the 1990s, actual mining activity had, to all intents and purposes, become insignificant in the regional economy of the Johannesburg Metropolitan Area. Manufacturing, although important in absolute terms, had dropped to a mere 18 per cent of the metropolis's gross geographic product (GGP). By contrast, the trade and catering sectors contributed 20 per cent of the local GGP, while the finance and business services sector made up nearly 30 per cent. Both the transport and communication sectors and the general government sector each contributed 10 per cent to the GGP (Beavon, 1997). These sectors thus contribute 70 per cent of the local economy. In the 1990s, informal trading became one of the most dynamic sectors, due to the desegregation of urban space associated with the end of the apartheid era (Tomlinson, Hunter & Jonker et al., 1995). Figure 3.2 illustrates the rapid development of Johannesburg from 1900 to 1992 (see appendix B).

3.3 Formal institutions of local government

The term governance encompasses the sum of the ways through which individuals and institutions (public and private) plan and manage their common affairs. Governance includes both formal institutions and informal arrangements, as well as the social capital of all the citizens in the designated area. South Africa's period of transition since the 1990s has included a massive local government transformation process, which has led to the decentralisation of powers and functions, and to the consolidation of the local authorities. The efficiency of local government determines whether the relationship between residents and the government is positive. One of the most dramatic changes in urban government has been achieved over the past ten years, during which it has progressed from being a racially divided and spatially fragmented arrangement to being an assortment of structures and systems more capable of managing current urban challenges (South African Cities Network, 2004). The *Local Government Transition Act* (LGTA) (Act 209 of 1993) outlined a three-phase transitional plan for the transformation of local government.

During the *first phase*, the pre-interim phase, negotiations were conducted that led to the establishment of pre-interim councils. Although this phase paved the way to the future, real change in local government was extremely limited. The *second phase* consisted of an interim situation, during which three important developments shaped the transformation of local government:

- First, the form and structure of the new system of democratically elected transitional councils were tested in practice. The new structure allowed for new Transitional Metropolitan Local Councils in six of the largest metropolitan regions in South Africa, Transitional Local Councils for the newly integrated urban areas in the larger cities and smaller towns, Transitional Representative Councils and Transitional Rural Councils with limited powers in most rural areas, and District Councils, which were indirectly elected and given their powers and functions by provincial proclamation.

- Second, a new policy framework was designed for local government. This policy process was initiated by the 1996 Constitution. It provided that a municipality must structure and manage its administration, budgeting and planning processes to give priority to the basic needs of the community. The following objectives were identified: to provide democratic and accountable government for local communities, to ensure the sustainable provision of services to communities, to promote social and economic development, to promote a safe and healthy environment, and to encourage the involvement of communities and community organisations in local government affairs.

- The third development involved the passing of new laws and the re-demarcation of local government boundaries to achieve a permanent form of local government. The most important legislation consisted of the *Municipal Structures Act* (Act 117 of 1998) and the *Municipal Systems Act* (Act 32 of 2000), which defined new institutional arrangements and new administrative systems. The Municipal Demarcation Board reasoned that developmental local government could not be realised within the fragmented boundaries of the previous local government system, and rationalised 843 municipalities into 274 more functional and viable jurisdictions.

The third and *final phase* was characterised by the testing of the transitional arrangements, by policy development that considered the weaknesses of the arrangements, and by the re-establishment of local government through the establishment of new structures and boundaries. During this phase, further local government change was promoted by helping municipalities to transform themselves within their new boundaries and by helping them to fulfil their developmental mandate. Even though the local government transition process has ensured that all cities are now governed by more appropriate institutional arrangements, some challenges will remain for some time to come. The metropolitan areas of Cape Town and Johannesburg developed in accordance with the above-mentioned local government structures and the following demographic profiles of the two cities will be interpreted within this framework.

The City of Cape Town has a population of 2.9 million people (2001 Census), making it the second largest city in South Africa. As in the rest of South Africa, the system of local government underwent a number of structural changes. The *Municipal Structures Act* stated that megacity governments were to be established in the major metropolitan centres at the beginning of 2001. This process replaced the former structure with a powerful and highly centralised metropolitan council that is better equipped to undertake programmes of city-wide restructuring and development. Two significant developments took place in the Cape Metropolitan Area (CMA) during the transitional period. First, an integrated development planning (IDP) approach was adopted. The approach seeks both to link planning directly to budgeting and implementation processes and to coordinate infrastructure and service provision systematically. The second major development is an attempt by the Cape Metropolitan Council to replace the discredited metropolitan guide plans with a comprehensive Metropolitan Spatial Development Framework (MSDF). Its objective is to provide an overarching plan for spatial restructuring aimed at reintegrating the fragmented urban system inherited from the apartheid era. A clear vision is formulated in the strategy document *Ikapa Elihlumayo*. The following issues are key priorities that need to be addressed in order for the CMA to function in line with the Western Cape Province in a developing and sustainable manner (Republic of South Africa, 2004b):

- building social capital with an emphasis on youth,
- building human capital with an emphasis on youth,
- strategic infrastructure investment,
- a micro-economic strategy,
- a spatial development framework,
- co-ordination and communication,
- improving financial governance, and
- provincialisation of municipality rendered services.

The Johannesburg Metropolitan Area has a population of 3.2 million (2001 Census), making it the largest city in the country. The city, which is the provincial capital of Gauteng Province, is the financial hub of Southern Africa. During the apartheid era, Johannesburg was divided into seven white and four black local authorities. The white authorities were 90 per cent self-sufficient and spent R600 per capita, while the black authorities were only 10 per cent self-sufficient, with an expenditure of only R100 per capita. The inequity in spending led to major inequalities in service provision for the city's racially diverse inhabitants (City of Johannesburg, n.d.). The present ANC-run city council has attempted to address the city's problems by adopting the slogan 'one city, one taxpayer'. Johannesburg was carved up into four regions governed by a central metropolitan council and four local regional authorities, which enjoyed substantial autonomy. The municipal boundaries were expanded to include wealthy suburb towns, such as Sandton and Randburg, poorer neighbouring townships, such as Soweto and Alexandra, and informal settlements, such as Orange Farm. The new structure soon experienced difficulties, as the inexperienced management led to over-ambitious spending, wasted expenditure, cases of fraud, and duplication of services. One of the most pressing problems was the difficulty involved in collecting revenue for services, as a 'boycott' culture had become entrenched after years of local citizenry involvement in apartheid defiance campaigns. By 1998, the city had a R300 million budget deficit, a R405 million overdraft, and a zero capital budget (City of Johannesburg, n.d.).

In 1999, Johannesburg drew up a blueprint called *Igoli 2002*, a three-year plan that called for the selling of non-core assets and the restructuring of certain utilities. The net result was that, in the space of two years, the management team took the city from the brink of insolvency to having an operating surplus of R153 million.

Johannesburg was not the only urban area experiencing problems. Countrywide, there were too many local councils, resulting in duplication of many functions. In late 2000, councils across the whole of South Africa were amalgamated in order to reduce the number of local authorities. In the process, large unicities were created in Cape Town, Durban, Pretoria, the East Rand, and Johannesburg. Johannesburg's boundaries were expanded from Orange Farm in the south to Midrand in the north. In December 2000, elections were held countrywide for all the new local authorities. A demarcation board divided the enlarged city into 109 voting wards, with each ward electing a councillor to head a local ward committee (City of Johannesburg, n.d.).

3.4 Differential population profiles of Cape Town and Johannesburg (2001)

The size, form, and character of a city's population have a direct impact on its development. Population *size* is affected by three variables: birth, death, and migration. The *form* of the population refers to the following characteristics: its age structure, life expectancy, family size, and household composition. *Character* refers to the relationship between population and place, and to the way in which the population regards itself as part of the city structure. Both Cape Town and Johannesburg have experienced significant population growth in the recent past. It has become increasingly necessary to look at the demographic composition of these two cities in order to determine whether post-apartheid changes have affected these patterns. Population variables of several types have been used to analyse the city profiles of these two metropolitan areas. In order to reduce the large number of tables and complex sets of results to a simpler pattern for the purposes of comparison, the dominant categories of each of the 13 variables have been extracted and summed up, offering generalised profiles of Cape Town and Johannesburg that can be compared with the national norm (see table 3.1 in appendix A). Illuminating similarities and differences between these two urban profiles emerge from such comparison.

Demographically, in 2001, Johannesburg had a slightly older population than that of Cape Town, the former consisting predominantly of black people (73%) and the latter of Coloured people (48%). For Cape Town, in cases of citizens born outside South Africa, the external place of birth is more often Europe as against Johannesburg's more African orientation. Culturally, Cape Town's residents are dominantly Afrikaans speaking (41%) and Protestant (29%), while Johannesburg displays a more cosmopolitan language composition, with isiZulu speakers (25%) forming the dominant group. In terms of socio-economic indicators, the education level of citizens in both cities tends to be low, with about 60 per cent of the population over the age of 20 years not having obtained Grade 12 (matriculation). Patterns of personal income are also consistently low in both cities, with 49 per cent of the population in Cape Town and 45 per cent of the population in Johannesburg earning between R800 and R3 200 per month. Employment patterns are particularly revealing in terms of global influences, since Johannesburg's dominant sector is in the trade sector (19%), while Cape Town's strongest category is the services sector (19%). Both sectors indicate a 'global city' orientation. In terms of housing, both cities clearly display their third-world developing context. While 'house as dwelling type', 'telephone in dwelling', 'electricity as energy source', 'piped water on property', and 'motorcar as travel mode' form the dominant categories, the percentages in both cities are low. In terms of the potential for social interaction, it is significant that 69 per cent of Capetonians and 58 per cent of Johannesburgers have telephones in their own homes.

Although there is still a long way to go in terms of development, there are, nevertheless, clear signs of globalisation present in the 'opening and diversified' profiles of Cape Town and Johannesburg. For in-depth insight into the finer structures of the respective profile compositions, each indicator and variable must obviously be analysed in detail. To illustrate this, the two variables, 'industry-employment' (table 3.2) and 'language' (table 3.3) are compared in terms of the ethnic population groups of Cape Town and Johannesburg (see tables in appendix A).

In both metropoles, the four industrial sectors (manufacturing, trade, finance, and services) are prominent, but with the difference that services features more prominently in Cape Town compared with the predominance of finance in Johannesburg. When this pattern is investigated within the respective population groups, black private household entrepreneurship features prominently in both Cape Town (17%) and Johannesburg (16%). In Cape Town, the coloured population group is more geared towards manufacturing (22%), while in Johannesburg this group has moved strongly into finance (26%). The trend for the Asian population group is notably towards trade in both cities, while the white population group in both cities is geared towards finance and services, which have the strongest potential for global interaction and worldwide connectivity. Language, as a cultural indicator, also shows divergent patterns for the ethnic groups in Cape Town and Johannesburg (see table 3.3). In contrast to Cape Town's strong isiXhosa concentration (90% of the black population group), Johannesburg has a more diverse language composition of English, isiXhosa, isiZulu, Sepedi, Sesotho and Setswana. Coloured residents speak mainly Afrikaans in both cities, while white people speak mainly English, the global language.

In both metropolitan areas there has been a sharp increase in the black population. This trend can be linked directly to cities in the post-apartheid era being regarded as centres of opportunity for previously disadvantaged groups. Migration of both African men and women to Cape Town and Johannesburg reflects departure from the apartheid practice of single men migrating to the cities.

Language composition suggests that there is a more diversified language spectrum among the black population in both metropoles (see table 3.3 in appendix A). Several research studies suggest that the use of Afrikaans has increased among whites while declining among the coloured population in favour of English. Although the language spectrum has become more diversified, the remnants of apartheid can still be identified when the geographical distribution of language is spatially illustrated, as can be seen in figures 3.3 and 3.4 (appendix B). In general, the three dominant languages of the cities under discussion are still distributed unequally and concentrated within specific areas of the cities. However, the socio-economic dispensation is becoming increasingly open and diversified among the respective categories. The industrial sector composition supports the definition and criteria of a global city, while the greater diversity of the population profiles of the respective ethnic groups indicates the post-apartheid city's greater openness and freedom of choice in terms of behavioural patterns.

3.5 Conclusion

Research results of this study represent a selection of initial findings regarding the differentiation of Cape Town and Johannesburg population profiles and the effects of post-apartheid restructuring on these demographic structures. Given the long period during which South Africa was isolated from much of the world due to the country's apartheid policy, Cape Town and Johannesburg are now showing promising strides in terms of changing their apartheid identity to a more openly global identity. However, it is still necessary to gather more information on the link between post-apartheid structures and demographic changes in these cities. The historical development of the two cities created a fairly unique character in each, and the differential population profiles are playing a role in creating the urban identity. It is important for municipal authorities to be sensitive to the distinctive character of their municipalities, while finding appropriate ways to eradicate the footprints of apartheid. Much research remains to be done before definite conclusions can be reached regarding the implications of these results on the identifying features of the respective cities.

Appendix A: Tables

Table 3.1: *Population profiles according to dominant group*

Indicator	Cape Town Dominant category (2001)	Johannesburg Dominant category (2001)	South Africa Dominant category (2001)
Demographic			
Population group	Coloured (48%)	Black (73%)	Black (79%)
Gender	Female (52%)	Female (50.2%)	Female (52%)
Age (years)	7–19 (24%)	20–29 (26%)	7–19 (29%)
Birthplace (excluding South Africa)	Europe (1.4%)	SADC countries (3.9%)	Africa (1.6%)
Cultural			
Language	Afrikaans (41%)	isiZulu (25%)	isiZulu (24%)
Religion	Protestant (29%)	No religion (23%)	Charismatic (23%)
Socio-economic			
Education level	Secondary (39%)	Secondary (35%)	Secondary (31%)
Industry sector	Services (19%)	Trade (19%)	Services (19%)
Income (Rand)	R801–R1 600 (26%)	R801–R1 600 (26%)	R801–R1 600 (22%)
Housing			
Dwelling type	House (59%)	House (51%)	House (56%)
Telephone	In dwelling (69%)	In dwelling (58%)	Nearby (52%)
Water source	On property (84%)	On property (84%)	On property (61%)
Travel mode	Motor car (19%)	Motor car (17%)	On foot (31%)
Energy source	Electricity (80%)	Electricity (79%)	Electricity (51%)

Table 3.2: *Cape Town and Johannesburg Metropolitan Area – Industry by population group (Census 2001)*

Categories	Black%		Coloured%		Asian%		White%		Total%		South Africa
	CT	Jhb	CT	Jhb	CT	Jhb	CT	Jhb	CT	Jhb	%
Agriculture	3.5	1.6	2.5	0.5	1.1	0.5	1.6	0.8	2.5	1.3	10.0
Mining	0.2	0.6	0.2	0.7	0.5	0.6	0.4	1.2	0.2	0.7	4.0
Manufacturing	9.9	11.5	22.5	16.6	12.6	12.6	12.1	11.8	16.6	11.9	12.6
Electricity	0.4	0.7	0.6	0.6	0.5	0.7	0.6	0.6	0.2	0.7	0.7
Construction	11.1	7.0	7.0	4.0	4.0	2.2	4.2	4.2	7.2	5.9	5.4
Trade	17.7	19.1	18.2	18.0	29.1	27.1	17.6	15.5	18.1	18.6	15.2
Transport	4.8	5.6	5.1	6.3	5.1	6.0	6.4	5.2	5.4	5.6	4.6
Finance	9.4	12.8	9.9	25.5	15.1	25.5	24.0	29.4	13.5	18.1	9.4
Community services	15.3	15.8	18.4	16.2	19.6	16.2	24.9	20.7	19.4	17.0	19.2
Private Households	16.8	15.6	4.3	2.2	0.8	0.5	0.5	0.6	6.3	10.5	9.8
Undetermined	10.9	9.7	11.3	9.3	11.6	8.1	7.7	10.1	10.3	9.7	8.9
Total%	100%	100%	100%	100%	100%	100%	100%	100%	100%	100%	100%
Total number	227 701	710 639	453 687	62 965	15 147	55 871	242 909	256 074	939 444	1 085 549	9 583 765

Table 3.3: *Cape Town and Johannesburg Metropolitan Area – Language by population group (Census 2001)*

Categories	Black%		Coloured%		Asian%		White%		Total%		South Africa
	CT	Jhb	CT	Jhb	CT	Jhb	CT	Jhb	CT	Jhb	%
Afrikaans	2.7	0.5	67.8	54.0	14.3	1.9	41.3	26.1	41.4	8.1	13.3
English	2.4	1.9	31.8	44.0	81.9	92.8	57.0	71.2	27.9	19.5	8.2
isiNdebele	0.1	1.2	0.0	0.1	0.2	0.3	0.1	0.1	0.1	0.9	1.6
isiXhosa	90.5	10.4	0.1	0.2	0.2	0.1	0.1	0.1	28.7	7.7	17.6
isiZulu	0.8	34.6	0.0	0.6	0.0	0.1	0.0	0.1	0.3	25.5	23.8
Sepedi	0.1	10.1	0.0	0.1	0.0	0.0	0.0	0.0	0.1	7.5	9.4
Sesotho	2.1	14.9	0.0	0.3	0.0	0.0	0.0	0.0	0.7	11.0	7.9
Setswana	0.4	12.3	0.0	0.3	0.0	0.1	0.0	0.1	0.1	9.1	8.2
Siswati	0.1	1.3	0.0	0.0	0.0	0.0	0.0	0.0	0.0	1.0	2.7
Tshivenda	0.1	3.6	0.0	0.0	0.0	0.0	0.0	0.0	0.0	2.7	2.3
Xitsonga	0.1	8.0	0.0	0.1	0.0	0.0	0.0	0.0	0.1	5.9	4.4
Other	0.6	1.0	0.1	0.3	3.3	4.8	1.4	2.3	0.6	1.3	0.5
Total%	100%	100%	100%	100%	100%	100%	100%	100%	100%	100%	100%
Total number	916 520	2 370 768	1 392 654	206 252	41 490	1 34 107	542 580	515 184	2 893 244	3 225 811	44 819 779

Table 3.4: *Population change (1996–2001) – Percentage increase between 1996 and 2001*

		Cape Town	Johannesburg
1996	Total	2 558 000	2 756 000
	Black	643 000	1 932 000
	White	543 000	528 000
	Coloured	1 236 000	172 000
	Asian	38 000	98 000
	Unspecified	98 000	26 000
2001	Total	2 893 000 (13.1%)*	3 225 000 (17.0%)*
	Black	916 000 (42.5.0%)	2 370 000 (22.7%)
	White	543 000 (0%)	515 000 (-2.5%)
	Coloured	1 393 000 (12.7%)	206 000 (19.8%)
	Asian	41 000 (7.9%)	134 000 (36.7%)

Appendix B: Figures

Figure 3.1: *City development of Cape Town during the twentieth century*

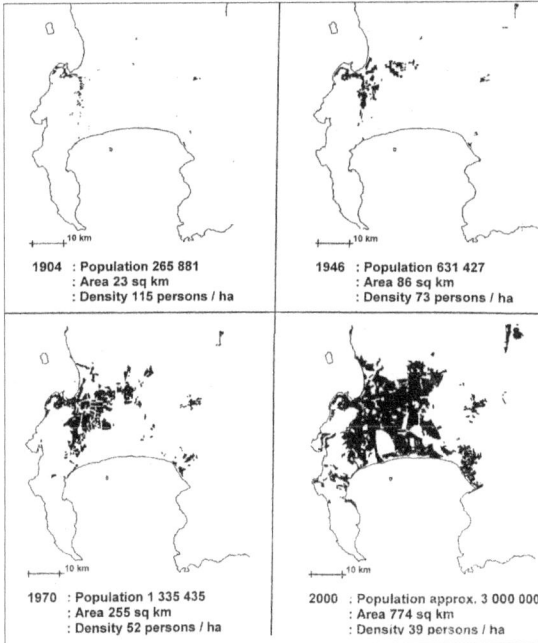

Source: Gasson, 2000

Figure 3.2: *City development of Johannesburg during the twentieth century*

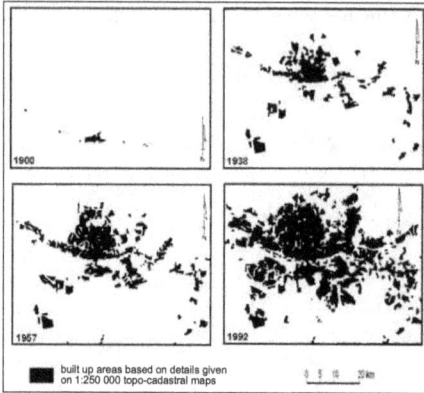

Source: Whitlow & Brooker, 1995

Figure 3.3: *Language distribution in the Cape Metropolitan Area*

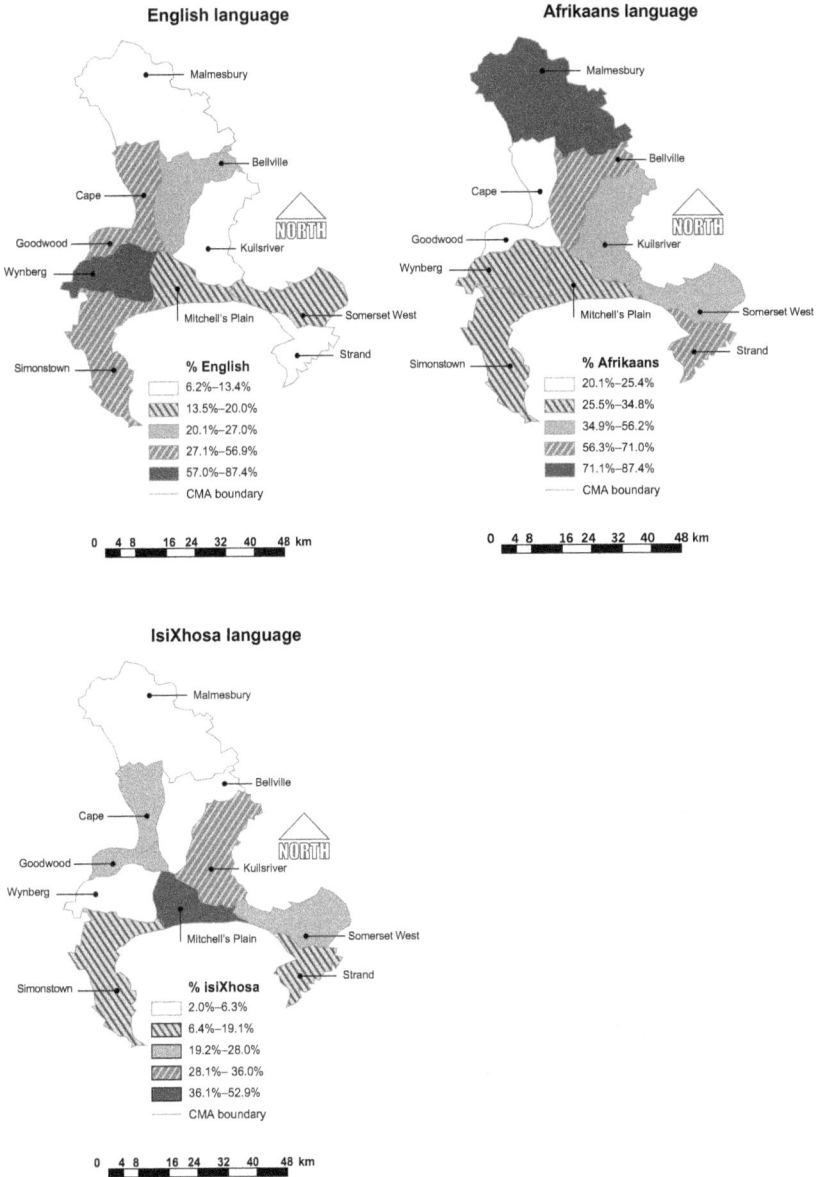

English language

Afrikaans language

IsiXhosa language

Figure 3.4: *Language distribution in the Johannesburg Metropolitan Area*

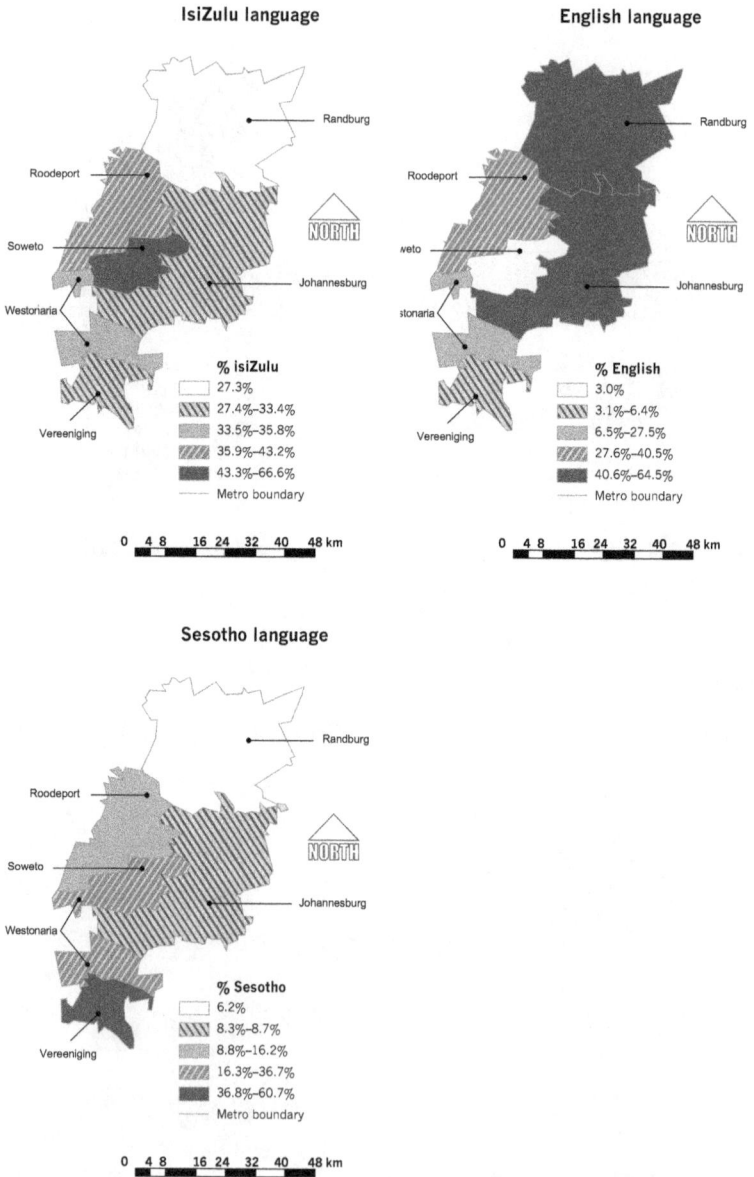

IsiZulu language

% isiZulu
- 27.3%
- 27.4%–33.4%
- 33.5%–35.8%
- 35.9%–43.2%
- 43.3%–66.6%
- Metro boundary

0 4 8 16 24 32 40 48 km

English language

% English
- 3.0%
- 3.1%–6.4%
- 6.5%–27.5%
- 27.6%–40.5%
- 40.6%–64.5%
- Metro boundary

0 4 8 16 24 32 40 48 km

Sesotho language

% Sesotho
- 6.2%
- 8.3%–8.7%
- 8.8%–16.2%
- 16.3%–36.7%
- 36.8%–60.7%
- Metro boundary

0 4 8 16 24 32 40 48 km

CHAPTER 4

Demographic profiles of Libreville and Lomé

Hugues Steve Ndinga-Koumba Binza

4.1 Introduction

The aim of this chapter is to present profiles of two capital cities on the western coast of the African continent, namely Libreville in Gabon and Lomé in Togo. It is mainly descriptive and covers the following topics:

- an overview of city development during the twentieth century,
- an outline of formal institutions of local government in these cities, and
- their separate population and linguistic profiles.

The first section of the chapter comprises brief histories of each city. Libreville is treated first, since data show that it was founded in 1849, significantly earlier than Lomé, which dates from 1877.

4.2 Location and brief history

Libreville
Libreville is the capital city of the Republic of Gabon. The Republic of Gabon, a French-speaking country, is located in Central Africa. It borders to the north-west on Equatorial Guinea, to the north on Cameroon, to the west on the Atlantic Ocean, and to the south and east on the Republic of Congo (Brazzaville). Gabon covers 267 667 square kilometres, most of which is dense tropical forest, interspersed with savannah, and fed by a river network of which the Ogooué is the most important. The country is administratively divided into nine provinces, which are further divided into districts (*départements*) and municipal areas (*communes*). The provinces are numbered according to an administrative order from one to nine. Province number one is called *Estuaire*, whose main city is Libreville. In the Estuaire province, Libreville

is located on the right bank of the Komo river estuary. The city and its environments occupy about 16 000 hectares on the northern shore of the estuary. Hills dominate the central part of the land of Libreville, whereas the north and the north-east are made up of plains. These hills and flat valleys produce physical constraints that determine the social geography and have orientated occupancy of the land of Libreville (Ndong Mba, 2004: 60). Libreville, which means free town or city in French, takes its name from the settlement organised by the French navy in August 1849 for 50 freed adult slaves and two children of Vili origin from the Congo who had been rescued several years before from the slaving ship *Elizia* (Gradinier, 1994: 204).

These newly arrived residents were given plots of land and huts in the Komo estuary between the lands of the Mpongwe, the Agekaza-Glass and the Agekaza-Quaben clans. The French colonial post (which was later moved to higher ground nearby – the so-called Plateau), the residence of the Sisters of the Immaculate Conception, and St. Peter's Church also came to be known under the name Libreville, and ultimately the name was applied to all the settlements on the right bank of the estuary. Libreville first served as capital of French Equatorial Africa until the function was moved to Brazzaville in 1904. In 1960, when the Republic of Gabon – with its current borders – attained independence, Libreville became its capital and rapidly developed into an important commercial centre.

Lomé

Lomé is the capital city of the Republic of Togo. The Republic of Togo, a Francophone African country, is located in West Africa. It borders to the north on Burkina Faso, to the west on Ghana, to the south on the Atlantic Ocean, and to the east on the Republic of Benin. Togo covers 56 800 square kilometres and is one of the smallest countries in West Africa. Most land in Togo is found on a large plain, which stretches out to the north. This plain is traversed by a single mountain range. The country is administratively divided into five regions, which are further divided into districts (*préfectures*) and municipal areas (*communes*). The regions are often named according to their respective geographic characteristics. Thus, the Savannas region in the North is covered by large savannah and plains; the Kara and Central regions are in the centre of the country and made up of mountains; the Plateaux region is characterised by mountainous plateaux; the Maritime region in the South is the sandy littoral zone containing the estuaries of a number of rivers. Lomé, in the Maritime region, is located on a sandy bar at the mouth of a lagoon of the same name (Lomé lagoon). The name of the city might have come from the presence of shrubs called '*alo*' in Ewe language: *Alo-mé* meaning 'in the midst of *alo*' (Marguerat 1992: 4). Founded in 1877 (Marguerat, 1985), Lomé owes its existence as a city to the displacement of a number of African merchants and

European trading houses to the Togolese coast from the Dahomey coasts during the second half of the nineteenth century (Haan, 1993: 58). First colonised by Germany and then by France, it was the south of Togo that enjoyed a measure of economic development (Haan, 1993: 5). Togo also became independent in the 1960s, and Lomé has remained the capital city since that event.

4.3 Local government

Local government in both Libreville and Lomé involves municipal institutions, namely the Municipality of Libreville and the Municipality of Lomé. Attention will be given here to their organisation, their rights and responsibilities, and to municipal services.

The city of Lomé was established as a municipality in 1932, while Libreville became a municipality immediately after its foundation. Its first mayor, M. Mountier, in fact, was one of the freed slaves mentioned above. Though legislation in both countries has been promulgated with a view to strengthening local government, the new institutions so established – that are spelled out below – are largely without real authority and tend to play the role of decentralised central state bodies. This dependent role is due to the fact that the two municipalities lack resources – there are no city-based rates and taxes collected and the absence of independent financial income robs city councils of legal authority to act autonomously. In the case of Lomé, for example, constitutionally provided legal and financial autonomy cannot be used due to the absence of financial resources, while, in Libreville, legislation promoting devolution of authority to city level (*loi sur la decentralization*) that has been passed some time back has yet to be fully implemented.

The Municipal Council of Libreville (Conseil Municipal de Libreville)

Libreville is administered by an executive mayor (*Maire Central*) elected from and by the 98 councillors (*conseillers municipaux*) of this Municipal Council. They in turn are chosen in a citywide election organised at ward level by residents. Six deputy mayors are also elected, and a secretary-general, appointed by the state, assists the mayor. The city is also divided into six districts (*arrondissements*), which are administered by a district mayor and councillors representing wards within this district.

The Municipal Council of Lomé

The city of Lomé is also administered by a mayor who is appointed by the central government and a secretary-general appointed, in turn, by the mayor. The city is divided along geographic lines into five districts (*arrondissements*), each of which is represented in the council by nine district councillors, selected in a citywide election organised at ward level by residents. These nine district councillors participate in District Councils in each of which a deputy mayor is elected to act as lead councillor. The councils of the city of Lomé currently play a consultative role in city affairs – the central government takes binding decisions.

Municipalities with little power

Both cities find themselves with councils that represent their residents but wield little real authority. In Lomé, for example, the municipality plays no role in monitoring urbanisation, in city planning, in land planning, in housing policy, or in the planning or supply of social services. In Gabon, the City Council of Libreville is not involved in the decision-making process for their city, which is guided by the central Ministries of Planning and Development Programmes, of Housing, Town Planning and Land Register, and of the Interior, Public Security, and Decentralisation. Accordingly, since both councils are not involved in decision making and decision taking, they do not feel bound to conform to these decisions. This leads, in turn, to continuing problems of accusation and counter-accusation regarding responsibility for planning and service delivery issues in these cities.

4.4 City development in the twentieth century

Since the early 1980s (when a major economic crisis took place in Togo), Lomé's informal economic sector (including *taxis-moto* and hawking) has been growing rapidly as the formal sector shrank. It is one of the African capitals with the lowest (per capita) municipal budgets (Nyassogbo, 1998), a financial situation that leads to severe difficulties in the delivery of sustainable basic services to urban residents. According to Danioue (2004),

> Lomé has been known for a long time for the absence of social spatial segregation. [Socio-economic] differentiation between neighbourhoods is difficult to establish as poverty lives next to wealth in the same neighbourhood and beside a nice villa, one can find an unfinished house or a house inhabited by low income residents. (Danioue, 2004: 8)

Accordingly, shantytown landscapes are largely absent in Lomé although, in the last decade, due to increased land speculation in the centre of the city, low-income households have tended to settle on the periphery. If social segregation is still limited in Togo, urban dwellers tend to settle according to their ethnic community

(François, 1993). While old inhabitants of Lomé have been granted property rights from the commencement of the colonial period, more recent urban migrants have decided where to settle by using ethnic and linguistic networks. A family is helped by kin to find a plot. Most recent migrants from the north of the country, for instance, occupy city space to the north of the Laguna (a principal wetlands area in the centre of the city) where land is cheapest. Voluntary neighbourhood differentiation of this sort has been accentuated in the last decade after the rise of ethno-regionalist tensions during the height of the 1990–1993 political crisis when members of the president's ethnic group were expelled from some neighbourhoods.

Lomé has a population of one million inhabitants (Danioue, 2004). There are 37 ethnic groups, speaking about 30 languages in the country (Lebikaza, 1997). These language groups may be categorised into two main families, the Gur group in the north and the Kwa group in the south (Takassi, 1983). The major ethnic groups are the Ewe (23.19 %) (a southern ethnic group), the Kabiye (13.79 %) (the president's ethnic group from the north), the Ouatchi (10.30 %), and the Tem (5.75 %) (1981 Census). Lomé, which is located on the coast, includes a population made up of 70% of the ethnic group Adja-Ewe (Danioue, 2004). As a consequence, Ewe-Mina (Mina being a form of Ewe) is 'the commercial language of South Togo' and of Lomé (Lebikaza, 1997: 157).

Libreville is the political and administrative capital of Gabon, while Port-Gentil is its economic capital (Ndong Mba, 2003). While Gabon has one of the higher per-capita incomes in Sub-Saharan Africa, income inequality is very high and finds clear expression in the structure of residential areas. Socio-economic spatial segregation is high in Libreville and, according to Bissielo (2001), 80% of Libreville's population live in under-equipped neighbourhoods, the 'matitis'. Migrants' access to the city is facilitated, as in the case of Lomé, by using ethnic and family networks (Kwezi Mikala, personal communication, 2004) so that neighbourhoods dominated by one language group still characterise the city's landscape.

Gabon has a population of 1.2 million inhabitants (Census 1993), including 200 000 foreign migrants (mostly migrants from neighbouring African countries and about 15 000 French expatriates). Its territory covers some 268 000 square kilometres (Idiata, 2002). There are 62 'linguistic entities' (parlers) in Gabon (Kwenzi Mikala, 1998), most of which include less than 10 000 members and which can be regrouped in ten bigger groups due to mutual understanding. The vast majorities of these languages belong to the Bantu linguistic family. Fang forms the largest language community and is spoken by 30% of the population. Ipunu and Inzebi are the two next largest language communities in the country (Idiata, 2002). Libreville itself has a population of 420 000 inhabitants, representing some 40% of the country's total population. In contradistinction to Lomé, there is no city vernacular language in Libreville. The Fang form the largest minority language

community (38%), and are followed by the Shira Punu (28%) and the Nzebi (12%).
It is worth noting that 24% of Libreville's population is of foreign origin, thereby
increasing the likely use of French as a vehicular language in Libreville.

4.5 Conclusion

Gabon is a richly endowed country – oil, manganese and uranium – with a tiny
population; unclear borders with Cameroon; and next to the highly unstable and
conflict-ridden Congo Brazzaville. Togo on the other hand is a small, poor country,
sharply divided on a North/South divide. McGowan (2004: 11) has argued,
recently, that the scramble for Africa during the second part of the nineteenth
century deeply influenced the nature of both Gabonese and Togolese societies.

> Gabon and Togo were both colonies of France, although for different periods of time
> – 1839 to 1960 for Gabon; 1918 to 1960 for Togo. France's African policy was to
> maintain the closest possible links with its former colonies after 1960 via cooperation
> agreements covering culture, economics, politics and military/security relationships.
> Both Togo and Gabon signed such 'accords de cooperation' with France. As a
> consequence, good relations with France remained both countries' most significant
> foreign policy relationship. This willingness to work very closely with France has
> produced real benefits for the ruling elites of both countries, but not for the people.

Both cities have experienced rapid growth over the past thirty years, in-migration
particularly from the north of Togo in the case of Lomé and migration from various
regions of Gabon and from neighbouring countries in the case of the more affluent
city of Libreville. This dimension should accordingly be added to the demographic
profiles drawn of these two cities. A summary of some of the primary features of
these profiles in tabular form brings this chapter to a close.

Table 4.1: *Demographic, ethnic and linguistic profiles of the two cities*

	Lome	Libreville
Population (census year)	1 million (2001)	420 000 (1993)
Significant ethno-linguistic groups (% in city)	Adja-Ewe (70%) Kabiye (20%)	Fang (38%) Shira Punu (28%) Nzebi (12%)
International language and (Lingua Franca)	French (Ewe)	French (French)
Recent urban in-migration (post-1995)	Significant in-migration from non-Ewe-speaking North	Significant in-migration from throughout Gabon and cross-border

PART 3: SPACE AND IDENTITY

CHAPTER 5

Space and identity
Thinking through some South African examples

Philippe Gervais-Lambony

5.1 Introduction

An identity is a social construct. It refers not to a given reality but rather to a discourse which is intended to bring order to things. It is a narrative, 'the function of which is to make normal, logical, necessary, and unavoidable the feeling of belonging to a group' (Martin, 1994: 23, author's translation). Identifying the origins of an identity discourse is not an easy task. With few exceptions, such discourses are not produced by a single actor. They occur in a diffuse manner within the society as a whole, having roots in political, religious, and scientific arenas, often in competitive mode. The role of an identity narrative is to construct a myth for individuals to accept as true, or untrue (as the case may be) – a myth, moreover, to be accepted at certain times of their lives (or of their day, depending on the time scale one refers to). This belief is a choice typically based upon interest, and, as such, the belief can be questioned at any time. Each individual moreover belongs to different identity communities and asserts his or her belonging to one or the other depending on circumstances. In addition, each such assertion not only identifies who one is but also simultaneously who one is not – an identity that one shares with some also sets one apart from others. Identity is therefore a complex concept. It refers both to the individual and to the collective. Does this in fact mean that an identity refers to an individual identification of who one is or to the feeling of belonging to a group with whom one shares this identity? Can one distinguish between the two?

Identity discourses often have a spatial dimension. If identity is a discourse which enables one to believe in an ordered world, it is an interpretation located in time and space. In other words, identity is 'a geography', an interpretation of spatial organisation. Conversely, living somewhere may contribute to the construction of an identity, and consequently we are able to conceive of 'an identity of locality'

(Levy, 1999) derived from the place of residence. In the third instance, we may even ask whether places themselves carry identities. This question raises the issue of the scale of analysis, since it seeks to explore the existence of an identity of places rather than that of individuals and of groups.

This brings us to the notion of territory (*territoire*) in French geography, a notion that I will use here.[1] The construction of territory is a form of identity construction. More specifically, it is one of the dimensions of identity narratives. Political discourse, in fact, is typically based on spatially delimited identity construction (at various spatial scales), on the construction of territories. South Africa offers an excellent case study of the construction of territorial identities both in the past (as apartheid territories) as well as in the present (as deliberate attempts to 'undo' these apartheid territorial identities). Spatial arrangements were aimed at fostering identities. Territorial identities were constructed in opposition or in reaction to such imposed territories. This country in fact is replete with spatial identity references. It is impossible to understand South Africa without resorting to this notion of territory, to the construction of territorial identities. And this in turn raises the question of whether South Africa represents a particular and unique case or, rather, a particularly clear case study of a more general phenomenon. I tend to believe the latter.

The aim of this chapter is to highlight the importance to geographical studies of the notion of identity by focusing on a few South African urban examples. The South African literature on identity studies is extensive and cannot comprehensively be surveyed here. References to studies in history (Harries, 1989 & 1994), in political studies (the ground-breaking works of Denis-Constant Martin (1998) on Cape Coloureds), in anthropology (Maré, 1992), in sociology (Bekker, 2001), and in geography (Mainet-Valleix, 2002) illustrate the range of research completed. It is apparent that the social sciences in South Africa share an interest in the notion. In fact, in a country where cultural identity appears to be the basis of much social organisation and where identities were manipulated, in the past, by a totalitarian regime (Meillassoux & Messiant, 1991), it seems normal that social science scholars persist in asserting that racial and ethnic identities were (and are) constructed rather than primordial. During apartheid, Marxist scholarship, which underlined this assertion, produced much of the best social science research on the period. This work revealed the manipulation of identities by the South African state in order to mask class cleavages and to foster cultural antagonisms that profited modern capitalism. While the thrust of this interpretation has been blunted by the demise of apartheid, its scholarly and activist value remains unblemished. A good illustration is found in work done on urban working-class unrest in the 1920s by historians who revealed that the white working class chose to defend its interest as a racial group rather than through seeking solidarity with others of their class (Bonner, 1994). Race, class, and culture are therefore the three most studied identities in South Africa. Most work singles out a specific ethnic, racial, or social group for attention. The approach in this chapter will be both more specific since attention will be given to the role space plays in identity construction, and more general since there will be no group pre-selected for analysis. Since I argue that the role of space in identity construction is essential to consider in South Africa, three dimensions of this issue will be explored here: first, an analysis of how the use of political power manipulates space to promote various identities (a South African-specific analysis); second, an analysis of how individual identities (in so far as they exist) are constituted; and third, an analysis of how places themselves acquire an identity (at a general level). The starting point of these analyses is the general hypothesis that territorial identities, beyond being simple political constructs, are the product of individual and collective processes taking place at different levels and converging to create the *essence* of a place, or of its territorial identity.

5.2 How politics uses space to create identities

The most common way in which politics uses space is found in the association attaching an identity to a spatial entity (and thereby establishing a territory). Politics proposes such attachments in order to convince individuals of their shared membership in a specific group. Society as a whole, together with those individuals, groups, and organisations that comprise it, conceptualises itself not only in spatial terms, but also in terms that reflect its interests. The spatial entities so established overlap, cut across each other, and often lead to ambivalent identities. This lies at the root of many spatial conflicts since territory is often both the basis for the construction of an identity as well as indicative of an interest. The function of political territory, according to Raffarin (1980), is control over both populations and resources (which are usually the real stakes). The main actor in this game, in its various guises, is the state, for it is the state that delineates external territorial limits and internal boundaries (such as provinces, counties, and municipalities). This, in turn, enables the state to diffuse and exercise its authority. The ideal from the state's point of view is that this imposition of territory on groups is experienced by these groups as constitutive of one of their salient collective identities. In the case of South Africa, in fact, apartheid (from 1948 to 1994) appears to have marked the society so deeply precisely because this ideology created sophisticated strategies of identity construction that were based on the belief that the manipulation of space would lead to the construction of pre-determined collective identities.

Before 1948, South Africans had experienced a classical colonial regime that distinguished human groups mainly according to racial criteria, setting apart whites and 'non-whites' and conferring privileges on the former while exploiting the latter. This was done primarily in the service of an economic system of colonial exploitation. The advent to power of the National Party in 1948, however, led to the creation of numerous territorial identities which went far beyond simple racial distinctions and employed the manipulation of space as an essential tool of control.

At the national level, apartheid imposed upon the country four 'white' provinces and ten Bantustans, which the state defined as 'ethnic' territories. The artificiality of these ethnic groups has been well argued by scholars: as colonial constructs often supported by significant missionary contributions (Harries, 1989), these ethnic groups were born, as elsewhere in Africa, during the nineteenth century and had new life injected into them by apartheid ideologists. The Bantustans became an essential tool for the apartheid regime for they rendered credible the claim that each ethnic group belonged to its own separate territory. These apartheid ethnic constructs were paralleled by racial constructs. The four 'racial' groupings that flowed from this process of construction are well known. What is of interest here is the spatial dimension of this classification: residential mixing was declared unlawful and urban municipalities were obliged to designate residential space as separate Group Areas defining where residents were required to live according to their racial classification. Simultaneously, public space was also delimited according to its separate use for members of different racial groupings. In short, spatial separation was instituted at all levels, from the Bantustan level down to the use of a beach or a post office.

Residential separation based on racial classification led to the construction of townships – areas reserved for 'non-white' urban residents. The notion of a township exemplifies the imposition at the local level of a territorial identity 'from above'. The township was invented in South Africa during the 1930s (Orlando, the first township of Johannesburg, was built in 1931–1932 according to Chipkin (1993) but only became the basic urban form of the apartheid city in the 1950s.) A township is a monotonous arrangement of small houses, lined up in straight streets, sometimes laid out in a star pattern. These vast housing schemes are surrounded by buffer zones that isolate them from neighbouring urban spaces. This residential urban strategy reflects both economic and security interests, but is first and foremost a device of identity construction. The urban form constituted by the township – associated, as it is, with European working-class suburbs (*cités ouvrières*) – may be thought of as a space of non-identity since accommodation is anonymous, landscapes are uniform and monotonous, and any indication of individuality is forbidden (as indeed were both private property and most commercial activities). The township differs fundamentally from the 'location' –

the 'non-white' residential space of the segregated city. Most locations were built at the beginning of the twentieth century and demolished in the 1950s or 1960s. They were characterised by their proximity to town centres, their significant degree of racial mixing, the possibility for 'non-whites' to be property owners, their very high levels of residential density, and their vibrant cultural life.

Two main sets of reasons explain the construction on scale of townships. In the first place, as industrialisation accelerated in the 1940s, a rapidly growing black urban population made it necessary to hasten the housing delivery process in the cities. Second, the apartheid regime needed an urban form that would facilitate control over the population while systematically imposing segregation in these cities. State security was ensured, particularly during periods of crisis, by the buffer zones which facilitated the encirclement of neighbourhoods by security forces, by the wide roads ensuring easy access by security force vehicles, and by the establishment of entry points of control that guaranteed the virtually complete isolation of the township when the need arose.

Townships were administered by central government bodies which entered into agreements with local authorities regarding service delivery and labour force matters. Accommodation was strictly on a rental base, thereby excluding blacks from property rights. Townships in this sense conformed to state ideology that defined Africans as rural dwellers and, accordingly, as temporary workers in the city. Forced population movement from location (where the Communist party had a strong presence, especially in the Witwatersrand) to township severely weakened communal structures and, more importantly, political structures. Finally, by keeping separate urban municipal and township budgets (which were financed by rents and taxes paid by residents and by municipal beer sales), the state established a financial system designed to offer cities cheap labour. By forbidding commercial activities to Africans in the townships, the system ensured a captive source of customers for shops in the white city. The township was therefore the key element in the political, social, and economic urban system of the time. But it was also a tool of identity construction: first, because it ensured the separation of racial groups as defined by the *Population Registration Act* of 1950 (which led to the creation of coloured and Indian townships as well) and second because of the laying out of ethnic neighbourhoods within township boundaries.

The township was, however, also the site of identity construction 'from below' since residents in these displaced populations recreated both territory and community in their township. Accordingly, social action in townships ended up being as strong and as dangerous for the regime as that of the former locations. In effect, the township was re-appropriated by urban residents.

Soweto is a case in point. On the morning of 16 June 1976, approximately 15 000 school students aged 10 to 20 were demonstrating against the imposition of Afrikaans as the main medium of schooling in black schools when the police opened fire. This police action changed the meaning these students had given to the protest: in a few hours, all state symbols in Soweto were attacked (buses, beer-halls, schools and, of course, security forces), thereby enabling these youths to claim control over their township space. The Soweto revolt marked the beginning of a new form of urban struggle: the systematic boycott of the apartheid city. This struggle was based on residents' resolution that the city itself, as the tool of their oppression, was to be rejected. Yet, at the same time, these 'Soweto riots' may be interpreted as a claim for recognition of the territorial identity of the township and for the right of its residents to control their own space. This explains why control over streets and other public spaces was symbolically so important, and why these actions may be viewed as a burst of joy as if to say 'this place is ours'. Violent political events in Soweto – clashes between youth and security forces, a succession of states of emergency, numerous arrests, and protests – enabled the realisation of this ultimate goal of taking control of a space and thereby transforming it into a territory, into a space with an identity. The township's identity imposed 'from above' and comprehensively rejected made way for a re-appropriated positive identity given it by its residents.[2]

Though it may appear that the apartheid regime produced identity discourses and constructed territories largely on its own, the state was rarely the only actor or the only vehicle of such discourses. Various political and economic elites revealed interest in adhering to, or promoting, apartheid social constructs. Ethnic divisions within the labour force coincided with 'white' business interests for a long time. Simultaneously, various 'resistance' identities were constructed in opposition to such identities imposed 'from above'.

I believe, accordingly, that it is not possible fully to understand South Africa without turning to such a notion of identity, for it provides an interpretation of South African spatial structure that was shaped in order to freeze imposed identities and privileged 'cultural' identification over other forms of social identification. Apartheid has gone, and yet these imposed identities appear to persist, implying that the process of imposition is more general than solely during the period of apartheid, implying in fact that apartheid may simply be a particularly salient example of a more universal process of imposition.

Since 1994, the post-apartheid government has been trying to reshape spatial organisation at various levels in order to alter former identities. At the national level, the aim is to build a new nation, a 'rainbow nation', according to Archbishop Desmond Tutu, a metaphor which points to South African society as comprising a number of communities that require mutual recognition. The metaphor of various tributaries flowing into a river is also used, where a tributary represents a community and the river the nation. (Alexander, 1998).

The new government has established new provincial and municipal boundaries. The country has been divided into nine new provinces, administratively reuniting former Bantustans and 'white provinces'. Each province has embarked on a process of identity construction at the regional level through the manufacturing of regional symbols, the adoption of 'official' languages in accordance with local linguistic groups, and the selection and development of a provincial capital city. However, new political and administrative boundaries have not modified inherited spatial organisation – they have merely redefined its limits. Can these new boundaries serve as the basis for new forms of identification? This question is beyond the scope of this chapter but is explored in other works by the author (Gervais-Lambony, 2002 & 2003). What I have said so far is aimed at showing why investigating the relationship between politics and space requires the use of the notion of identity.

The argument so far flows from a classical approach to politically shaped identities. Studying identities in a spatial context, however, also implies going beyond such an approach so as to reveal life's complexities and the unordered character of identity construction. Moreover, it is important to move beyond simple opposites: individual–collective, spatial–time-bound, past–present, social-cultural. Identity construction is a process that transcends such opposites and mixes various registers and markers. Such complexity comes to light when one investigates the identities constructed by individuals. I address this issue in the next section.

5.3 Space and individual identity

An issue related to 'individual' identities is whether such an identity can exist separately from a collective identity. One could easily side-step this question through claiming that individual identities do not exist since individual identities are always collective in nature. As an illustration, '[t]he individual is, according to sociology, a relational object' (Vuarin, 1997: 48) and always belongs accordingly to a 'social configuration' (Elias, 1939) through which the individual is intrinsically linked to others. The individual can only be defined through the collective.

It may be argued, however, that identity always involves individual choice, leaving an important role for the individual to play as actor:

> [I]n each case, the individual is, at the beginning, attached to a plurality of groups: choice is made more or less easily, riskily or painfully according to the situation within which the individual finds himself, by the events which occur successively in time; all these, however, never obstruct the possibility for some kind of choice. (Martin, 1994: 22, author's translation)

Identity is never static, never fixed. One construction might indeed be replaced by another when the individual enters another age category, another social group, or another living space, or when he or she alters his or her identity choices. Identities are therefore multiple.

To illustrate this multiplicity, the migrant labour system implemented in Johannesburg during the second half of the twentieth century exacerbated the already fragmented nature of black urban residents' identities. A domestic worker, a mine worker, or an industrial worker could very well have been an important person in her or his original rural community; in the city, however, this worker had to be anonymous, defined exclusively by her or his employment status (which was typically the single qualification legalising residence in the city). Accordingly, a married man, a father, would have been regarded in official eyes as barely adult – as a single man in the urban setting.

The questions I pose here are how an individual with an individual identity is taken up into a collective entity, and subsequently, how this transformation influences (and how is it influenced by) his or her relationship to space. In order to address these questions, one also needs to explore how individual choices lead to territorial identity construction, to the allocation of meaning to places. The account and analysis of two individuals' life journeys below reveals how complex the discussion of these questions becomes and how important it is to embark upon such a line of questioning.[3]

S is the child of a mine worker, of a migrant. His father was a Mozambican citizen who came to work on the Witwatersrand's gold mines. Upon his arrival in 1949, he was employed and given shelter by a mining company in the Benoni municipality (situated to the east of Johannesburg, in the East Rand). After having lived in a mine compound, he settled in Daveyton Township, following his marriage in 1953 to a Xhosa-speaking South African woman. S's mother was an urban dweller throughout her life, she was born in the East Rand, but her Tswana-speaking father had emigrated from Botswana to work in Johannesburg in the 1920s, and her Xhosa-speaking mother had come from the Transkei.

Let us first consider the multiplicity of S's father's identities. Being black, he had to live in a specific area and was very strictly limited in his access to the labour market. Being 'foreign', he was not subjected to a South African Bantustan authority but belonged to that extraordinary category invented by apartheid: 'native alien'. Being Shangaan, he belonged to an ethnic group originating from the north-west of South Africa and the south-east of Mozambique. Finally, as a mine worker, he belonged to a well-delimited social group in South Africa. These identities are not organised according to a hierarchical order, as the individual chooses one or the other according to circumstances, or has to refer to one or the other depending both on the place he finds himself in and the company he finds himself with.

Crucially, despite the imposition of apartheid-defined identities, this man made choices; he chose, for instance, not to marry within his ethnic group. The Witwatersrand is in fact a cosmopolitan region where ethnic mixing is common. It attracted migrants from the whole of South Africa and from the Southern African region, as well as a variety of people from different regions of Europe. What real meaning then is attached to so-called 'ethnic' identities in such a context? Public meetings that are currently taking place in the Witwatersrand are characterised by what I would like to call 'linguistic freedom': Anyone may use the language of his or her choice (which is not always mother tongue, for there are tactical considerations that rule the choice of language depending on the context).

So who is S? A Shangaan-Xhosa-Tswana? A mine worker's son? A black South African? An East Rander? The language spoken in his family is Xhosa. He lived in Daveyton,[4] in a neighbourhood reserved for Xhosa speakers and was taught in this language at school. This was a choice made by his father who gave up his Mozambican-Shangaan identity to facilitate integration.

In 1984, S's family bought a house in the Vosloorus Township,[5] part of the Boksburg Municipality, where his parents passed away and were buried. S's mother died in 1996 and his father three years later. The father left his children the following instructions: I want to be buried next to my wife in the Vosloorus cemetery and, since there is no room left in the vault, I wish to be cremated so that the urn may be placed next to my wife's coffin. Cremation is unusual in the Dutch Reformed Church, the family church, and is almost unknown in rural South African traditions. The eldest son was obliged to carry out his father's wishes against the traditions of the church, and, more importantly, the family. His late father had made a strong identity choice, privileging his identity as an urban dweller over all others since that was the identity that linked him forever to his beloved wife.

In 1984, when the family moved to Vosloorus, S was 24 and had ended his studies seven years earlier. While working as a 'tea boy' in the company club of East Rand Proprietary Mines (ERPM), he had tried to achieve his personal dream of becoming a musician and had taken music classes in Johannesburg, in a voluntary institution that was offering art training to 'non-whites'. Involved in the youth protest movement that followed the Soweto unrest in 1976, he acquired a new identity, that of a township youth militant. He signed up to the ANC youth league, became involved in the civics movement and thus became a member of the 'lost generation', youth that sacrificed both education and personal future prospects for the struggle. As a result, S experienced all the facets of life of a young political activist, including protests, strikes, clashes with security forces, clandestine activity, conflict with hostel-based Inkhatha militias, door-to-door mobilisation, and the organisation of local networks. He describes this period of his life as his 'twenty years in the wilderness'. Such a choice of words also refers to something else: the rejection of ethnic, familial, and socially ascribed identities. It led the little 'boy' of the ERPM to become the president of the civics in Vosloorus and subsequently to be elected an ANC municipal councillor in 1995, during the first free municipal elections in South Africa. He was re-elected in 2000. Now aged 42, S dreams of quitting political life and returning to music. He also dreams about how to complete his education while remaining politically active and earning a living sufficient to sustain his family (his wife and his three children). In addition, he is investigating the origins and ties of his mixed family background. But what is clear to him is the central importance of being an 'East-Rander'. He expresses this in simple terms: 'I have no other home', an expression pointing to a primary territorial identity.

Other individuals make different choices. M hails from Giyani in the former Gazankulu Bantustan. His wife still lives there with four of their eight children; the four remaining children live with him in Johannesburg in a rented room in a former white suburb in the north of Johannesburg. He 'chose' to live 'one foot inside, one foot outside' in order to sustain his household in Giyani, which he visits over two weekends each month. But this choice is as contingent as the identity that flows from it. M came to work in Johannesburg for the first time in 1981. Having obtained a driver's licence, he worked as a driver for white private companies and for foreign diplomatic missions. With this relatively good salary, he managed after seven years to save enough money to open, in 1988, a 'general store' in Giyani. His customers were mainly public servants of the ex-Bantustan of Gazankulu. The demise of the Bantustan in 1994 and a subsequent period of local settling of scores put an end to his business. In 1994, he returned to Johannesburg to take up employment once more as a driver. M has, therefore, had several successive identities: that of a rural dweller from Gazankulu, a migrant worker in Johannesburg, a small shop-owner, and a driver. But the use of the term 'successive' fails to capture the multiple nature of M's identities. He is perhaps more aptly described as the resultant sum of this past.

These two individual trajectories reveal the complexity and fluidity in time and space of identities, as well as the often strong spatial dimension of these identifications. They also show the importance of individual choices, whether they are choices taken under strict structural constraints or otherwise. The sum of these choices make up the city and, in the case of the Witwatersrand, a common denominator is prominent: The city is made up of the personal histories of those migrants who came in search of jobs and in search of freedom. These multiple choices over a long period of time have created a territorial identity for the Witwatersrand, an identity for the city itself.

5.4 A territorial identity?

For each of us, the present contains the sum of our past. Our identities, however, are not chronologically layered but rather a mixture of our memories. Such influence of the past upon a personalised present holds true for places as well. This is what Marcel Roncayolo (2002) suggests when he refers to urban places developing territorial identities over time. Is it appropriate to apply the notion of identity to places as well as to people, or is this simply a geographer's bias, a linguistic short-cut, or a literary metaphor? Julien Gracq (1990), for instance, when describing his feelings about the town of Nantes, reveals how individuals' identities converge with those of the place where they live. Though each interpretation of a city is individual, the city may be viewed as a prism through which its residents see the world and from which residents are influenced by their urban space. The fact that writers and travellers often describe the city as a living object is not simply a question of style, since the city exists through the imaginations of those who live in it. The city, therefore, has its own unique identity. Augustin Berque (1993) refers to a process of 'connivance with the place' when he argues that urban society fuses with a built environment and thereby establishes a new identity.

It appears appropriate then to accept the existence of a territorial identity. But where does one look for its roots? In the first place, the answer is in the unique relationship that links residents to their place of residence. I hypothesise in fact that this relationship is formed by the past of individuals, of society, and of space. The weight of the past is what makes the identity of a place possible.

In a global context, urban studies currently focus on the fragmentation of urban forms, on the disappearance of city-wide social life, on the end of the city. Urban South Africa experiences similar processes. In Johannesburg, for instance, the development of local and neighbourhood identities is said to be directly related to deepening social inequalities, to criminal activities, and to feelings of fear among residents. Residents are fortifying themselves either in luxurious gated communities or in deprived informal settlements. On the other hand, Johannesburg exists. More than a century of being has enabled the growth of a specific territorial identity that has survived this socio-spatial fragmentation. South Africa is a country with a haunting if largely silent past; its history is built on displaced populations, on stolen lands, on altered names, and on manipulated spaces. The past of its cities appears in the landscapes, in individual memories, and in the collective representations of its residents. This past, moreover, is compressed since the national time scale is that of a young country and time scales at city level are those of very short cycles of development.

Rusty old iron, red trams with the appearance of fire-engines, mahogany bars with
polished brass rails ; brick-built warehouses in deserted streets, where there was only
the wind to sweep away the rubbish ; rustic parish churches standing at the foot of
offices and stock-exchanges built in cathedral style; mazes of seedy buildings looming
over intersecting valleys of trenches, swing-bridges and footbridges; a town being
piled ever higher, since the vestiges of old buildings are constantly used as a basis
for the new. Such was Chicago, the very image of the Americas. No wonder the New
World cherishes in it the memory of the 1880s; the only antiquity to which it can
lay claim in its thirst for renewal is this modest gap of half a century, too short to be
a criterion for our ancient societies, but enough to give it, with its lack of temporal
perspective, some little opportunity to sentimentalize about its transient youth.
(Levi-Strauss, 1973: 96)

The history of Johannesburg (van Onselen, 1982; Chipkin, 1993) is one, even
more so than Chicago's, of the successive demolition of neighbourhoods, the
scars of which remain palpable. Johannesburg was one of the cities in the world
where growth was extremely rapid since soon after its establishment it became
an important centre of the global economy. Johannesburg is characterised
by rapid changes and by a taste for modernity: posterity appears to be of little
importance. Once gold was discovered on the Witwatersrand in 1886, a mining
compound developed, a town of tents and ox-wagons emerged, and streams of
gold prospectors arrived. Men were in the majority: Anglophone mine diggers
from the United Kingdom, Australia, and other regions of the British Empire; a
minority of Afrikaners arriving from rural areas to work in the brick or transport
companies; African mine workers from Mozambique, the Transvaal, and the
Cape, and Africans from Natal employed as domestic workers or launderers. The
discovery of gold also led to a large influx of prospectors who worked the wider
region to the east and the west of what is now Johannesburg.

The Witwatersrand (now renamed Gauteng) has retained the characteristics of
a mining town, a frenetic and violent city where one comes primarily either to
enrich oneself or to seek means to survive. There is also a deep shared sense of
nostalgia for a time when Johannesburg embodied capitalist modernity at the tip of
Africa. Johannesburg was connected from its beginnings to international finance
centres, and especially to the City of London. Though its inner-city residential
areas are today characterised by decay with entire buildings standing vacant of
residents, the city continues to convey memories of a time when it aspired to be
the New York of Africa.

Simultaneously, Johannesburg is populated by the ghosts of neighbourhoods
demolished to suit successive segregation policies. The oldest of these, The Kaffir
Location, to the west of the city centre, was razed to the ground at the beginning of

the century. It was at that time that private housing developments for 'non-white' residents emerged: Alexandra (from 1914), Sophiatown (from 1905), Martindale and Newclare (1912), while racially mixed slums were developing in the inner-city. Subsequently, residential access for 'non-whites' in Johannesburg was marked by the progressive demolition of old neighbourhoods in proximity to the city centre and the development of Soweto townships. The destruction of Sophiatown (from 1955 to 1959) was a most striking event in this history. The white neighbourhood of Triomf was subsequently built on the site. The symbolic value of Sophiatown – the nostalgia it conveys to Johannesburg residents – is both deep and enduring. This 'myth of Sophiatown' is, to my mind, an essential element of Johannesburg's identity as a place, as a territory. It is worthy of a little more exploration.

Sophiatown is the symbol of an urban culture based on racial mixing, freedom, music, and alcohol consumption in the *shebeens*, an alternative black culture captured in *Drum*, an influential black magazine of the 1950s. All the former locations of the Witwatersrand, although physically demolished today, are kept alive by the image of Sophiatown in the memories of residents. One of the most famous paintings of Gerard Sekoto, a South African black painter, depicts a street of Sophiatown. At the beginning of the 1960s, Myriam Makeba was singing 'the streets are sad and lonely, the old Sophia is gone ...'. Almost 40 years later, publications praising the inventiveness of and feelings of joy aroused by Sophiatown abound, and Triomf has been renamed Sophiatown.

Sophiatown was overcrowded, dirty, and dilapidated, and many of its activities were controlled by criminal street gangs, but it embodied 'The City', an identity subsequently forbidden to Africans in Johannesburg and in South Africa. Hence, the urban myth that echoes far beyond Johannesburg. Moreover, the nostalgia associated with Sophiatown is anything but passive, since the myth has influenced the territorial identities of other urban neighbourhoods where different communities meet and mingle. Hillbrow, for instance, the first desegregated neighbourhood in Johannesburg, was for a time 'another Sophiatown', a place of freedom, of mixing, and of intellectual vitality. Yeoville then took over and continues to a certain extent to play this role. But these spaces are fragile – diminished by crime, redlined by the banks, often deserted by prominent residents who move to another neighbourhood when decay reaches, for them, a point of no return. Sophiatown, on the other hand, is indestructible because it embodies a way of city life, a way of life constantly reasserted and reconstructed. Guillaume (2001) has argued that, though Soweto inherited over time many of the functions of Sophiatown, some of these elements may be found everywhere in the city. The reality of a neighbourhood is one thing, but the myth and nostalgia it conveys remains alive through Sophiatown memories. Such a process relates to what Berque (1993) called an 'arch-landscape' (*arché-paysage*), which plays the role both of myth and of identity narrative in the city. The process continuously identifies what the city should aspire to, and accordingly brings together urban space and those who inhabit it. It exemplifies the ways a territorial identity is constructed by uniting past memories and nostalgia with present ideals in a shared urban space.

5.5 Conclusion

Let me attempt to summarise the arguments I have made.

Identity is informed by time. 'People look back for various reasons, but shared by all is the need to acquire a sense of self and of identity. I am more than what the thin present defines' (Tuan, 1977: 186). And this applies to both individuals and places.

Identity is informed by choice. Offered a menu of identity choices, we make choices to assert ourselves as one or the other, either consciously or as a result of structural contingencies. These choices vary over time depending on circumstances, on the company we keep, and on the possibilities available.

Identity is informed by politics. Each human group is involved in power relationships, and each individual belongs to various groups. Political power proposes or imposes identity narratives which continuously influence the identities of individuals.

Does space inform identity? Yes, because time, choice, and politics are 'spatialised'. Time is inscribed into space, in the natural environment for Australian aborigines, for example, or in the built environment in the metropolis for modern urban dwellers. In the case of South Africa's former locations, it is the memory of a place that no longer exists that informs the construction of an identity. But time is also relevant on the scale of an individual's lifetime, a lifetime marked by various places of residence and by various attachments to different places. Identity choices, moreover, are informed by space – by places known or imagined, by places where one has lived, which one has visited, or even dreamt of. And, to return to the issue of power, politics in its efforts to impose identity 'from above' often manipulates space, by defining and delimiting it.

The South African urban examples I have presented support these hypotheses. I conclude therefore that research on spatial organisation cannot avoid reference to the notion of identity and, conversely, that identity studies cannot avoid the spatial dimension.

Finally, it is useful to reflect on the way individual and collective identities that meet in the same space merge with this space and produce a unique and identifiable geographical object which is the constantly changing construction of the interaction between human beings and the place where they reside.

Notes

1 I say 'in French geography' because Anglo-Saxon geography does not need such a concept. This is an interesting question that goes beyond the scope of this chapter – why the term 'territory' as it is used by French geographers cannot be translated into English, the term 'place' being a poor substitute, referring rather to 'lieu' (see Tuan, 1977). In this text, 'territory' will be used in its French meaning.

2 Soweto, however, is far from homogeneous. Its two million residents have very diverse regional origins, speak different languages, and have different standards of living. A specific Sowetan identity did emerge during the 1976 unrest, typified by a process of crystallisation of all identities during a territorial crisis. It did not last; currently, there are a number of internal local identities in Soweto and territorial conflicts occur frequently (see Guillaume, 2001).

3 Case studies in this chapter are based on field research conducted by the author during the period 2000–2003. Interviews were organised with 25 residents of the East Rand (Ekurhuleni Metropolitan Area) and Johannesburg, and were repeated every year in order to obtain 'life stories', two of which are referred to directly in this chapter. Interviewing was as informal as possible so as to establish rapport with informants.

4 Built in 1955 to relocate residents of a squatter camp and of the former Benoni location, Daveyton was described by Verwoerd as a model for the rest of South Africa, presumably because of its strict ethnic separation of residents. The case of S's father reveals the futility of such a project.

5 Political reforms in the 1980s allowed black urban residents to acquire property rights in the townships.

CHAPTER 6

Domestic workers, job access and work identities in Cape Town and Johannesburg

Claire Bénit & Marianne Morange

6.1 Introduction

Domestic work is one of the largest job sectors for low-skilled workers in South African cities. However, it is difficult to evaluate accurately how many people, mainly women and some men, are employed as domestic workers in South Africa – one estimate is that their number is close to 900 000. This figure tends to be fairly stable. In 2000, the number varied from 940 000 in February to 952 000 in September. In 2001, it was estimated to lie between 870 000 in February and 880 000 in September (Statistics South Africa, 2001; 202; 2003). Such a difference, from one year to the next, reflects difficulties of evaluation in a job sector known to be very *discreet*.

Domestic work is a hidden form of work, involving tasks that workers have to complete at their employers' homes. The hidden nature of the work makes it difficult to control, to manage and to register, which explains why South Africa lacks reliable official data on this sector. More importantly, domestic work is scattered throughout the urban space, generating diffuse mobility patterns that are hard to detect.

Under apartheid, mobility patterns were not as developed as they currently are for the following two reasons. First, the *live-in* or *sleep-in* arrangement was widespread until the midnineties (Le Roux, 1995). This arrangement declined after influx control legislation was abolished in 1986, opening the way for migrant workers' families to join them in the townships. Second, the job market is currently becoming increasingly flexible, due partly to a rising unemployment level. Rising unemployment has led to a diminishment of job security, associated with a growing demand for piece work and the scattering of job opportunities throughout the urban space. Urban migration is becoming less circular; multiple and scattered labour mobility patterns are becoming more common in a job market transformed both by de-industrialisation and the transition to post-Fordism.

In both cases, domestic workers relate to the urban space in very specific ways. Being isolated from one another, they struggle to find ways and means to integrate into the social fabric of the city and to perceive themselves as members of a clearly identified social group, with a specific identity. This might be one of the reasons why domestic workers are neglected worldwide by researchers in the social sciences, although they play a major role in the national economy of many countries (Destremau & Lautier, 2002). It also explains why research has so far focused on other aspects of domestic work: a recent issue of the French journal *Tiers Monde*, dedicated to the study of domestic workers (Destremau & Lautier, 2002), focused on the mobility of migrant domestic workers elsewhere in the world, as they move from rural to urban settings, and on their social trajectories in cities, while, in South Africa, the focus lay on their conditions of work (Cock, 1980).

The authors of this chapter have chosen to broach the subject from an urban perspective, by analysing the way in which domestic workers relate to urban space. The success of charring (Breitenbach & Peta, 2001) makes domestic work a near-perfect prototype of what has been called globalised salary employment (*salariat mondialisé*) (Destremau & Lautier, 2002), which refers to the way domestic workers deal with the flexibility of the job market and to the way that this flexibility influences the way they relate to urban space. This concept, therefore, reflects the impact, on an urban scale, of what Bourdieu has called site effects (*les effets de lieux*) (Bourdieu, 1993) on the rapidly transforming conditions of work and on increasing access to work opportunities, as well as on the new nature of urban mobility.

However, increasing enforcement of legislation relating to domestic workers' conditions of work and wage levels, in contrast to mere flexibility of work, can play a key role in encouraging the formation of a new social identity for domestic workers. This may especially be so if they find themselves capable of joining trade unions and of working in a more formalised environment.

To explore these concerns, the authors base their study on a series of 33 interviews, held with domestic workers in different areas of Cape Town and Johannesburg.[1]

6.2 From paternalism to flexibility: The influence of post-apartheid transformation on the domestic work environment

Relationships between employers and domestic workers are still based on archaic paternalistic practices that are a direct continuation of the *live-in* system established during the apartheid era (Friguglietti, 1989). The system aimed to bridge the divide between black and white areas, so that the demand for full-time domestic workers in the white residential areas could be satisfied. In the 1960s, the employer was considered as 'an urban father who makes sure of feeding his children before catering for the other children in the rural areas'.[2] The metaphor reveals the importance of influx control and of the exclusion of black people from urban areas, while it also confirms that paternalistic patterns of relationship in the social field were particularly well developed and rooted in the domestic arena.

Employers' paternalism: A traditional, arbitrary, and alienating form of regulation

The ongoing tendency for employers to provide accommodation for domestic workers means that domestic workers are still entitled to a certain number of benefits, just as they are compelled, in turn, to abide by certain rules and fulfil certain duties. Rights and duties are often implied, and can be confused in a system based on personalised relationships, clientelism, and favouritism. Employers decide arbitrarily whether to pay transport fees for their domestic workers' annual Christmas visit to the workers' families, who may live in remote rural areas; whether to pay for medication, whether to pay for accommodation, if the workers do not live on the premises of their employers, and whether to provide their workers with any other kind of help, such as financial assistance with the tuition fees of the workers' children. The majority of domestic workers are, in fact, indebted to their employers, which makes the workers even more dependent on them (*Cape Times*, 2002b). Sometimes a woman passes on a domestic worker to her daughter.

Live-in domestic workers can, therefore, be considered to be held captive, both by their jobs and their employers. They have difficulty in accessing other job opportunities and neighbourhoods for a variety of reasons. First, they find themselves isolated and confined to their employers' backyards (Lessie, one of the domestic workers we interviewed, complains: 'We just have to be there, by the back door. I see myself as a little mouse, quiet and lonely at the back of the yard.') and separated from their families. They have to recreate a social network in order to gain a sense of solidarity and support in the immediate neighbourhood, such as in the housing block or street in which they live. Such links are often reinforced by means of participation in communal religious practices, such as attending church (the Sunday service may provide the only opportunity for socialising and be regarded as a valued occasion to escape from their employers' backyards). Such expressions of solidarity are extremely valuable in dispelling the feeling of isolation experienced by domestic workers. However, they also help to reinforce a sense of spatial captivity. Domestic workers are often informed of other job opportunities by means of verbal interchanges with other domestic workers in the areas in which they work, so that, despite the contact, they are still, in fact, confined to a very narrow local job market. Deprived of everyday township socialising, they have little hope of entering another spatial network.

Second, employers usually tend to employ *live-in* domestic workers, who they expect to be available most of the time. Working under such conditions, domestic workers have little personal time in which to look for another job.

Third, domestic workers depend on their employers for their accommodation, and have to secure another place in which to live before being able to quit their current employment. Free accommodation may at first look like a valuable option in terms of saving both time and money, but it costs a great deal in terms of spatial and social mobility, as well as in terms of psychological and emotional security.

YVONNE
A product of 15 years of paternalistic behaviour, spatial captivity and social stagnation

Yvonne was born in Durban, where she started making a living from doing piece jobs, before she found a permanent position as a cashier in a supermarket. When she lost her job following a conflict with the manager, she decided to become a domestic worker. She secured a position through her mother-in-law, who was herself a domestic worker. Since then, Yvonne has been working for the same family for 15 years.

Over the years, Yvonne followed her employer from Pietermaritzburg to Johannesburg, and then to Cape Town, where she arrived in 2001. She was separated from her son during most of this time, as he stayed in Durban with her sister. When he turned 11, she brought him to join her in Cape Town. Yvonne lives in a cottage in Kenilworth and is satisfied with her free accommodation: 'I have no one to feed and my salary is so little' (R800 a month). She works from Monday to Friday from 6.30 a.m. to 7 p.m., and she also sometimes works extra hours on a Saturday or Sunday, for no additional pay. Her employer pays for her bus fares to and from church on Sundays. However, she usually walks everywhere else, including to the local shopping centre.

Yvonne lacks the time to look for another job and is reluctant to do so, because she considers herself too old to be able to secure other work, although she is only 46 years old. She has tried unsuccessfully to find additional charring to do on Sundays. Employers do not usually want occasional domestic workers to work over weekends, because the employers are often then away from home, she says. With no job contract, no other job possibility, and very limited mobility, Yvonne is unable to negotiate a raise, and has only received a salary increase of R200 over the past 15 years. She is unable to save money, she is not registered with the unemployment insurance fund, she is neither a member of a medical aid scheme nor a pension fund, and she depends on her employer's goodwill to pay for her medication when she falls ill. Like many other domestic workers, she repays a substantial amount of her salary (R300 a month) on her television set.

Towards a greater flexibility: Freedom or precariousness?

The live-in system is currently declining as it becomes more and more contested by domestic workers who consider it to be a 'modern form of slavery' (Destremau & Lautier, 2002: 258), and who see the stability it offers as coming at too great a cost. The demise of the apartheid regime, the advent of freedom of movement, and the reuniting of families who had been forcibly split up led to the development of charring, which allowed workers to free themselves to a certain extent from the effects of paternalistic alienation. However, charring is a precarious form of work.

JESSICA
The flexibility of work – the price of a relative freedom
Jessica has been working as a domestic worker for 30 years. At the moment, she is working in five different places: in Kuils River on Mondays, in Brackenfell two Tuesdays a month, in Pinelands on Wednesdays, and in Montevista on Thursdays for one employer and every second Friday for another. She opted to work in different places after she lost her full-time job, when her previous employer passed away, leaving her overnight without a source of income. She feels more secure not having to depend on only one employer. Having several different employers also reduces the risk of workplace tension and enables her to avoid developing close relationships with children other than her own. She does not want to be dragged into a situation where patronising employers would expect her to be devoted to their children and work after hours, whenever the children would need her.

She would rather char on the other side of the city from where she lives than turn down a job, even if she has to take seven different kinds of transport to her different jobs. She is too afraid to be tempted to go back to a full-time job, which she sees as a form of slavery. Although it takes her a long time to commute, she finds that she is more capable of organising her own schedule so as to take care of her own children.

Though Jessica asserts that charring has a positive impact on her family life, she also complains that 'charring is not a real job'. She claims that she is tired of having to spend such a long time on trains and buses: all her workplaces are far away from Guguletu, to where she and the rest of her family were forced to move in the 1960s.

However, live-in domestic work still has an important role to play in providing those migrating from rural areas with employment and in integrating them into the urban economy. Domestic work requires no more than a minimal education, and employers of domestic workers often provide accommodation for their workers. Newcomers with scant knowledge of the urban environment are often eager to save money on accommodation and transport, as they often wish to send at least part of their earnings back to their families on their rural holdings.[3] Of the 11 women interviewed in Cape Town, nine were migrants from rural areas, small Eastern Cape towns or the former Transkei.[4] All had at one stage been (or are still being) accommodated by their employers.

Circular migration and family division, entrenched by the apartheid system, are still in existence today, creating tensions between *newcomers* and long-standing *urban-dwellers*, who call themselves the *Cape-borners*, meaning people who arrived a long time ago, or who were born in Cape Town. The *Cape-borners* complain of the unfair competition that newcomers provide in the job market. Isolated in their backyards and stuck in a precarious situation, newcomers are more flexible and their lack of resistance and of protest make them open to exploitation by their employers. Such exploitation contributes to further destabilisation of a job market that longstanding urban-dwelling domestic workers, especially unionised women, try to change and make more bearable. When they want to do several different part-time or charring jobs in order to become more independent and to earn better pay, *Cape-borners* have, to their disadvantage, to compete with women coming from rural areas. The newcomers are prepared to work for minimal wages if they receive free accommodation, and have usually not yet come to realise the advantages offered by the flexibility of charring in comparison to what they see as more stable positions.

MARY
A domestic worker who is aware of being exploited

Forty-three-year-old Mary lives in a shack in Kliptown (Soweto) and has always worked as a domestic worker. She secured her first job by canvassing door-to-door for work in the neighbouring township of Eldorado Park. After 14 years of working for them, Mary claims that her employers, a couple of coloured teachers, fired her overnight, without any explanation of why they were doing so.

After remaining unemployed for two years, she found another job as a domestic worker in Eldorado Park, thanks to a friend. However, she quit this job after five years because her wages were too low (R300 a month for full-time work). At the time, she also helped to launch a domestic workers' trade union in Kliptown. However, the union did not last long. Currently, she has two part-time jobs in Eldorado Park, which she once again found by going door-to-door throughout the neighbourhood. She currently earns R530 a month for five days' work, and is unhappy with her working conditions but cannot afford to quit at the moment. When asked about the new minimum-wage legislation, she replied that she was concerned about domestic workers losing their jobs if they insisted on being paid at least the minimum wage. Mary no longer expects any improvement in her situation, in spite of her strong personality that led her to take initiatives to find a job, to protest when working conditions were exploitative, and to start becoming politically involved. Her economic context prevents her from being more successful: The difficulty in finding a sufficiently well-paid job, or in finding enough part-time jobs to secure a decent income, shows how precarious domestic work can be as a source of income, rather than how flexible it is.

The growth of domestic work: A consequence of rising unemployment
In the urban environment, which is currently characterised by decreasing opportunities for formal employment, domestic work provides employment opportunities for low-skilled black jobseekers. Domestic work has come to offer more job opportunities than industrial work in many low-income areas of Johannesburg (Bénit, 2001). Indeed, many life trajectories reflect the shift from industrial to domestic work.

DORIS
Victim of de-industrialisation and spatial distance
Forty-two-year-old Doris has been working as a domestic worker for only two years. She was born in Kliptown (Soweto), where she still lives. Her father was an industrial worker and her mother a domestic worker. In 1991, she found a job, which paid R100 a month, in a clothing factory in Fordsburg in the Johannesburg inner city. However, when the factory closed down two years later, she lost her job. She found another job, which paid R150 a month, in a second-hand clothing factory, from which she was later also retrenched.
After remaining unemployed for two years, she was hired by a drycleaner in

the inner city. When she started work, she tried unsuccessfully to negotiate her schedule, so that she could leave work before six p.m. in order to avoid taking the train at night, as she regarded doing so as 'too dangerous'. After she was mugged while disembarking from the train in Soweto one night, she resigned from her job.

Another period of unemployment followed, until she found a job as a domestic worker in Pimville (Soweto), with her children's schoolteacher. She is currently working full time for R300 a month, on which she has to support both herself and her husband, who is an unemployed factory worker, as well as their six children and four grandchildren.

Informal trade as a means of coping with de-industrialisation and growing unemployment worldwide is only an inadequate and temporary solution. Many informal traders categorise themselves as unemployed jobseekers, as they are involved in an ongoing search for domestic positions.

HELEN
Domestic worker and landlady

Forty-year-old Helen was born in KwaNdebele and moved to Johannesburg, where she found a job as a hardware factory worker in Strijdom Park, north of Johannesburg. She lost her job after two years, and stayed unemployed for two years ('That time was bad time'). She survived by selling fruit and vegetables in Diepsloot, an informal neighbourhood in northern Johannesburg, where she was given a plot on which to live. She made about R900 a month at the time.

For five years now, she has been working as a domestic worker in three different part-time jobs in the northern suburbs. She found these jobs thanks to her neighbours in Diepsloot. Currently, she earns R1 200 a month. Moreover, she leases five shacks on her plot, for which she charges the average rent of R90 a month per shack. Her overall monthly income, therefore, amounts to R1 600. However, she claims that she is very unhappy, as her elder son is in prison after having been involved in a hijacking, and her second son has since become a drug addict.

Though Doris's and Helen's trajectories represent the most common, becoming a domestic worker is not necessarily considered to be a social or economic decline. Domestic work is even sometimes described as less tiring and better paid than industrial work. Rebecca, for instance, who was born in the Transkei in the 1940s, refused to take the conventional route of seeking employment in Johannesburg: 'Gold mines had a very bad reputation, and I did not want to go to

Johannesburg, when I left the Transkei to go to Cape Town.' Janie also decided to take up employment as a domestic worker, in preference to becoming an industrial worker.

JANIE
The flexibility of charring in comparison with the rigidity of a more conventional factory job

Janie worked for a long time in factories before she chose to become a domestic worker. She found that factory work was too hard and incompatible with her family life: 'I used to work in a printing works, then I worked in soldering, then in a sweet factory, but it was too hard. My children were still young and I had to start working at five a.m. It was too difficult, too early: you cannot do that if you have young children, especially babies.'

Janie left the factory to work for herself, charring in Rondebosch, Observatory, Claremont, and Mowbray. She is satisfied with the work that she currently does, as it gives her time to take proper care of her children, as well as to look after her husband, who is severely ill. When it takes the form of charring, domestic work may be defined as provision of services in a free market by a person who works for himself or herself.[5]

6.3 Place matters: Spatial segmentation in the domestic labour market

The working conditions of domestic workers are so diverse that it is hard to define the meaning of the category *domestic worker*. The authors of this study have so far explained this diversity in terms of differences in personality patterns, in terms of residential history (migrant or non-migrant), and in terms of professional and family history (domestic work after the loss of an industrial job or in line with the type of work held by the mothers of domestic workers). However, another, more unexpected, reason for these differences should be stressed: site effects (Bourdieu, 1993).

Site effects can be defined as the impact that space and place of residence have on the individual's integration into the job market, in two ways. First, living at a distance from wealthier neighbourhoods, which contain residences of potential employers, increases the risk of unemployment. Domestic workers undergo more frequent and longer periods of unemployment when they live in Kliptown (on the southern periphery of Soweto) or in Diepsloot (on the remote northern periphery of Johannesburg), than they do when living in Alexandra or Zevenfontein, which are much closer to suburban malls and middle- to high-income residential areas.

Figure 6.1: *Domestic work in Johannesburg: A segmented labour market*

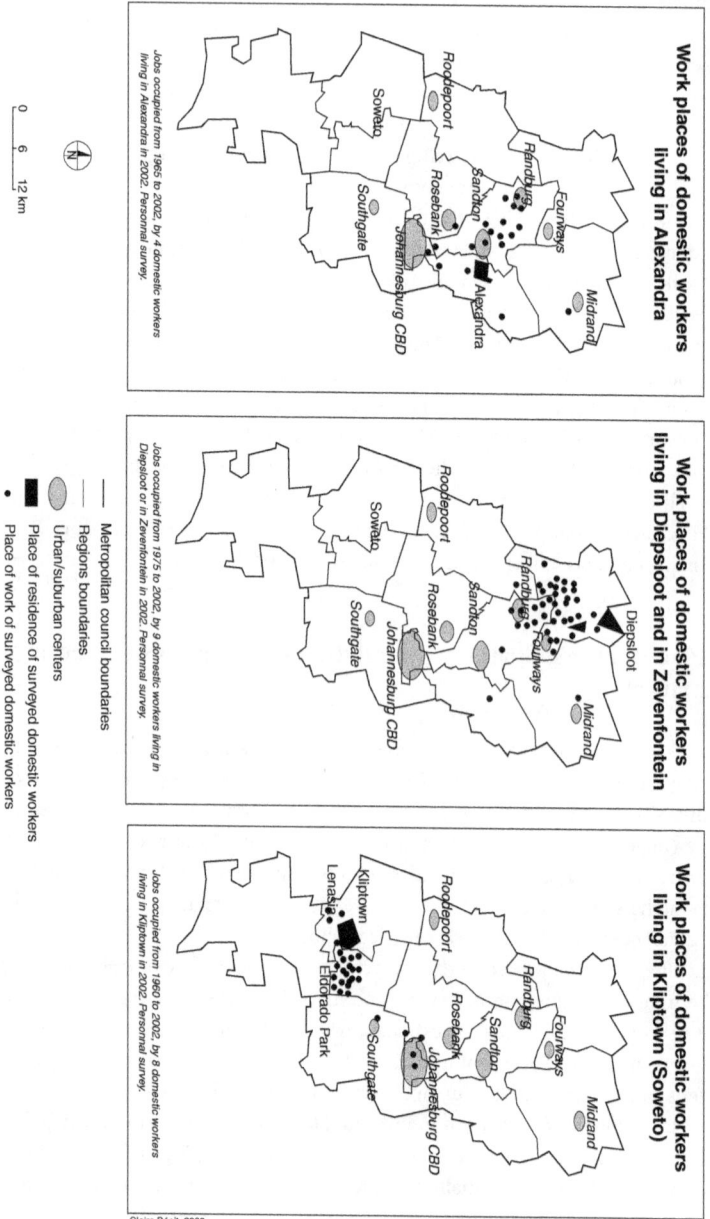

Work places of domestic workers living in Alexandra

Roodepoort
Soweto
Randburg
Sandton
Fourways
Rosebank
Southgate
Johannesburg CBD
Alexandra
Midrand

Jobs occupied from 1965 to 2002, by 4 domestic workers living in Alexandra in 2002. Personnal survey.

Work places of domestic workers living in Diepsloot and in Zevenfontein

Roodepoort
Soweto
Randburg
Sandton
Fourways
Rosebank
Southgate
Johannesburg CBD
Diepsloot
Midrand

Jobs occupied from 1975 to 2002, by 9 domestic workers living in Diepsloot or in Zevenfontein in 2002. Personnal survey.

Work places of domestic workers living in Kliptown (Soweto)

Roodepoort
Kliptown
Lenasia
Eldorado Park
Southgate
Randburg
Sandton
Fourways
Rosebank
Johannesburg CBD
Midrand

Jobs occupied from 1960 to 2002, by 8 domestic workers living in Kliptown in 2002. Personnal survey.

— Metropolitan council boundaries
— Regions boundaries
⬭ Urban/suburban centers
● Place of residence of surveyed domestic workers
• Place of work of surveyed domestic workers

0   6   12 km

Claire Bénit, 2003.

Figure 6.2: *Spatial mobilities of domestic workers in Cape Town*

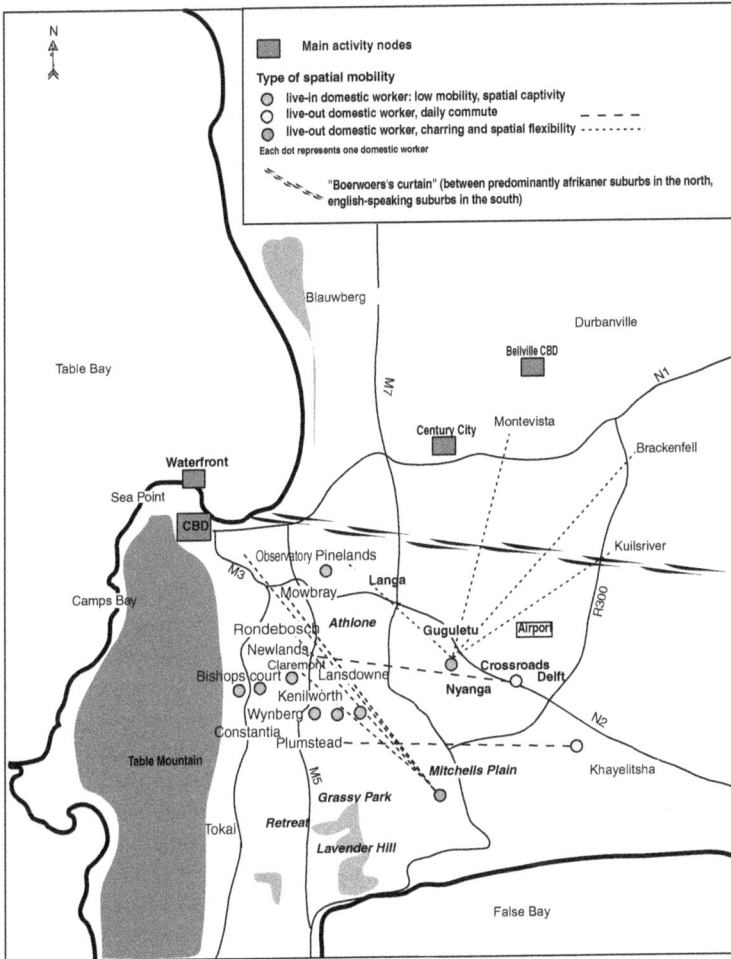

Marianne Morange, 2003

Second, an awareness of whether the place of residence is central or peripheral[6] is crucial to understanding the diversity of available jobs, and the spatial extent of the labour market for each individual. As can be seen from the maps of Johannesburg, Kliptown residents work almost exclusively in the neighbouring townships of Eldorado Park and Lenasia; Zevenfontein and Diepsloot residents tend to work only in the adjoining northern suburbs. On the contrary, Alexandra residents can choose from a far more diverse and widespread range of job opportunities.

Their place of residence plays a major role in the ability of individuals to find a job, to access transportation, and to negotiate wages and working conditions. Indeed, domestic work, as an essentially spatially scattered and relatively invisible form of employment, relies, more than other forms of employment, on spatial proximity and the existence of social networks.

Transport, an important limitation to job accessibility

Distance is a primary constraint to access to jobs, in terms of both time and cost. This is obvious in Doris's case, as she has given up a formal job in the inner city for domestic work in Soweto, due to the distances that she would otherwise have had to travel and the insecurity that she would have experienced in having to use public transport. Therefore, distance adds to the perception of a *ghetto effect*, and further confines residents to a particular neighbourhood.

One might argue that distance is one of the reasons why *live-in* arrangements remain important for domestic workers, although such arrangements can be considered as an anachronism in the current job market. Domestic workers usually prefer not to be separated from their families than to live in relative isolation in their employers' backyards. However, the latter option allows them to save on transport costs and to accept jobs that may be spatially far apart from their families. *Living in* is sometimes the only means of securing accommodation in a city, especially for recently arrived migrants. As in the case of Doris in Johannesburg, Mary in Cape Town turned down a job opportunity in Sea Point because accepting the job would have meant that she would have had to travel too far to get to work. After having remained unemployed for a long period of time, she felt obliged to accept a position in Claremont, though the job required almost as much travel as the one in Sea Point. However, the Claremont position at least offered free accommodation.

The cost of transport forms a major part of the monthly expenses of workers who do not live in. One must also take into account such indirect costs as time consumption, which has a direct impact on the quality of life, especially as far as the care and education of children is concerned. By way of illustration, Cecilia earns R950 a month, which she spends in the following way:

Table 6.1: *Cecilia's monthly expenditure*

Item of expenditure	Cost in rands
Train	88
School transport for her daughter	233
School fees for her daughter	120
Accommodation	452
Electricity	100
Water*	182
Total	993

Source: Cape Times, 19 August 2002

* The amount that Cecilia spends on water is a theoretical amount, as effectively she does not pay her water bills. Her non-payment of her water account seems to confirm that the so-called 'boycott' of urban services is at least partly due to poverty (Morange, 2006).

Inadequate transportation systems increase the time spent on travelling to work. In Johannesburg, physical access to domestic jobs – especially in the residential suburban areas – requires that workers use minibus taxis more than any other mode of transportation. Therefore, in this regard, the place of residence matters a great deal. Alexandra township, which is central to the Johannesburg urban-growth corridor, is well connected to the rest of the city by virtue of its being on the routes of three different taxi associations.[7] This explains the wider spatial scale and the greater diversity of Alexandra residents' job locations. Diepsloot and, *a fortiori*, Zevenfontein (a so-called *temporary* informal settlement) are less well supplied with taxi services, but are close to the residential suburbs where workers can find employment. Kliptown, which is linked to the inner city by train (as a leftover from Fordist apartheid times, when Soweto's residents were largely workers in the industrial parts of the city centre) has become much more peripheral to the new low-skilled job market: Kliptown domestic workers seldom find a job in the northern suburbs.

The time spent on commuting increases with the number of taxis that domestic workers have to use in order to reach their workplaces: many of them use three different taxis, which is extremely costly, both financially (there is no general taxi *pass,* since no agreement is in place between the various taxi associations) and time-wise (the waiting time for a taxi can be more than one hour). Domestic workers also have to walk long distances from taxi stops to the suburban houses where they work. Public transportation cannot fully accommodate the spatial scattering of jobs: most domestic workers have to walk about 30 minutes each way to and from work (accounting for one hour a day spent just on walking). The walking time is currently rising, because of the increasing number of road closures in Johannesburg, and workers have to take long detours, as well as cope with changes in taxi routes. Martha, who lives in Zevenfontein and works in the northern suburbs, now has a 30-minute walk each day, instead of a five-minute walk, as she had previously, due to the development of gated communities.[8]

In Cape Town, domestic workers often have to use three different kinds of transport network to get to work: trains, buses, and taxis. In addition, they often have to combine the use of these networks with long walks. However, they still do not have to cope with as many difficulties as do domestic workers in Johannesburg, for three reasons: the public transportation network is more developed in Cape Town, especially in the *white northern and southern suburbs*; the metropolitan area is not as widespread as it is in Johannesburg, so that the distance to work is usually shorter; and access to public spaces is not widely impeded by private closure of roads and entire areas. However, domestic workers in both cities have, in certain respects, to cope with the same kinds of difficulty: long, time-consuming queues at bus and taxi stations, an irregular train service (few trains run outside peak hours), and numerous changes of trains that they have to make due to having to pass through the city centre or a secondary station, in order to commute from the townships where they live to the residential areas where they work. Rebecca, like many others, has to live such a nightmare each day.

REBECCA
Transport – fast, secure, or cheap? A hard-to-make choice

Rebecca works five days a week in Plumstead. She stays in Khayelitsha (Site C). To go to work, she can choose from one of three different options.

Her first option involves her walking in the morning to the nearest railway station, which is only a five-minute walk from her house. A train journey to town would take her approximately 35 minutes. She would have to change trains at the central Cape Town station and board a second train for Plumstead, where she would arrive approximately 20 minutes later. From Plumstead station, she would need to walk to work, which would take her approximately another 15 minutes. As the train service is unreliable, according to her own experience, her first option would take her more or less one hour to complete, and would cost her R88 a month.

Her second option involves her taking a taxi in the morning (for R6) to Wynberg station. The taxi ride would take her 40 minutes to complete. The taxi does not leave as early as the train, so if she were to choose this option, she could sleep later. However, she would have to walk for longer in order to reach the taxi rank, as it is further away than the Khayelitsha train station. Otherwise, she could take another taxi for another R3. From Wynberg station, she would then have to take another taxi (costing her R6) that would get her to Plumstead in approximately 20 minutes. When taken altogether, Rebecca's second option would cost her between R12 and R15 one way (depending on whether she were first to take a taxi or walk, taking into account that if she does not take a taxi she is likely to be late for work). If Rebecca were to make use of taxis every day that she goes to work, she would spend R120 to R150 a month, which amounts to 10% of her current monthly income.

Rebecca's third option involves her taking a bus to Wynberg station, which would take her approximately one hour. She could then take a second bus, by which means she would reach Plumstead in about 15 minutes' time. However, the bus service is infrequent and unreliable, as it is affected by the amount of traffic on the roads. Moreover, if she were to make regular use of buses, it would cost her R175 a month, since she would have to buy two different *clip cards* (monthly tickets) for the journey. Although the municipality is responsible for the bus service, the bus fares are not standardised. Each bus network determines its own fares, so that there is no general metropolitan pass that might otherwise help to reduce the cost of commuting by bus. The fragmented pricing system is the result of the outmoded urban migration pattern between townships and factories in an industrial city where workers had only, in the past, to use one train or one bus to get to work.

Upon consideration of her three different options, Rebecca has decided to take a taxi to work in the morning and a train home. The result is that she has to pay more in order to ensure that she is on time in the mornings, but is able to cut her costs to a certain extent by returning home by train in the evenings, when she has more time for the journey. Nevertheless, she still finds it necessary to buy a monthly *clip card*, which she only uses 50 per cent of the time.

Finding a job: Spatial proximity or social networks?
Nonetheless, the authors' findings show that concentration of jobs around the place of residence has more to do with the way in which domestic workers actually look for, and eventually find, employment, than with the inadequate transportation networks.

Melanie Jacquemin, in her paper on domestic work in Abidjan (Jacquemin,

2002), stresses that 'the most common way of finding a domestic job is through one's social network' (2002), consisting of family, ethnic or regional kin, friends, and neighbours. She compares this model to that of using a more formal and collective labour organisation – the labour bureaus (both formal and informal), currently developing in Abidjan. As such labour bureaus are not commonly found in Johannesburg and Cape Town, the authors will further analyse domestic workers' access to job opportunities in terms of the so-called spatial proximity hypothesis. According to this hypothesis, domestic workers find their jobs through direct, physical contact with their future employers. In highly segregated cities, such as Johannesburg or Cape Town, and in cities lacking employment nodes, such direct contact seldom occurs. It requires that workers have the opportunity to leave their *ghettos* in order to visit the shops, to attend schools, or to work at their first job. Direct contact with prospective employers can also occur when jobseekers canvass door to door for work in residential suburbs, or when they visit suburban malls. However, approaching prospective employers in this way is an extreme measure, and occurs, most of the time, in neighbourhoods where the jobseeker already has a practical knowledge.

According to the social network hypothesis, domestic workers find their jobs through their networks, whether they are personal (involving friends, other family members, neighbours, or even former employers, who liaise on behalf of the workers with prospective employers), or through impersonal means (such as through placing or answering advertisements in the media, or through labour bureaus).

In both Johannesburg and Cape Town, domestic workers reported that they found employment more easily through their social networks than they did through making use of spatial proximity to prospective employers (see tables 6.2 and 6.3). In more than half the cases that the authors investigated, domestic workers found a job by using their personal networks (other family members and friends). In the other cases, job access relied heavily on former participation in the job market: in many cases (20% in Johannesburg and 24% in Cape Town), the employers found new work for their employees. Utilisation of past participation in the job market appears to be important and largely underestimated, since door-to-door canvassing for work often occurs in the vicinity of the current employer's residence. The securing of new work tends to depend more on the knowledge of potential employers than on their actual physical accessibility.

In Johannesburg, door-to-door canvassing and direct encounters with prospective employers represent an important way of finding a job for domestic workers, comprising approximately 25 per cent of the cases that the authors investigated. Use of such a *modus operandi* can be explained in terms of the less spatially segregated structure existing at metropolitan level, which allows for direct contact between potential employers and jobseekers. However, this important means of finding work is highly compromised by current urban development in Johannesburg, which is characterised by gated communities and road closures.

Table 6.2: *Finding a job in Johannesburg*

Means of finding a job	Number of cases	Percentage
By means of spatial proximity	16	24
Direct contact	7	10
Door-to-door canvassing	9	13
By means of social networking	51	76
Family members and friends	34	51
Employers	13	19
Labour bureaus	2	3
Advertisements in newspapers	2	3
Total	67	100

Table 6.3: *Finding a job in Cape Town*

Means of finding a job	Number of cases	Percentage
By means of spatial proximity	3	8
Direct contact	1	3
Door-to-door canvassing	2	5
By means of social networking	35	92
Family members and friends	20	53
Employers	9	24
Labour bureaus	1	3
Advertisements in newspapers	5	13
Total	38	100

Sources: Bénit and Morange, Personal surveys, August 2002

Note: The people whom the authors interviewed reviewed their entire working histories and related how they found each job in turn.

If social networks are more important for finding a job than spatial criteria, one could expect live-in domestic workers to be freed of the *ghetto effect*, of feeling trapped in their employers' place of residence. However, social networks themselves have a very strong territorial basis: they are spatially segmented, as can be seen from the details depicted on the maps included in this chapter. Personal networks of family and friends have a very narrow spatial scope, though they play an important role in accessing housing, as well as work, in local townships and informal settlements.

Even employers' recommendations within their own networks of neighbours, family members, and friends are often surprisingly spatially confined in quite narrow spaces. The spatial segmentation of urban networks and practices, not only at the lower but also at the upper urban social extremes, may be explained by the excessive social and ethnic specialisation of urban space inherited from the system of apartheid, even if it is undergoing some change in the current post-apartheid era. In Johannesburg, Sandton's residents have traditionally been wealthier and predominantly Anglophone, while the residents of Randburg have tended to be more middle income and Afrikaans speaking. The middle-income residents of Eldorado Park (a former coloured township) and Lenasia (a former Indian township) still appear predominantly ethnically segregated. A similar ethos of segregation can be found in Cape Town, with Anglophone middle-to-upper-income neighbourhoods prevailing in the southern suburbs, and Afrikaans-speaking middle-income neighbourhoods predominating in the northern suburbs, behind what is sometimes nicknamed the 'boerewors curtain'. This spatial segmentation is relevant to both personal and impersonal networks, of which the latter consist of job agencies, newspaper advertising,[9] and churches,[10] which, most of the time, have a very local scope.

Finding a job as a domestic worker ultimately depends on many different factors. While the jobseeker's personality obviously plays a role (Amelia and Sina reflect their personal abilities in the way in which they found their jobs – by showing that they are clever, mobile, creative, determined, cheerful, and extrovert),[11] knowledge of urban space is crucial to successful job hunting. A prolonged presence in an urban environment and possession of a good education are key elements to building what Jacques Lévy (1994) has called *spatial capital*, borrowing from Bourdieu (1993). When this spatial capital is lacking, as in cases of recent migration to the city, use of regional or family networking is the only means of accessing the job market, while those jobseekers who have been living in the city for a long time can use a variety of means to find work. Amelia, who has spent the last 15 years in Johannesburg, knew immediately in which newspaper to publish her job advertisement; her understanding of the local job market and of available training opportunities and costs is quite accurate. Johanna, born in Alexandra (Johannesburg), was also able to use a whole range of means (advertising, social networking, door-to-door canvassing, and church contacts) to find her various jobs. She also benefited from being able to use her training as a nurse to offer a specialised service (medical assistance) to her future employer in order to secure a higher wage (R1 440 a month). Being able to find a job easily, she has also always been able to quit when she found working conditions to be unsatisfactory (such as in the case of overly fussy employers, racist behaviour, or low wages).

However, knowledge of the urban environment is not enough in itself to secure employment, but has to be combined with a certain level of literacy and education. Mary, who has been living in Kliptown (Johannesburg) for 22 years, but who is illiterate and speaks little English, is not as confident as the other Johannesburg-based women whom the authors have already discussed. Thanks to her outgoing personality and knowledge of the city, she can complement her social network with door-to-door canvassing, but her canvassing remains limited to the neighbouring suburb of Eldorado Park where her employer imposes harsh working conditions on her – a very low wage of R300 a month for a seven-hour working day six days a week.

Segmented labour markets: Varying working conditions in the workplace

The spatial proximity and social network hypotheses combine to form the concept of a spatially segmented job market for domestic workers in metropolitan areas. Not surprisingly, working conditions differ greatly due to job location, as can be seen in figure 6.3. Domestic workers' wages in northern Johannesburg can amount to three times the wages of domestic workers in the southern part of the city. This difference can be explained by the difference in the income of employers, who, in the northern suburbs, tend to be largely in the high-income group and, in the southern suburbs, middle income. However, the difference in wages is also due to the varying ability of domestic workers to negotiate their working conditions in the local job markets, which the workers experience as differing widely – as being flexible in Randburg, secure in Sandton, and captive in Soweto–Lenasia.

The most extreme contrast in employment patterns lies between northern and southern Johannesburg. Working in the southern part of Johannesburg generally means having a single low-paid, full-time job. Daily wages are, on average, four times lower than those generally paid in Randburg and Sandton, as can be seen in figure 6.4. The lower wages reflect the lower income of employers living in Eldorado Park or Lenasia, who largely belong to the Indian or coloured middle-income group. However, lower wages also reflect the very tense interracial relationships that prevail in the area and that are much more tense than the relationships experienced between black domestic workers and white employers in the northern suburbs. Many domestic workers actually complain about being despised and ill-treated, or even of being treated as slaves, by their employers.[12]

In contrast, as can be seen in figure 6.5, Randburg has a larger number of employers (per domestic worker), resulting in higher autonomy for domestic workers and the beginning of professionalisation (Destremau & Lautier, 2002).

Figure 6.3: *Domestic workers' average monthly wages, depending on workplace*

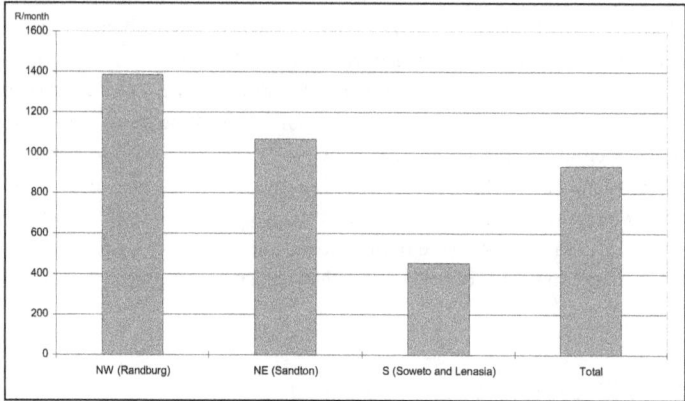

Source: Claire Bénit, Personal survey, Johannesburg, August 2002

Figure 6.4: *The average daily wage of domestic workers in Johannesburg*

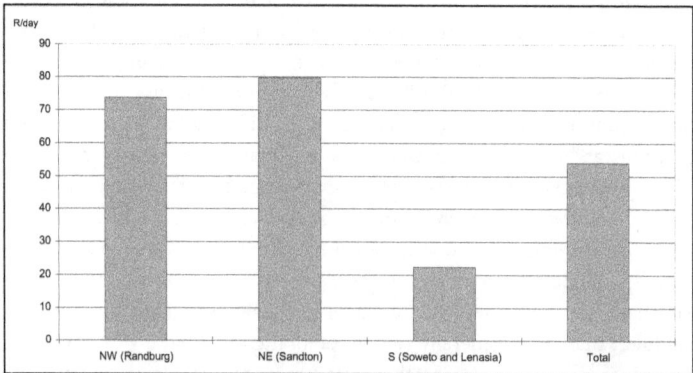

Source: Claire Bénit, Personal survey, Johannesburg, August 2002

Average total wages are higher, giving greater bargaining power to domestic workers, as it is easier for them to quit one of their part-time jobs if they have several others. The network of potential future employers is also larger. Amelia, who has two part-time jobs in Randburg, says: 'My mother was a domestic worker in the old days, in Kimberley. She wasn't free. I am free.'

Figure 6.5: *The average number of employers per domestic worker in Johannesburg*

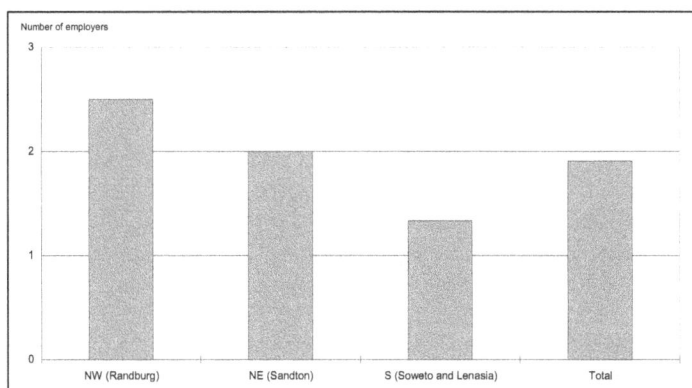

Source: Claire Bénit, Personal survey, Johannesburg, August 2002

6.4 Regulating domestic work: The emergence of a professional identity?

Domestic work appears to be a sector of the job market that is extremely diverse in terms of situations and arrangements. It is highly flexible, diluted, and scattered throughout the urban space, informal and unregistered. In such conditions, regulation of the relationship between employers and employees, and of conditions of work, seems unfeasible. Traditionally, domestic work was regulated by the paternalistic attitudes of employers toward their employees, whom they considered to be personally bonded to them. Such conditions are no longer clearly apparent in the charring system, but have not yet been replaced by another form of control. That is why, initiated by both public authorities and trade unions, (SADSAWU, 2002a) new legal and official rules were voted for and implemented between 2002 and 2003 in a sector that had up until then been relatively neglected by legislation.[13]

The challenge of unionising scattered and fragile employees

The first South African trade union, formed in 1943, to focus on the needs of domestic workers is the African Domestic Servants Trade Union, one of the oldest of South African trade unions. However, very few domestic workers are, even now, actually unionised, due to their relative social invisibility, and to the fact that they have been subjected to paternalistic practices that continue to rob them of their independence. Unlike factory workers, they do not usually meet and socialise at their workplaces. Although they can be verbally encouraged to join a union, such verbal encouragement takes a very long time and is relatively unrewarding, as it requires going from door to door, handing out pamphlets, organising meetings, and convincing often intimidated and exploited workers to attend the meetings in order to end their social isolation. By 1994, only 20 000 domestic workers (around 2% nationwide) had joined a union. By 2002, that number had more or less stabilised. Currently, the number is somewhere between 20 000 and 25 000 members, who actually pay their subscriptions to the main union, SADSAWU (the South African Domestic Service and Allied Workers Union) (see SADSAWU, 2002b), according to its main Somerset West-based rival, the South African Domestic and General Workers Union (SADAGWU), which splintered away from the Congress of South African Trade Unions (COSATU).

SADSAWU has been weakened by its stormy history and lack of financial resources (see Naledi, 1996). Created in 1984 from the merging of several locally based organisations, which joined COSATU in 1989, SADSAWU only managed to remain active until 1994, due to the financial support of a number of foreign NGOs. In 1994, when the financial support came to an end, all 13 local bureaus closed down. After additional foreign financial resources had been found, SADSAWU reopened in 2000. However, its fluctuating history reveals the structural weakness of a union that depends on the goodwill of a distant foreign sponsor. In 2000, only 10 000 members were recorded as regularly continuing to pay their monthly R10 subscription fee.

Despite their structural weaknesses, unions, by means of formal wage claims, try to ensure a R1 200 a month minimum wage for all workers. Domestic workers are traditionally among the most poorly paid workers in South Africa: in 1995, the median national income was close to R1 400 a month, whereas the median national domestic worker's income was only R333 a month (including both rural and urban areas) (Bhorat, 20009). The unions also insist that employers pay transport costs and school fees for domestic workers' children, when they have to attend expensive formerly white local schools. The unions also support new migrants, who run the risk of being victimised by their employers, especially when they have been hired by means of suspect labour bureaus. Some labour bureaus charge potential employers a R100 fee for recruitment of a domestic worker from the rural areas of South Africa. The employer also has to pay for any train, taxi, or bus fare to bring the worker to town. Some employers recoup the money spent on bringing employees to town by not paying the employee for his or her first couple of months' work. Unions also play an important role in denouncing domestic violence against live-in domestic workers.

Significant changes, at least in the law

In 2002, full-time urban domestic workers obtained a minimum wage of R800. Moreover, since 2003, employers have been obliged to register their employees with the Unemployment Insurance Fund. Registered domestic workers are entitled to financial support for a six-month period if they lose their jobs. Finally, the *Basic Conditions of Employment Act* (BCEA) of 1983 (that has covered basic conditions of domestic workers since 1994) currently regulates their conditions of work, redundancy, and dismissal, as well as their right to strike.

Conditions of work, the right to leave and vacation benefits according to the BCEA

Conditions of work, the right to leave, and vacation benefits, according to the BCEA, include the following:[14]

- A 45-hour work week prohibits domestic workers from having to work more than nine hours a day for five days a week, or for more than eight hours for a period of six days per week.
- A domestic worker may not work more than 12 hours in any one day.
- All domestic workers are entitled to 36 continuous hours off per week.
- Domestic workers may not work more than three hours a day overtime, and 10 to 15 hours' overtime in any one week.[15] Employers must pay their domestic workers one and a half times their normal wage for any overtime that they work.
- Employers must increase their workers' hourly rate if they require them to work before six a.m. or after six p.m.
- A lunch break of 30 minutes is compulsory for every five hours of non-stop work done by domestic workers, if their entire workday does not exceed six hours.
- No employer can expect a worker to work on a Sunday without the worker's agreement. If a domestic worker agrees to work on a Sunday, his or her employer must double his or her hourly rate.
- Employers must provide female workers with unpaid maternity leave for four months.
- All workers are entitled to three weeks' leave a year, as well as sick leave.
- No person may employ a child who is younger than 15.
- All employers must sign a written contract with all their workers.
- The *Labour Relations Act* strictly forbids firing someone with no reason and without notifying him or her in advance. The act also protects the right of all workers to strike.

For several reasons, the legislation currently in place was criticised even before being voted in (see Bhorat, 2000 and *Cape Times*, 2002a).

First, such rights remain largely theoretical, since the law relies on the employer's goodwill for their implementation. Physical and social isolation hamper controls on the application of the law. If a conflict arises, it is up to a judge to decide on which one of two opposed versions he or she should trust. Determination of how conditions of work and rules regulating labour practice are applied in the privacy of employers' residences is problematic. Employers can still discriminate against domestic workers by insisting that they hold an access card to fenced, high-security complexes, or by insisting that they undergo HIV/Aids testing (*Cape Times*, 2003a). The registration of domestic workers for UIF, which started in March 2003, was widely publicised in national and local newspapers, which also contained application forms to encourage employers to apply for registration of their domestic workers (*Cape Times*, 2003b). However, only 34 000 employers had registered their employees by the deadline, though 800 000 employers had been expected to apply for registration.

Second, the latest legislation is said not to be protective enough, since it aims mainly to encourage a mental shift among employers: The minimum wage is far below the mean level of wages currently being offered in Cape Town and Johannesburg.[16] For four hours of work in the Cape Town city centre, a domestic worker should earn at least R18, but the taxi fares alone (to and from Khayelitsha) were as high as R17 in August 2002.[17] Transport costs have clearly not been taken into consideration in the legislation. Therefore, the value of setting a minimum wage rate is debatable, since domestic workers include the cost of transport when they calculate how much money they can earn and whether it will be worth their while to accept a specific job offer.

Third, legislation does not currently cover part-time work: the BCEA only covers employees who work more than 24 hours a month. Therefore, conditions of the act do not cover employers who only make use of domestic workers once or twice a week. The question has been raised as to whether fiscal deductions for employers would not be more efficient in such a situation.

It is difficult to take stock of recent reform: is the glass half-full or half-empty? A total of 34 000 domestic workers emerged from the shadows when they were registered for UIF, but it is estimated that 750 000 people are *still* working in complete darkness.

6.5 Conclusion: The rise of a collective identity for domestic workers?

Domestic work in South Africa has undergone important changes since the collapse of the apartheid regime. Domestic workers now have increased autonomy, since they are able to work part time and to escape the live-in system imposed by employers, which often resulted in the splintering of families. The increasing professionalisation of domestic workers has been encouraged by several attempts to regulate the conditions of domestic work, despite the high flexibility and spatial scattering of the sector. The growth of domestic work, however, is also linked to post-Fordist de-industrialisation and the rise of unemployment, which has been accelerating since the 1990s. Both full-time and part-time domestic work constitute the major response to the threat of long-term unemployment, which is particularly serious in the townships and informal settlements of Cape Town and Johannesburg. These changes reflect normalisation of the conditions of domestic workers in South African post-apartheid cities.

In spite of its inefficiencies, the new legal framework being built to protect domestic workers makes them more visible to society as a whole, and is in the process of raising, if not a shared class consciousness, at least a *social-group* consciousness. In Johannesburg, for instance, some local security initiatives have set up a Domestic Workers Watch, enabling domestic workers to gather to discuss security issues and to receive some training from the watch, in conjunction with assistance provided by the South African Police Services. Though setting up such a watch may be seen as a way of accessing domestic workers as a source of information, the process involved also acknowledges the workers' role as that of a collective, networked, and important urban stakeholder in residential middle-income and upmarket neighbourhoods.

Legal debates might also encourage domestic workers to organise themselves, to join trade unions, and to become more aware of their social rights, as well as to build new collective initiatives. As an example, recently in Sea Point – a mixed suburb adjoining Cape Town's inner city – a group of domestic workers, supported by the NGO Development Action Group (DAG), united to explore the feasibility of a social housing programme dedicated to their specific needs. This was made possible through the provision of an institutional subsidy by the South African government to housing associations and NGOs for building and running social housing complexes (see DAG, 2003 and RHC, 2003a). This is the first time that such an initiative has been envisaged in South Africa. Even though the project is still far from getting off the ground, the fact that domestic workers have engaged in difficult negotiations with local authorities in order to buy a plot with significant site value, opposite the renowned Cape Town Waterfront, shows that their perception of their place in the city, and of their own social importance, has greatly improved. Their self-image as a social group has increased both their social capital and their ability to negotiate. Their perception of the urban space and of the advantage of a much sought-after location in the city also proves their increasing *spatial capital* (Lévy, 1994), a form of urban integration that one would not have expected after such a long confinement in their employers' backyards.

Notes

1   The in-depth interviews were conducted during August 2002, with 22 domestic workers in Johannesburg, and with 11 domestic workers in Cape Town. In Johannesburg, interviewees were selected according to their place of residence, while in Cape Town they were selected among those known to the main trade union. The questionnaire dealt with the domestic workers' personal trajectories and histories, the way in which they found their jobs, their conditions of work, and their choice of transport to and from work.

2   Bantu Affairs Commission, Domestic Workers in Urban Areas, Dagbreek, Doornfontein, Johannesburg, quoted by Radebe, 1995: 19.

3   This is especially true of women who had to leave their young children at home, because the employers refused to allow them to bring their children to town with them.

4   Between 1994 and 1998, it is estimated that 22 000 black people and 8 000 coloured people moved to Cape Town, after a peak period between 1989 and 1993, when 37 000 black people and 10 000 coloured people made the same move (see Cross, Bekker & Eva, 1999).

5   Theoretically, casual domestic workers (unlike independent contract workers) are entitled to the benefit of the Unemployment Insurance Fund as long as they work more than four hours per week for a given employer. However, most of them do not access this social net, as their working conditions are generally precarious and their employer seldom complies with the legal requirements.

6   In multi-centered cities, such as Johannesburg, the concepts of *centre* and *periphery* seem inappropriate. However, it still makes sense to talk of *centrality* in reference to the conjunction of density and diversity (see Lévy, 1994), and also the ability to link and to be linked to many different places in the city. We use *centrality* in the latter sense.

7   Not to mention the Gautrain, which is being planned to link the Johannesburg central business district (CBD) to Pretoria by way of Sandton and Alexandra, despite the realisation that the route will inevitably have some problems.

8   Road closures and the development of gated communities do not only increase the walking distances to jobs, they also prevent jobseekers from going door to door to look for jobs, which we see as an important way of accessing domestic workers' jobs. Moreover, domestic workers often have to prove their identity at gates to closed-off

neighbourhoods, as they had to show passes under the apartheid regime. Some domestic workers working in Hurlington Manor, a gated community in northern Johannesburg, protest against such practices: 'It is like apartheid all over again,' one domestic worker says. 'It is as if they are expected to produce a dompas to go through a public road again,' says Jody Kollapen, Human Rights Commission chairperson (Cape Argus, 2003: 7).

9   Advertisements for domestic workers appear more often in local newspapers, such as the Sandton Chronicle, than in a national newspaper, such as The Star.

10 The role that the church plays in enabling domestic workers to secure other jobs requires further study. Some researchers suggest that the role played by the church might be important in enabling jobseekers to secure domestic work (see Dolbeau, 2000).

11 This self-promotion of personal qualities is also a means by which the domestic workers whom we interviewed reconcile themselves to the low social status attached to their social condition – and by which they strove to gain the respect, personal, if not social – of the interviewer, which they probably do not receive in their everyday experience (see Vidal, 2002).

12 Allegations of slavery are more common, surprisingly, than are complaints regarding the apartheid era.

13 Domestic workers were mentioned in none of the following acts: the first Wage Act of 1925, the Workmen's Compensation Act of 1941, the Labour Relations Act of 1956, the Wage Act of 1957, the Unemployment Insurance Act of 1966, and the Basic Conditions of Employment Act of 1983. No legal framework regulated hours of work or minimum wages. However, trade unions were, at least theoretically, allowed, and domestic workers had access to the courts in respect of disputes concerning minor claims for payments of less than R2 000. The Manpower Training Act of 1981, the Guidance and Placement Act of 1981, the Machinery and Occupational Safety Act of 1983, and the Small Claims Courts Act of 1984 contained minor rules regarding domestic workers. However, generally speaking, domestic workers' conditions of work were defined by common law: an employer had to pay his or her domestic worker a salary, which both parties negotiated fairly. The wage negotiation implied that the two parties were equal, though this was far from being the case (see Delport, 1994).

14 For more details, see Kehler, 2002.

15 The exact number of overtime hours was still being debated at the time of completion of this chapter.

16 The BCEA and the Labour Relations Act both prohibit arbitrary and sudden decreases in salaries.

17 An employer is forced to pay half a day's work on the basis of a minimum of four hours.

CHAPTER 7

When shacks ain't chic!
Planning for 'difference' in post-apartheid Cape Town

Steven Robins

7.1 Introduction

Walking through Joe Slovo Park,[1] a low-income housing scheme situated in the historically white middle-to-upper income suburb of Milnerton, Cape Town, provides a rude reminder of the failure of planners, policy makers, and developers to acknowledge the complexity and heterogeneity of everyday social life and lived experience. In the early 1990s, an ambitious housing scheme had sought to transform the 'chaotic' shack settlement of Marconi Beam[2] into an orderly low-income suburb, Joe Slovo Park (JSP). However, instead of the anticipated neat rows of brick houses with grassed front lawns, this housing scheme is now barely distinguishable from the informal settlement that had been demolished to make way for Slovo Park. Peering behind the high walls surrounding Slovo Park reveals the full extent of the disjuncture between the planners' idealised model of 'suburban living' and the actual lived reality of this low-income housing scheme. While planners and developers envisaged a highly regulated formal housing development devoid of backyard shacks, shebeens,[3] and spaza shops,[4] Slovo Park's core brick structures ('RDP' subsidy houses)[5] have been swamped by informal structures built from corrugated iron and a mixture of other improvised building materials. It appears as if these brick and mortar houses have been re-colonised by corrugated iron, plastic, and wood. In other words, the 'formal' suburb of Joe Slovo Park seems to have reverted back to its original 'unruly' state. While there are significant improvements in the living conditions, infrastructure, and amenities at Joe Slovo Park as compared to the former informal settlement, elements of informality have nonetheless come back to haunt planners who envisaged a neat and orderly low-income suburb.[6] Why is it that the desires of city planners for socio-spatial order so often collide with the desires and realities of those who walk the streets of planned cities? Is this simply a case of the 'clashing cultures' and 'conflicting rationalities' (Watson 2003: 395) of planners and citizens, and is multicultural planning part of the solution or part of the problem? The following section addresses these questions by interrogating dominant theories of cultural difference that animate much contemporary planning discourse on 'culture' and multiculturalism. This discussion begins with a brief historical account of the cultural politics of an informal settlement in Cape Town. It focuses on changing forms of state intervention in urban residential areas in terms of planning and tenure.

7.2 Changing state discourses on urban planning and tenure

In June 1986, I witnessed the South African Defence Force (SADF) arming Xhosa-speaking vigilantes in a bloody battle against anti-apartheid activists in Crossroads, a shantytown settlement on the outskirts of Cape Town. I was working with an international television crew determined to obtain incriminating footage of security force complicity in fuelling inter-community violence in Crossroads. The SADF and South African Police had clandestinely armed a large group of Xhosa-speaking vigilante elders, referred to in the media as the *witdoeke* or 'fathers', in an attempt to violently purge Crossroads of ANC activist organisations that had established strongholds in the informal settlement in the early 1980s. Divisions had emerged in Crossroads as a result of struggles over access to housing, development resources, and growing tensions between militant youth who took control over the Peoples' Courts,[7] and who enforced consumer boycotts and work stay-aways. These actions alienated and antagonised many of the elders who participated in the neo-traditional headmen structures (*izibonda*) that existed in many of the migrant hostels and informal settlements in Cape Town's townships. The security forces exploited these tensions between 'fathers' and 'sons' by supporting these conservative elders in a violent struggle against anti-apartheid youth activists in Crossroads. Driving through Crossroads on a misty morning in June 1986, we managed to film police and *witdoeke* collaborating in the torching of hundreds of corrugated-iron shack homes. We also filmed the charred human remains of 'necklacings' and the dozens of corpses lying alongside the road, the casualties from the previous night's fighting between the *witdoeke* and the ANC comrades or *amaqabane*. A day later, the South African-based journalist George D'Ath was killed by machete-wielding *witdoeke*.

A decade later I spent four days at the Truth and Reconciliation Commission (TRC) hearings into the role of the military in the Crossroads violence. I heard one of the elderly *witdoek* warlords of the 1980s, Sam Ndima, telling Advocate Dumisa Ntsebeza, the TRC's head of the investigations unit, that he was simply a victim of the apartheid state's duplicitous machinations and manipulations.

Ndima was now wearing an ANC T-shirt instead of the widely feared white head-scarf (*witdoek*) he had worn in the 1980s. Ndima spoke about how the youth had usurped power, 'necklacing' *impimpis* (police informers), and undermining their traditional authority by setting up their own Peoples' Courts. He also claimed that his *witdoeke* soldiers had been manipulated by the apartheid security forces. Ndima managed to reinvent himself as both a victim of apartheid and a loyal ANC member.[8] He had created a new political identity for new political times. Clearly, Ndima and residents in informal settlements in South Africa and elsewhere are often 'moving targets'; they are seldom straitjacketed into the moulds of liberal democratic citizenship and subjectivity that planners imagine, but neither are they so fundamentally 'other' that they cannot participate in modernist planning interventions and the liberal democratic game. It will be argued that the urban poor, whether in South Africa or elsewhere, are not necessarily locked into development encounters characterised by clashing cultures and conflicting rationalities. Instead, their capacity to engage with these processes is usually limited by the material resources at their disposal rather than 'cultural' factors.

How deep is 'deep difference'?

Writing about the continuation of violent patronage politics in Crossroads after apartheid, Vanessa Watson (2003) draws attention to the conflicting rationalities of modernist planners and Crossroads residents. She argues that conventional understandings of 'multicultural planning'. as a rational and consensus-building process that encourages cultural tolerance and the accommodation of difference – cannot account for the politics of 'deep difference' which, she argues, accounts for the continuing violence and political culture of patrimonialism in Crossroads. Whereas planners envisage 'proper' and 'responsible' citizens who arrive at rational planning solutions through consultation and consensual politics, the realities on the ground suggest that alternative political rationalities exist in places like Crossroads that are inherently incompatible with the liberal democratic conceptions of citizenship and civic participation. Watson's analysis of conflict in Crossroads in the post-apartheid period implies that there is an insurmountable impasse between liberal and illiberal political rationalities. But how deep is this 'deep difference'?

My brief account of Sam Ndima's appearance before the TRC suggests that political cultures, rationalities, and identities can be deployed situationally. In the 1980s, Ndima and his neo-traditional lieutenants had aligned themselves with the apartheid security forces in a violent campaign to reassert 'traditional' authority. By 1996 Ndima had changed his tactics, allegiances and political identity. Ndima's wearing of an ANC T-shirt at the TRC hearings in the mid 1990s suggested that he had switched his political affiliation. He now identified himself with a democratic political organisation that was busy reassessing the place of traditional leaders within a modern constitutional democracy. Switching sides was relatively seamless for Ndima and his lieutenants. It would seem that people living in Crossroads, and elsewhere, are not necessarily trapped within the straightjacket of political identities and rationalities, but are instead usually capable of switching registers, repertoires, and identities depending on the specific contexts, audiences, and political objectives. If this is indeed the case, what then are the implications of this for planning and for theories of multicultural planning?

The trouble with multicultural urban planning

Writing about cultural diversity in Sydney, Sophie Watson (1996) draws attention to the homogenising impulse of the modernist legacy of a predominantly British planning tradition. It is a tradition that, she argues, disavows difference. Despite occasional contestations of public spaces in Sydney by Aboriginal groups and non-Anglo migrants, Watson argues, contemporary Australian planning discourses and practices seem to have been affected only marginally by multicultural debates. South Africa, as a former British colony, has also inherited this homogenising modernist planning and architectural tradition. However, in the 1990s we have witnessed the arrival on our shores of a global discourse of multiculturalism alongside calls for Africanisation in all spheres of South African culture. Architects, for instance, have sought out vernacular African architectural styles and aesthetics, while heritage professionals have been called upon to identify and conserve African 'sacred spaces' such as initiation sites. In 1996 I was commissioned by the Cape Town city planning department to identify precisely such places of African cultural significance. Although the urban landscape has been profoundly shaped by the more mundane and banal apartheid spatial legacies of racialised segregation and poverty, there seems to be an extraordinary degree of interest in more 'exotic' urban spaces. While this exotic notion of African culture does not by any means reflect the perspective of the entire Cape Town city planning department, it is nonetheless foregrounded in debates by culture and heritage policy makers and planners at both national and city levels. It is also within this multiculturalist milieu that ethnic tourist villages and township tours are flourishing in various parts of the country.

South Africa's embrace of the rainbow nation metaphor is perhaps the most visible sign of the significance of multiculturalist discourse in the post-apartheid era. However, as many cultural critics have pointed out, multiculturalism tends to become a homogenising strategy that defines and demarcates the limits within which difference is permitted. Watson (1996) points out that multiculturalism is generally regarded as benign by Anglo-Australians as long as the exotic 'Other' can be packaged and transformed into folkloric spectacle and tourist dollars: Little Italy, Little China, the Jewish Quarter, the Malay Quarter, and so on. However, difference is viewed with less appreciation if it threatens homogenising notions of national identity. Similarly, there tends to be tolerance for cultural diversity and multicultural planning as long as the uniform built environment of suburbia is not compromised or 'polluted', for instance by informal building materials and mixed land use such as the running of informal businesses from suburban homes. In South Africa, black South Africans have managed to evade all such regulations as long as these activities have taken place in the townships. Yet, as the case study discussed in this chapter demonstrates, these informal building practices 'sometimes spill over' into the historically white parts of the city. The following section investigates the historical legacies of contemporary urban planning discourses and suggests reasons for forms of popular resistance to these interventions.

Back to the future: The perennial quest for urban order at the Cape of Storms

In the early decades of the last century, South African urban planners drew inspiration from Le Corbusier's 'Surgical Method' in their attempts to radically reconfigure the urban landscape. They appear to have shared Le Corbusier's modernist faith in rationally conceived 'master' plans and urban designs that would create social order by means of 'proper' zoning of land use and the segregation of different social groups. In the name of social order and racial harmony, South African urban planners appropriated Le Corbusier's notion of planning as a rational, technical process that could be divorced from politics. It is worth quoting at length from Norman Hanson's introductory remarks made at the 1938 Town Planning Congress in Johannesburg:

> It is possible to achieve this radical reorganization by drastic methods only, by a fresh start on cleared ground. This ruthless eradication directed towards a revitalizing process we have, following Le Corbusier's lead, named the Surgical Method ... through surgery we must create order, through organization we must make manifest the spirit of a new age ... (Hanson, cited in Jensen & Turner, 1996: 85)

This modernist utopian faith in the capacity to dramatically transform 'disorderly' urban environments reflects the thinking of influential planners and architects going back to Baron Haussmann's mid nineteenth-century renovation of Paris. These ideas emerged in the nineteenth century in response to the problems of social disorder and threats to public health that came to be associated with the working-class neighbourhoods of industrial cities. These planning interventions all share the assumption that it is possible to radically redesign the built environment in ways that improve the social fabric of 'dysfunctional' communities and neighbourhoods. In other words, planners believed, and continue to believe, that social behaviour could be strongly influenced by urban form. The case study in this chapter draws attention to the limits of such 'physicalist' thinking, which continues to animate post-apartheid planning discourses. This will involve interrogating some of the underlying assumptions of urban planning in relation to questions of housing and built environment, and citizenship and governance.

In the late 1930s, Le Corbusier's (1929) *The City of Tomorrow and its Planning* was hugely influential in planning circles in South Africa. This modernist manifesto called for radical intervention in the urban landscape:

> The city is dying because it is not constructed geometrically. To build on a clear site is to replace the 'accidental' layout of the ground, the only one that exists today, by a formal layout. Otherwise nothing can save us ... Surgery must be applied to the city center ... We must use the knife ... (Le Corbusier, 1929, in Steinberg, 2004: 111)

In Cape Town in 1940, 'surgery' took the form of the Foreshore Project that sought to modernise and 'sanitise' the inner city. This involved three slum clearance projects in the predominantly coloured areas of District Six, the Malay Quarter, and the Docklands. Coloureds were resettled in the bleak and windswept Cape Flats. Jonny Steinberg (2004) eloquently describes the devastating impact these modernist ideas had on tens of thousands of coloured people forcibly removed as part of 'slum clearance projects'. It is worth quoting at length from Steinberg's account of these spatial legacies:

> Flying over the Flats on the descent into Cape Town International Airport, you can see ... concentric layers of streets, turned in upon themselves, forming tight, hermetic circles, each surrounded by a barren wilderness of no-man's-land ... Driving through Manenberg, or Heideveld or Hanover Park, one feels as if one has been locked into a maze, as if the ghetto is a dense universe ... The satellite towns are 15 minutes from downtown. But this is premised on the universality of the family car; [many of] the working class families of the Flats have no cars. Moving in and out of the satellites is a costly expedition ... Most important of all, perhaps, the Flats neighbourhoods were built on the premise that coloureds lived their lives in nuclear families. Indeed, it was the conceit of modernism that the nuclear family was synonymous with the twentieth century, that other forms of kinship were the residues of more primitive times. Yet the coloureds of the inner city had lived their lives in extended families ... And so, between 1966 and the early 1980s, tens of thousands of people were wrenched from their lives in the inner city and dumped in the satellites on the edge of town. Extended

families were dispersed to all four corners of the Flats, and everybody shared their
cramped streets with strangers ... (2004)

Planners sought to create new spatial orders as an antidote to the disorder and
unruliness of modern urban life. However, their interventions were only partially
successful. In Cape Town, for example, tens of thousands of poor and unemployed
coloureds (and Africans) have indeed become virtual prisoners of the Cape Flats
ghettoes. Yet, the Cape Flats is also home to powerful gangs such as the Firm,
the Americans, and the Hard Livings, whose drug, taxi, sex work, and abalone
enterprises stretch out from the Cape Flats to include Cape Town's inner city and
plush suburbs as well as the small rural towns and fishing villages of the Western
Cape (see Steinberg, 2004). Notwithstanding these messy urban realities, post-
apartheid planners and policy makers continue to fantasise about creating ordered
urban environments. At the heart of these fantasies are the following: home
ownership, the idea of the nuclear family, and the dream of virtuous citizens living
in suburban order.

What these Cape Flats planners failed to take cognisance of was the
extraordinary power of 'alternative' social, economic, and cultural realities. For
example, Jonny Steinberg's *The Number* (2004) shows how members of prison
gangs create all-consuming rituals of commitment and belonging that take on
life-and-death meanings and consequences and which, over a period of many
decades, have become deeply embedded in the streets of the coloured townships
of the Cape Flats. Steinberg (2004) suggests that, in the absence of formal
employment opportunities, these gang cultures are unlikely to be dislodged by
dreams of home ownership and suburban living. It is precisely street realities
and underground economies of this kind that tend to be elided in planning
processes.

Planners in the Development Action Group (DAG), an NGO, were responsible
for facilitating and coordinating the implementation of the private-developer-
driven Joe Slovo Park upgrading scheme. They comprised a group of progressive
planners who were acutely aware of the need to consult with communities. They
were also aware of disastrous modernist legacies of apartheid state housing
development interventions, and sought to distance themselves from these top-
down technocratic interventions. Despite this awareness of the traps of modernist
planning, they unwittingly found themselves reproducing certain key assumptions
of this planning tradition. The following section examines the seductive power
and longevity of these ideas and practices. These planning discourses, I argue,
persistently underestimate the social and cultural consequences of historically
produced conditions of poverty and inequality.

Fantasies of suburban living for a new South Africa: Modernist state interventions and the magic of title

One of the most sweeping policy visions for such projects of urban transformation has been put forward by the much-celebrated Peruvian economist Hernando de Soto. De Soto (2000) has boldly claimed that Third World poverty can be eradicated by transforming 'extra-legal' ownership of property – i.e., illegal informal housing – into legal ownership, with the Deeds Registry proposed as the vehicle. De Soto's recipe for promoting people's capitalism and empowerment throughout the developing world relies upon 'the magic of title deed' (see De Soto, 2000). This strikingly seductive idea – that title provides collateral for poor people to access bank loans and thereby convert 'dead capital' into business opportunities – has been embraced by donors and government-sponsored think-tanks throughout the world. De Soto's ideas about title have been around for at least two decades. In post-apartheid South Africa, De Soto's magic formula is seen to offer an instant solution for creating a formal secondary housing market in South Africa's black townships.[9] Title, individual home ownership, and access to a suburban housing market are seen as the key for creating a stable, upwardly mobile, and virtuous citizenry. This suburban model is also seen as a way of eradicating informal settlements, which are seen to represent spaces of disorder and stagnation.

De Soto's magic bullet solution seems highly plausible and desirable to South African housing policy makers despite the existence of a body of research indicating that there are numerous financial, legal, social, and cultural obstacles[10] to the creation of a viable township housing market, and that most owners of old township stock built in the 1960s are reluctant to sell their homes for economic, social, and cultural reasons (Robins, 2004).

These obstacles include the following: Owners of these houses are unlikely to find buyers with access to cash or bonds, and, even if they could, they would struggle to find another affordable home. The lengthy struggle of many township residents for urban rights and access to a house during the apartheid period means that, even if they have title deeds, they are unlikely to want to sell. Houses are often part of a family's social and political biography. Also, township houses are often a family asset rather than individually owned. To unilaterally sell such an important social asset could unleash serious family conflict. In addition, township houses are often part of 'stretched households' that straddle urban and rural areas and have a role in multi-sited livelihood strategies. Finally, selling a township or RDP house can be risky, as sellers and buyers could be caught in a debt trap when they buy a replacement house. Clearly, title deed and home ownership is far more complicated than De Soto and market fundamentalists assume. Title deeds may, under certain circumstances, provide collateral for loans.[11] Yet, as millions of unemployed and workers know, having title deeds in a redlined urban township can be meaningless as collateral.

Despite this growing evidence of the limits of title as the vehicle for the creation of a secondary housing market, De Soto's argument remains seductive precisely because of its elegant simplicity and millenarian promise to eradicate global poverty. It claims that legal reform can magically solve Third World urban poverty with minimal disruption or cost to the owners of global capital. Not surprisingly, many government officials, planners, academics, and NGOs desperate for instant solutions to grinding poverty and massive unemployment have fallen under his spell.[12]

The case study discussed in this chapter follows the implementation processes of low-income housing schemes based on an individual home-ownership model. It examines the underlying assumptions of models of housing delivery in relation to broader national questions of governance, citizenship, and 'the formalisation of the informal'. The chapter takes as its starting point the view that *houses are much more than bricks and mortar*; housing development is highly political and deeply embedded in ideological processes aimed at building good and virtuous citizens out of the raw material of 'the unruly masses' (see Robins, 2002). In fact, it would seem that planners, policy makers, city managers, and activists have always conceived of housing in relation to broader issues of citizenship and governance. Informal settlements are generally viewed by planners and the state as the antithesis of modern and virtuous urban living. These also tend to be perceived by city managers and planners as dangerous and 'unruly' spaces that defy state surveillance and the 'rectangular grids of civilization' (Comaroff & Comaroff, 1991; Crush, 1995; Dubois, 1991, Escobar, 1985, 1988, 1995; Mitchell, 1988; Robins, 1994; Scott, 1998). Tim Mitchell's *Colonising Egypt* (1991) and James Scott's *Seeing Like A State* (1998) show how urban planners have sought to render these 'unruly' urban populations more visible and legible by creating a system of regular, open streets and re-ordering space and the surveillance and control of its occupants (Mitchell, 1991: x). Similarly, colonial administrators and planners sought to spatially reorder and regulate what were perceived to be essentially unruly African landscapes. In Southern Africa, colonial spatial planning interventions such as 'betterment' and centralisation schemes – which attempted to re-order African land-use practices and establish linear and grid-like residential settlements – provoked intense anti-colonial resistance and political opposition to colonial rule (De Wet & McAllister, 1984; De Wet, 1986; Drinkwater, 1989; Robins, 1994). In Joe Slovo Park there were also signs of evasion and popular resistance to planners' conceptions of the neat and rectangular grids of suburban built environments.

7.3 Post-apartheid planning: The case of Joe Slovo Park, Cape Town

Planning interventions tend to elide difference in the name of a homogenised 'target population' (see Ferguson, 1990). This will become clear in the case study (see below) of Joe Slovo Park, a low-income housing scheme in Cape Town's historically white suburb of Milnerton. Planners and administrators waged a losing battle to enforce building and trading regulations, and residents continued to build corrugated iron shacks and run informal businesses (e.g., spaza shops and shebeens) from their Slovo Park homes. Housing schemes such as Slovo Park tend to be designed and implemented with a range of homogenising assumptions about 'proper' citizens based on the suburban property model. It was assumed at the Slovo Park project, for instance, that the 'target population' of shanty-town squatters who qualified for the government housing subsidy would in fact want to settle in small low-income houses. Planners were shocked when some home owners began selling their houses and moving back into shanty settlements where they could continue living in shacks and running informal businesses without having to pay taxes, licences, rates, and levies. This case study demonstrates that it was largely material constraints, rather than 'cultural difference' or conflicting rationalities, that prevented 'beneficiaries' from living out planners' fantasies of suburban order in Slovo Park.

Given the size of their extended families and their limited household income, the majority of residents could not afford to build brick and mortar extensions to the tiny core structures at the formal housing scheme of Slovo Park. Therefore, they could either build their extensions in corrugated iron or else move back into informal settlements where they were able to accommodate all the members of their large households. Instead of having to pay large sums of money to build brick extensions to the core houses, they could simply extend their shacks with limited costs using cheap (informal) building materials. In addition, many ran shebeens and spaza shops from their homes and some were involved in illegal activities such as gun smuggling and dagga (marijuana) dealing. In other words, there were sound material reasons why the new Joe Slovo Park settlement was 're-informalised'. It was largely as a result of chronic poverty and limited access to income, rather than cultural difference, that Slovo Park was so dramatically re-informalised. Yet, multicultural planning discourses often end up reifying and exoticising cultural difference in ways that obscure these more banal and mundane material realities.

While there seems to be growing concern amongst planners to address cultural difference (Sandercock, 1998) and 'conflicting rationalities' (Watson, 2003), these concerns have often been de-linked from the more material consequences of poverty and the informalisation of everyday life in shantytown settlements and urban ghettos. Addressing cultural difference and 'conflicting rationalities' in South African cities, I argue, needs to take cognisance of these more mundane material legacies of apartheid. These material realities may in turn be the ground upon which Vanessa Watson's 'deep difference' lies. Without such attention to materiality, however, planners will continue to flounder in their attempts to re-imagine urban futures in South Africa and elsewhere.

When shacks ain't chic: 'Reinformalising' Joe Slovo Park

In addition to the 'return to informality' – the endless shacks built next to formal brick houses – that is so evident at Joe Slovo Park, the planners' utopian vision of a harmonious 'multi-cultural', multi-economic class and non-racial housing scheme is contradicted by socio-spatial segregation and the tensions that have emerged between the mostly Xhosa-speaking lower income Slovo Park residents and the predominantly coloured and white residents of the middle-income Phoenix housing development adjacent to Slovo Park. Although Phoenix was planned as an integral part of the upgrading scheme, tensions along race, ethnic, and economic class lines surfaced, culminating in the erection of high concrete walls between Slovo Park and Phoenix. How did this planners' vision of multicultural planning and integrated urban development collapse like a pack of cards? Did planners imagine that individual home ownership alone could extract poor residents from 'thick' social ties and kinship and patronage networks, and recreate them as autonomous and virtuous citizens committed to all the trappings of suburban living?

7.4 Selected problems with state interventions in planning and tenure

Development interventions often fail precisely because they are based upon planners' fantasies and utopian visions, and misplaced conceptions of homogeneous 'target populations' (see Ferguson, 1990; Robins, 1994; Crush, 1995). Such assumptions draw upon the notion of a decontextualised group of individual beneficiaries with similar circumstances, needs, and aspirations. Whether one is talking about housing or literacy provision, rather than imagining a static and uniform 'target population', it would make more sense to think of residents of informal settlements as 'moving targets', constantly making and remaking their lives and circumstances in relation to the contingencies of the present and the future. This 'ethnographic' approach also draws attention to divergent identities and practices, and the competing understandings of 'development' held by planners, community brokers, and 'beneficiaries'.

'Target populations' and 'moving targets': Some of the challenges to urban planning

Planners seldom acknowledge the complexity and heterogeneity of communities and actual social practices in their standardised policies and 'one-size-fits-all' master plans and blueprints. Investigating the actual lived experience of these communities could bring to the surface submerged or hidden forms of social differentiation and everyday practices that are so evident in informal settlements. It could also draw attention to the limits to state-led efforts to 'formalise the informal'.[13] The building of informal structures at Slovo Park – despite community agreements that this would not be allowed – draws attention to the disjuncture between the world of planners and that of the urban poor. It was therefore not surprising that city officials fought a losing battle to enforce regulations that prevented people from running informal businesses (e.g., spaza shops and shebeens) from their homes in Joe Slovo Park. In addition, planners and housing officials were taken aback when some home owners sold their new houses for a fraction of their value and moved back into shanty settlements where they could continue living in shacks and running informal businesses without having to pay taxes, licenses, rates, and levies.

Soon after people moved into their new houses, building inspectors and housing officials abandoned the impossibly difficult task of monitoring and regulating building standards at Slovo Park. This meant that spaza and shebeen owners were free to build corrugated iron structures next to their brick houses and run their businesses from home. Many poorer households sublet backyard shacks to people seeking accommodation close to the city centre and employment opportunities. For example, significant numbers of African immigrants and refugees moved into Slovo Park because of its geographical location and to avoid growing xenophobia in the established African townships. These unintended outcomes draw attention to the limits of planning interventions.

Rick de Satge (1997), an urban development consultant who worked with DAG, in a study of the upgrading of informal settlements in KwaZulu-Natal and Gauteng provinces, comments on the striking mismatch between housing policies and actual social realities. De Satge identifies the problem of policy inflexibility that is built into the private ownership tenure regimes ('suburban property models') that underpin housing upgrade interventions.

> Effective strategies for upgrading informal settlements demand policy flexibility and the recognition of informal systems developed by ordinary people with great experience of survival on the margins … There are informal tenures systems [that] have been developed around a recognition of transience, of the need to move on, which the systems facilitate while simultaneously trying to cushion some of the negative effects of this instability. The upgrading of informal settlements has to intersect meaningfully with these realities. *An inflexible approach premised solely on the suburban property model is doomed to failure.* (De Satge, 1997: 4, emphasis added)

The Joe Slovo Park housing development encountered similar problems to those identified by de Satge in KwaZulu-Natal and Gauteng. For example, the lack of information and understanding of tenure issues, the high land-registration costs of the private property model, and a maze of legislation and regulations were all significant obstacles. Informal property markets – as opposed to the 'normal' housing market – may be able to reduce costs and unnecessary red tape, but they are nonetheless generally unstable and prone to contestation and conflict. Obstacles to 'formalising the informal' include migration, mobility, and the fact that growing numbers of residents (including 'illegal aliens', criminals, gangsters, shebeen owners, and shacklords) are dependent on the weak state surveillance and poor policing of informal settlements, and therefore have 'vested interests in the status quo' (de Satge, 1997: 6).

During the course of fieldwork in Joe Slovo Park, I came across 'tsotsis' and 'skollies' (gangsters)[14] who appeared to be completely invisible in the neatly drawn plans and blueprints of developers, NGOs, and officials. These individuals were part of a subterranean underworld of informal operators who live their lives beyond the reach of formal political and state development discourses and institutions. The civics, ANC branches, NGOs, and local government agencies seldom factored these elusive and shadowy figures into their plans. Yet, given the disproportionately large number of unemployed people in informal settlements, these underworld figures probably constitute a significant minority. The interests, agendas, and lifestyles of these individuals and the gangs they belong to do not generally conform to planners' imagined communities of virtuous citizens. Although these people are seldom seen or heard at local meetings and development forums, their invisibility *vis-a-vis* the state, civics, and NGOs does not mean that their actions do not significantly impact upon the outcomes of development projects. Yet, these informal social actors and illegal economies can make or break development projects. While wishing to avoid both romantisising these individuals as 'social bandits', or characterising Joe Slovo Park as a space saturated with social pathologies (e.g., crime, illegality, and violence), it is nonetheless necessary to take cognisance of the existence of these subterranean activities, violent economies, and counter-cultures. It is perhaps time that such shadowy figures, and numerous other aspects of everyday social life in poor communities, find their way into the neat and orderly sketches of planners and architects.

Dreaming of suburban order, living in poverty

The planners' conceptual sketches of the new suburb of Joe Slovo Park reveal a utopian vision of a neat and orderly built environment diametrically opposed to the images of anarchic and 'chaotic' informal settlements such as 'Cukutown' (Marconi Beam).[15] Nowhere in these planners' drawings of the future Joe Slovo

Park do we see the informal structures and corrugated shacks that have come to characterise the built environment at the new housing scheme. Instead, the sketches convey the image of an idyllic suburb comprising neat rows of houses, three-storey walk-ups with tidy shops. As Rick de Satge, a former member of the Development Action Group (DAG), the NGO that was responsible for the implementation of the Marconi Beam upgrading scheme, put it:

> The planners focused on spatial design and assumed that these planned spaces and architectural forms would shape how people actually lived. But nobody at DAG really understood the complicated social dynamics and livelihood strategies of the community. We made some effort to research these issues but we never really came close to understanding the social complexity. Perhaps the DAG project leaders did not really want to be held back by these complications. They simply wanted to get on with implementation, even if this meant getting the community to buy into the project by means of patronage networks and community brokers who did not fully represent all sectors of the community. Perhaps some of the planners felt that if all this social complexity was fully revealed it would blow away political and public support for the project. Everybody desperately wanted to believe we could create this model low-income suburban development. (Rick de Satge, personal communication)

It would seem that if it were widely known that Joe Slovo Park would undergo a process of 're-informalisation' characterised by corrugated iron shebeens, spaza shops, and shacks, as well as drug dealing and gang activities, it would have been difficult to find buyers for the middle-income homes at the neighbouring Phoenix development. The image of a disorderly Joe Slovo Park would also have generated considerable unease and opposition from the neighbouring (mostly white) middle-income ratepayers associations of Milnerton, who were in any case against the Marconi Beam development scheme from the start. The Local Authority was equally uneasy about initiating a low-income scheme in the middle of an upper-to-middle income suburb. It was therefore perhaps not strategic, nor in the interests of Marconi Beam beneficiaries and their NGO allies, to publicly disclose the complex character and problems facing this community. This was meant to be a post-apartheid showcase of how to do integrated multi-income-level and multi-racial housing development. What was required was nothing less than a suburban dreamscape.

Internally circulated DAG reports did, however, draw attention to some potential difficulties. The report identified the following potential obstacles:

> From the perspective of Milnerton as a whole the fundamental problem is one of integrating a new dimension of society into existing ones. It is expected that the 50 hectares designated for houses in Marconi Beam [i.e., Joe Slovo Park] are likely to

accommodate over 3 000 households. The population is likely to have a very different profile to that of the existing [upper-to-middle income] areas. It will be more dependent on walking and public transport to get to work. It will require substantial education and health and welfare facilities and services. It will require new work opportunities at a low level. All of these are perceived as a threat by the [mostly white, middle-to-upper income] Milnerton residents. (Development Action Group, 1994a)

The report also noted that none of the 'appalling' physical conditions at the informal settlement could be addressed without a dramatic improvement of the economic base of the community.[16] It was these problems of livelihoods and affordability that would come back to haunt DAG planners' visions of an orderly and standardised suburban built environment.[17]

Whether DAG and the planners anticipated the extent of the re-informalisation process or not, it is clear that the dominant planning discourse within which the NGO operated did not allow for any serious contemplation or official acknowledgement of such a future scenario. As a result, the planners' sketches represented the future Slovo Park as an idyllic suburb, much like any middle-income suburb elsewhere in the world. The 20-hectare site was to be a mixed-use development, with a one-third residential component, while commercial, industrial, and recreational uses would make up the balance. This would provide the opportunity for small-scale and home-based industries and enterprises. According to a DAG Project Description Report (1994), 'There will also be a mix of house types to suit incomes at the lower income levels ranging from R0 to R3 500 monthly income with a bias towards the lower end, thus avoiding both monotony and the ghetto syndrome' (Development Action Group, 1994b: 10). However, this planners' vision was unrealistic given the specific socio-economic needs and livelihood strategies of the people living there. For instance, a 1992 Urban Foundation survey discovered that, of the 70.7% of the people in the economically active age group, 47% were unemployed.[18] How were unemployed Marconi Beam residents going to afford the high costs of living of suburbia? Would they not need to rent out backyard shacks and build shebeens and spaza shops in order to survive economically?

7.5 Conclusion

Planners often fail to realise their utopian and technocratic plans and blueprints in the face of everyday struggles by the urban economic underclasses. Instead of planned, formal development based on home ownership and dreams of suburban living, housing schemes are often captured by informal housing and economic activities that deviate dramatically from 'the plan.' While both planners and many of the 'beneficiaries' may share these dreams of suburban living, there are a variety of reasons why poor communities are generally unable to realise these utopian visions of 'modern' urban living.

Despite the hybrid and improvisational nature of the building styles of brick and corrugated iron of poor communities in the developing world, South African planners and policy makers continue to have fantasies of dramatically transforming and standardising the everyday urban spaces of 'the poor'. For example, the current Minister of Housing, Lindiwe Sisulu, stated in 2004 that she was determined to completely eradicate informal settlements, a goal that no developing country has yet managed to achieve. The South African government, it would seem, is reluctant to fully accept the long-term realities of informal settlements because these spaces are perceived to be places of endemic poverty, disease, crime, violence, and instability. These settlements also question South Africa's vision of itself as *the* quintessential modern African state. Informal settlements are also perceived to constitute a challenge to the state's authority and control over its population, land uses, and the built environment. This explains the undying commitment of the South African government to the bureaucratic dreamscape of properly planned and ordered suburbs with neat houses, fenced lawns, and virtuous citizens. But where do the millions of very poor South Africans fit into this fantasy of suburban living?

Joe Slovo Park can be seen as a monument to the problematic nature of utopian and rationalist tendencies of planning that fail to anticipate the unintended and unexpected (Ferguson, 1990; Holston, 1998; Scott, 1998). In this particular case, it ought perhaps to have been anticipated that many 'beneficiaries' would have to continue to rely on informal economies and corrugated-iron building materials once they moved to Slovo Park. This sociological blind spot perhaps represents the folly of the masterplan that 'excludes social conflict, ambiguity and indeterminacy characteristic of actual social life' (Holston, 1998: 46; see Scott, 1998). As James Holston notes,

> modernist planning does not admit or develop productively the paradoxes of its imagined future. Instead, it attempts to be a plan without contradictions, without conflict. It assumes a rational domination of the future in which its total and totalizing plan dissolves any conflict between the imagined and the existing society in the imposed coherence of its order. (Holston, 1998: 46)

Holston suggests that these masterplans attempt 'to fix the future ... by appealing to precedents that negate the value of present circumstances'. What is required, according to Holston, is the inclusion of the 'ethnographic present' in planning.

In other words, planners need to anticipate the possibilities for change in *actually existing social conditions*. I would argue that what is also needed is that planners recognise the highly improvisational and fluid character of everyday life, especially amongst working-class and poor people. Whereas the middle- to upper-income classes may be able to plan and routinise their lives and built environment in ways that can be more readily anticipated, predicted, and captured by master plans and standardised solutions, this is generally not the case with poor people who are constantly on the move, seeking out *ad hoc* solutions to everyday problems of shelter and livelihoods.

These 'solutions from below' tend to draw upon whatever materials happen to be available, thereby creating an aesthetic of the improvised 'ready-made' that defies the planner's totalising vision of a neat, orderly, and predictable suburban landscape. These highly improvisational and situational practices of the urban poor are not adequately captured by notions such as 'deep difference', 'culture', or alternative political rationalities. Resorting to static, bounded, and essentialist conceptions of multicultural planning that valorise exotic otherness will not help either. Instead, the Slovo Park case study highlights the need to recognise the recurring mismatch between utopian master plans and the mundane material realities and everyday practices of the poor. It draws attention to the situational character of the cultural politics of 'informality' in ways that go beyond notions of multiculturalism, conflicting rationalities, and 'deep difference'. [19]

Notes

1   This housing scheme was named after the first ANC Minister of Housing, Joe Slovo, who in the early 1990s introduced the National Housing Subsidy Programme. By the late 1990s, the scheme was well under way in terms of its target of 2 000 housing units.

2   Marconi Beam is a 256 hectare site located in the centre of Milnerton, five kilometres from the Cape Town CBD. About 900 households moved onto the land during the late 1980s and early 1990s. The first 'squatters' to settle at the Marconi Beam Transit Area were the families of the workers at the adjacent Cape Turf Club (Milnerton Racecourse) who were only provided with single hostel accommodation. This Transit Area site, referred to as 'Cukutown' by local residents, was eventually cleared of shacks when 'squatters' moved into new houses in the adjacent Joe Slovo Park housing scheme in the latter half of the 1990s.

3   A shebeen is a 'speakeasy' or illegal drinking club. In informal settlements, these drinking spots are usually in shacks.

4   Spaza shop is the term for small, informal, 'general dealer' stores that can be found in large numbers in South Africa's townships. See Andrew Spiegel's (1996) analysis of the elusive etymology and contemporary meanings of the word 'spaza'.

5   The national housing subsidy is R16 000, plus an additional amount of R2 400 addressing
    locational, topographical, or other geotechnical difficulties. This applies to households
    earning between nought and R1 500 per month; the subsidy is less for higher income
    earners (Kecia Rust, personal correspondence).

6   Marie Huchzermeyer (personal correspondence) suggests that this obsession with orderly
    built environments is not simply an expression of a planner's vision of suburban living, in
    terms of which there would be a need to cater for consumers' individual choices. Instead,
    these interventions are generally more concerned with the imperatives of social control
    and the standardisation of housing products and built environments. Huchzermeyer
    also suggests, quite rightly, that these rigid and orderly housing interventions tend to
    be strongly supported by poor and low-income communities that are driven by a sense
    of individualised entitlement and a desire for freehold title and ownership of a 'proper'
    house. It would appear that 'beneficiaries' of housing subsidies are 'seduced' into certain
    'modern' and 'civilised' modes of consumption, including the desire to own a 'proper'
    house. This insatiable desire for the fruits of 'modern' suburban living is evident in the
    fascinating research findings of Helen Meintjes (2000). As Meintjes notes, 'whatever the
    preferences of people in all the areas sampled, those living in formal housing structures
    experience the greatest pressure to conform to the principles of proper living, despite
    not necessarily being financially better-off than those living in shacks ... In effect, it
    appears that people's expectations about the equipping of houses varies with the nature
    of house structures, which in themselves are also symbolically significant' (Meintjies,
    2000: 66–67). For instance, Meintjes found that, unlike those living in shacks, most of
    the households in formal housing displayed four-plate ovens and large colour television
    sets, whether or not these were functional. This, and other studies, suggests that this
    voracious appetite for 'modern' commodities and 'proper' appliances and lifestyles is
    often unsustainable, and poor people soon discover that they cannot afford the hidden
    costs of formal suburban living, hence the process of 're-informalisation'.

7   These were the forms of popular justice that emerged in many townships in South Africa
    as a result of the attack on the legitimacy of any apartheid state institutions. The People's
    Courts sometimes alienated elders by inverting 'traditional' generational hierarchies and
    delving into the domestic sphere. Many male elders were publicly flogged as a result of
    allegations of domestic violence and this contributed towards a backlash against these
    community policing and popular justice initiatives.

8   Xhosa traditionalists of the 1980s such as Ndima managed to reinvent themselves as loyal
    members of an African nationalist organisation that had once labelled traditional leadership
    as an outmoded, anti-modern, anti-democratic, and sexist institution whose incumbents
    had collaborated with the colonial and apartheid authorities. These dramatic shifts in
    political identity and allegiance became increasingly common as South Africa settled into
    its new democracy. Former enemies, including members of the Afrikaner National Party,
    joined the ANC, and traditional leaders who had participated in the Bantustan system

became card-carrying members of the organisation that they had fought and denounced during the apartheid years. It was equally intriguing in 2004 to hear President Mbeki and former President Mandela praise the late Transkeian Paramount Chief Keiser Matanzima at a funeral in which the former Bantustan collaborator and 'enemy of the people' was represented and eulogised by the ANC leadership as a 'man of the people'.

9   A secondary housing market is seen from this perspective to provide the necessary conditions for the upward social and economic mobility of the urban poor: With title, they can obtain bank loans by using their house as collateral, and this creates business opportunities which in turn enable households to buy into better neighbourhoods. This economic mobility, it is believed, facilitates greater political and social stability and economic growth.

10   For example, for township residents and communal farmers to take advantage of title and benefit from trading and accumulating assets, measures would be needed to facilitate easier access to credit, information about markets, and a sufficient supply of marketable and affordable housing.

11   Legal recognition of the houses and shacks of the poor can, in certain circumstances, provide secure tenure. The return of District Six residents to their homes shows that title deeds can provide security for citizens dispossessed under apartheid. What is needed is a realistic assessment of the transforming power of legal title in a situation where millions of South Africans are jobless and chronically poor. Title, it would seem, is not a sufficient condition for the creation of new economic opportunities and a vibrant secondary housing market in townships and communal areas.

12   Critics like Alan Gilbert and Peer Smets remain deeply sceptical of the sweeping claims, providing compelling counter-evidence from developing countries that little formal finance is forthcoming after legalisation. Latin American governments have given out hundreds of thousands of land titles, but this has not necessarily improved security of tenure, facilitated access to formal credit, or stimulated the emergence of vibrant secondary land and housing markets. Also, the housing needs of the poorest in developing countries are generally not addressed by formal market mechanisms – housing is usually self-supplied. And residents of slums and informal settlements are generally priced out of the formal housing market. These obstacles are evident in South Africa's informal settlements and townships.

13   After having been mugged by gun-wielding youths in Joe Slovo Park in November 2004, I realised that even the 'formalised spaces' of Joe Slovo Park had been captured by gangsters.

14   In this chapter, the words *tsotsi* and *skollie* (gangster) reflect respondents' own usage of the term to identify themselves. I am not suggesting that *tsotsis* and shebeen-owners are representative of the Marconi Beam or Slovo Park community. These are not homogeneous communities with uniform common cultural practices, identities, and understandings. They comprise individuals and groupings with distinctive agendas,

needs, and understandings. I draw on the voices of cultural brokers and *tsotsis* to encourage planners to acknowledge that social and cultural identities shape orientations to and away from 'development', and that this heterogeneity needs to be addressed when planning interventions.

15 See Sample Modules A, B, and C, Conceptual sketches, in Development Action Group, 1993, pp. 74–75.

16 Reports spoke of the need to begin long-term sustainable economic development. To achieve this, it was necessary to do the following: 'Create formal jobs through industrial and commercial developments within the Trust site and in the area generally. Create self-employment opportunities through training and small business support. Build real construction capacity in the community and in the black construction sector broadly through the initial house building process. Ensure community control over housing, industrial and commercial land to internally subsidise the housing' (Development Action Group, 1994a: page number not available).

17 Although significant commercial and industrial developments did take place in the area surrounding Slovo Park, in many instances these jobs did not go to members of the beneficiary community. In addition, there was substantial training of local construction workers, and local contractors were appointed by CONDEV. However, in most cases, such jobs were of a short-term nature. The Development Action Group (1994b) was, however, extremely optimistic that long-term jobs would be created on a 'significant scale' in the construction sector. The report went on to claim that 'the housing project will be used to train people from the community in both artisan skills and business management. Those who meet the required performance standards could become sub-contractors or even contractors in their own right. There will be at least R0.5 billion investment in construction over the next ten years in Marconi Beam so opportunities will not end when the housing project is completed' (Development Action Group, 1994b).

18 An Urban Foundation survey done in 1992 found that Marconi Beam was in many respects a typical Western Cape informal settlement. The survey covered 820 out of 834 households in a total population of 2 835 people. The survey found that 70.7% of the people were in the economically active age group. Of these, 47% were unemployed, 32.7% were permanently employed, and 20.2% were casually employed. Of the employable people, 18%, or 360, were employed as grooms at the Cape Turf Club (Milnerton Racecourse) and most of the remaining employed people worked as domestic workers, gardeners, and casual labourers. In addition, of the 820 households surveyed, 122 (14%) had a regular income, 533 (67.4%) earned less than R1 000 per month, and 165 (17.6%) earned more than R1 000 per month. The average household income was R576.80 per month, while the average individual income for those employed was R462.35 per month. Finally, of the 2 835 residents, 55% were found to be 'functionally illiterate', 30% of children of school-going age did not attend school, the average level was standard 4 (grade 6), and only four residents were at university. The survey went on to note that community

organisations were generally weak and that very few people attended general meetings. This was attributed to a number of factors, including the lack of credible and prominent community leaders. It was also observed that there were large numbers of commercial enterprises, including sophisticated provision stores and shebeens. Alcohol and drug abuse and violence against women were identified to be widespread (Development Action Group, 1994a).

19 The research in Marconi Beam was done over a period of five years. It began in 1994 when I was involved in an ethnographic research project in Marconi Beam on the social uses of literacy. This project was initiated by Martin Prinsloo, Department of Adult Education, University of Cape Town. The research involved interviews with residents, planners, and officials, as well as observations at development and planning meetings. Some of the interviews were done together with Amon China, a researcher at UCT's Department of Adult Education. I also benefited from discussions with Robert Mongwe, a social anthropology student at the University of the Western Cape, and later at Stellenbosch University, who did his post-graduate research at Marconi Beam/Joe Slovo Park.

PART 4: CLASS, RACE, LANGUAGE AND IDENTITY

CHAPTER 8

Discourses on a changing urban environment
Reflections of middle-class white people in Johannesburg

Charles Puttergill

8.1 Introduction

White residents have constituted a dominant group in the city of Johannesburg since the beginning of its establishment. Their control over political, economic, and cultural domains has ensured prime location and infrastructure for their residential areas. The city developed an extensive suburban sprawl to accommodate the more affluent white population north of its central business district (CBD) and an agglomeration of black townships that were, comparatively speaking, materially deprived, and located in the south-western periphery of the city (Lemon 1991; Parnell & Pirie 1991).

The demise of apartheid at the end of the twentieth century transformed this ideological and political context in South Africa. Political change and the concomitant economic liberalisation have been described as a double transition. This has offered the city an opportunity to remodel itself again. Thirteen apartheid-based local government structures merged to form a unified non-racial city with a single tax base. The growth of the city has not been matched by a corresponding growth of resources. Service delivery to residents and residential areas is accordingly under significant strain. Moreover, by implementing policies geared towards equity and inclusion, local government has shifted attention from the servicing of privileged, previously white group areas to addressing the needs of the urban poor, albeit within the constraints of powerful vested interests (Bekker & Leildé 2003; Seekings 2003).

This chapter examines responses of middle-class white people in an interview-based study to the changes they observe occurring within their neighbourhoods and the city (see appendix A). The racial categories referred to in this chapter reflect usage within contemporary South African society. It is the legacy of past policies and relations and does not imply fixed and timeless categories. The focus is on discourses of the interviewees on changes in the suburbs in which they live. Since they often spontaneously raised issues relating to changes in the inner city and in informal settlements as well, discourses on these changes are discussed separately. Crime, a topic often raised, is only addressed indirectly since it is an issue beyond the scope of this chapter. The chapter begins with a brief overview of changing government policy on racial residential segregation in the country. Subsequently, research addressing the changing racial consciousness of whites in South Africa is introduced in order to establish a context within which the discourses of interviewees may be interpreted. Interpretation then follows within three sections: change in own suburbs, change in the inner city, and informal settlement. The chapter closes with a brief conclusion and a methodological appendix.

8.2 The context of change

Residential segregation has characterised Johannesburg since its establishment. Before the unification of South Africa in 1910, numerous regulations governed the settlement of Africans on the outskirts of towns. The 1914 Tuberculosis Commission highlighted squalid living conditions and health risks posed by the lack of even rudimentary infrastructure. To address these risks, the Stallard Commission proposed measures to regulate African migration, settlement, and employment (Davenport 1971; Davenport 1987; Hindson 1987; Lemon 1991; Parnell & Pirie 1991). As segregationist pressure from white people grew, a national policy of residential segregation was enforced more consistently from the 1920s. Stallard (1922, in Bloch & Wilkinson 1982: 4) argued that 'it should be a recognized principle of government – [African] men, women and children ... should only be permitted within the [white] municipal areas in so far and for as long as their presence is demanded by the wants of the white population'. These principles guided the *Natives (Urban Areas) Act* of 1923, which was amended and consolidated several times.

The ascendancy of the National Party in 1948 set the stage for the implementation of apartheid as a comprehensive policy framework. The *Population Registration Act* and the *Group Areas Act*, both passed in 1950, enabled the government to reserve occupation and ownership in residential and commercial areas for a statutorily defined group. This provided a foundation for implementing a policy of complete segregation between white people and other race groups. The *Separate Amenities Act* of 1953 and the *State-Aided Institutions Act* of 1957 enforced segregation in service delivery (Bloch & Wilkinson 1982; Davenport 1987; Hindson 1987; Horrell 1978).

Greater control was exercised over the processes of urban settlement under apartheid. Stringent regulation limited opportunity for black settlement in white urban areas. Two interviewees' descriptions of the implementation of apartheid reflect the determination with which officials applied the policy objective of shaping the city as the preserve of those classified white, with the consequent division, exclusion, and marginalisation of those deemed 'non- European':

> I experienced the brunt of apartheid on a daily basis, because I lived with a coloured family as a member of that family and served a community which was an excluded community, although they had more privileges than the Africans. [#10A]

> But you also saw the horrific effects of the uhm Group Areas Act, [10A: Yes] where a lot of [Q: people were removed] people, no if you could … if you looked white then you could say that you had white friends and you could … pass, so-called, they deemed that you had white values, you could get re-classified. And so families were split on the basis of colour and so really the colour uh issue became very much more sharper because, okay black was beautiful, but brown was convenient. [#10B]

> And so I had to go uhm to confront uh the uh local people who were moved, and say to them [to the officials], look uh, this family you're going to divide, because in Kliptown they were white railway workers who had lived and married a black woman and their children were living in the same house which they had been involved in and this young man was saying, 'because you're white and because you're coloured you'll have to split this family' you, you know … [#10A]

The conversations in these excerpts refer to the harsh excesses of apartheid in maintaining a race-based hierarchy and determining access to resources. The process of establishing segregated townships and administratively controlling people's daily lives draws attention to the racialisation of social relationships. Interviewees describe the devastating impact that the implementation of the *Group Areas Act* had on the coloured community and the identity choices available to those who could pass as white. Passing as white, closely guarded against by officials, demonstrates that race is constructed.

The fluidity of race is apparent from interviews. Many recall the English–Afrikaner schism and the marginalised status of some who were classified white. An interviewee remembered the Portuguese being called 'white kaffirs'. All examples underscore the sense that whiteness had to be produced and reproduced.

At the turn of the nineteenth century, 'the racial question' in South Africa referred to putative 'ethnic' cleavages between Afrikaans- and English-speaking white people. The 'native' policy of these two groups was informed by their respective material interests. As the crisis of legitimation regarding the racial order in South Africa increased, cleavages within the 'white' community faded and they rallied to defend their privileged position (Thompson 2001; Schutte 1995). Goldberg points out that

> [r]ace is not a static concept with a single sedimented meaning. Its power has consisted in its adaptive capacity to define population groups and, by extension, social agents as self and other at various historical moments. It has thus facilitated the fixing of characterisations of inclusion and exclusion, imparting [to] social relations an apparent specificity otherwise lacking. (Goldberg, 1993: 80)

The attempt to establish an exclusive white group led to proscriptions on fraternisation across racial lines. Decades of strict residential segregation, together with the development of separate institutions such as churches and schools, resulted in an isolation from other racial groups. Yet white people had choices, as two interviewees point out:

> In South Africa, you couldn't choose to suffer, in a sense, if you were black. But your blackness made you suffer, but the difference is that if you were white, you had a choice and I think you always had to be aware [10A: That's true] that you always had a choice. [#10B]

According to these two interviewees, it was convenient to go with the flow, a flow that created barriers between white people and other groups. Two other interviewees resisted going with this flow. One became a conscientious objector to national service conscription and the other developed an extensive friendship network across the colour line. Most interviewees, on the other hand, regarded racial divisions in society, at the time, as normal and natural.

Why the focus on middle-class white people in the city of Johannesburg at the beginning of the twenty-first century?

The legacy of past stratification and domination continues to structure the prevailing conceptual order in South Africa. This has made racial consciousness an important marker of social relationships in contemporary South Africa. Redefining societal inclusion as a result of political transformation undermines the privileged position of white people under the previous dispensation. This loss of hegemony disturbs the assumed normality of past practices and privileges and transforms the significance of race (Bekker 1996; Goldberg 1993).

Several studies suggest that the shifting dynamics of class within the politically dominant group during the apartheid era created structural conditions amenable to change. At the end of the 1960s, the popular cross-class Afrikaner alliance that culminated in the implementation of the policy of apartheid found itself under increasing pressure. This alliance started to unwind in the 1970s. A numerically significant proportion of Afrikaners started acting in terms of class rather than ethnic interest and, by the 1990s, the more affluent became firmly orientated towards consumption. With the economic position of white people securely established, relying on race to maintain privilege became less crucial and led accordingly to greater flexibility in public policy (Hyslop 2000, Seekings 2003; Tomlinson 1990). Lemon (1991: 15) for example, observes that, by the 1990s, 'the government must have realized its own interest in making it easier for middle-class and upwardly mobile blacks, especially Africans, to move out of segregated townships.' Seekings (2003) suggests that a shift from race towards class as an organising principle within society occurred by the 1990s. According to Hyslop (2000), white people increasingly identified themselves as 'middle class' as the appeal of defining themselves collectively in racial terms waned.

In spite of this argument that class had replaced race, 'class'-based concerns remain central to the way in which the racial groups perceive each other. What such a 'middle class' identification means, and the extent to which it is deracialised, is one of the questions this chapter will examine. Schutte (1995: 330) argues that 'many decades of apartheid had seriously impaired the ability [of whites] to cross racial barriers. ... [and that some whites realised] that they would never be able to rid themselves of their white racial visibility and ascriptive identity'.

A key dimension of post-apartheid urban policy is to redress racial segregation (Tomlinson 1990). In describing their experiences of change, most interviewees spoke from a context of segregation. The descriptions of the city by Mabin (2001: 183) aptly capture the current context: 'Johannesburg is really a remarkable place from which to view the urban world. It is a "suburbanizing world city in an urbanizing poor country" ... From its very high density but troubled inner city, through bourgeois suburbs of last century to symbols of extraordinary suburban ("edge city") investment.'

8.3 Changing demographics of suburbs

The discussion in the preceding excerpts reflects how segregation was enforced in Johannesburg during the apartheid era. A consequence of these processes is that suburbs in which interviewees live continue to reflect this segregation. They are aware nonetheless of the changing demographic composition of suburbs in the city and how this impacts differentially on suburbs, in some instances changing their character.

Commenting on the change they observe, interviewees directly or indirectly allude to differences between the suburb they live in and other areas of the city.

More than two-thirds compare the demographic composition of other areas within the city to their suburb. Less than one-third focus on the changes they experience in their suburb. All interviewees mention crime and that people of other racial groups are increasingly settling in their suburb. Rising levels of crime are a common concern and generate insecurity.

The level of crime within the city is high, compared to other cities in the world. A cursory glance at official statistics available confirms that incidents of crime are many, and that they increased after 1994 and then stabilised. The trend of a rising crime rate was already apparent in the 1980s. This crime wave can be attributed, in part, to instabilities accompanying the double transition brought about by political and economic change. Suburbs have been affected differentially in this regard (Isserow 2001; Parnell & Pirie 1991).

Change in own suburbs

A changing demographic composition of suburbs was an emerging theme. Two-thirds admitted that their suburbs remained primarily white but were aware that people belonging to other racial groups were settling in them. Instances where interviewees thought demographic change in their suburb was significant probably reflected an overestimation due to the greater visibility of newcomers. The viewpoint on the impact a changing demographic composition would have on their suburb was not determined by whether they thought such changes were considerable or not.

Two strands of thought emerge on the consequences of changing demographic composition. Those emphasising the shared middle-class position of black people moving into their suburb predict minimal changes. Others believe that cultural difference could cause some tension.

The following response reflects some key arguments typically made about ways in which shared class interests minimise the impact of changing demographics on lifestyles in the suburb:

> I haven't seen as much of a change, in the area in which we live. Uh, because most
> of the homes are established and with still the same white people basically who
> lived here, except the house across the road which has been to let and uhm for two
> lots of six month leases there've been black people living there, but not bothering
> anybody or you know and they in fact, they didn't even really integrate, either. We
> did invite them once to tea, the one lot … No, I, I think there are still many carry,
> carry-overs from the old apartheid regime. Key people still tend to largely live in the
> communities in which they formerly lived, although those who are more upwardly
> mobile, especially in the rural, in urban areas, have moved into other areas and you

do see them, you know and and people seem to find that quite okay ... Uhm, you
see them, in the dress of the, the girls, very westernised. And none of us walking
around with doeks and things like that ... So what the apartheid regime did wrong I
think is that they did not develop the African middle class. So now we've got masses
of uneducated people whom we're sitting with and causing a huge problem for us.
And and I think that the diverse, the difference between people is going to be class
... and not race, because a black person and a white person who are of the same class
are going to find it quite easy to mix, because they have lots of things in common ...
But now you can see the levelling of the class issue. If you go to any traffic light here
in Joburg and I am sure probably in Pretoria, you'll see lots of whites, poor whites
and they're poor people. It's just another thing of the white thing. Like my friend, my
one white friend, she said to me, 'I don't give to white beggars' So why? I also don't.
Because they had all the benefits of the past. They had a council house, they had
welfare, they all this and they had like all the opportunities and they blew it. They
did. [#4]

The notion that class interests and values are shared across racial lines is reflected in
responses of many other interviewees. In the conversation cited above, references
to 'upward mobility', the importance of developing an 'African middle class', having
'things in common', sharing 'middle-class values', and 'levelling of the class issue'
underline the importance attributed to class in solving the racial problem. The
interviewee concedes that middle-class black people in her suburb have not yet
really integrated, due, in part, to 'carry-overs from the old apartheid regime'. In
spite of this, she emphasises that white and black people in the suburbs share
middle-class interests.

The possibility of class becoming a more acceptable, less contentious basis for an
exclusionary discourse and defence of relative privilege arises. In this regard, 'poor
whites' are dispensable. In fact, their existence contributes to a 'levelling of the
class issue', just as the upward mobility of black people serves the same function.
Hence class difference and privilege are deracialised. There is a clear preference
for differentiation by class to differentiation by race, with the former viewed as
less problematic than the latter as upwardly mobile black people join the middle
class.

Interviewees accept that the middle class increasingly will be multiracial as more
black people enter it. They express a desire to maintain a middle-class sameness
within this changing context in the suburb. Sameness is achievable by upholding
shared middle-class values, as an interviewee suggests:

Oh, we have seen changes occurring in, as to the fact that there are a lot of uhm,
Indians and blacks buying the houses. Uh, they are of course probably uhm, of our

financial status, [Q: Yah, yah] because if you look at the cars they drive and the uh the the way they're dressed and the way they speak and the way they, what they're paying for the houses ... But there's no change, in that the area's deteriorating, not at all, not at all. I would say the houses round here that look as though they need uhm renovating outside are very much more the that belong to the white people. And uh the funny thing is Charles, the houses that have got the biggest locks on the gates are the Indians and the co, the black people, not the white people, Eh eh eh, because they obviously uh uh, I personally think they don't trust their own, [Q: Yah] that's my personal feeling, they don't trust their own, and we've never been broken into, we had one attempt, but hence I mean, you see the way we live [Q: Yah], but I feel perfectly safe, I'm not concerned that my uhm neighbour here is Indian and my neighbour diagonally across the road is black, I'm not concerned at all, and of course you see a lot of children here very nicely dressed in their school uniforms ... And uh wherever you go the the shopping centres, the uhm the schools, the uh especially the uh uh recreational uh like the botanical gardens, there are many many uh you know blacks, coloureds and Indians walking around there and my personal opinion is, that frankly, they are very very well behaved. [Q: Yah] That's one of the things that, because, this is the circle I moved in, you know what I mean, I couldn't tell you what it's like in Turffontein because I have got no idea. [#1]

The reference to 'of our financial status' – underpinned by the clothes, cars, and homes – describes a similarity between white and black residents. These patterns of consumption suggest a shared class position. The comment that it is often white people whose homes may need renovation reflects their potentially precarious class position. Hence the increasingly multi-racial composition of the suburb does not threaten its class base. The comments that their 'children [are] nicely dressed' and they are 'very, very well behaved' in public areas frequented by her white middle-class 'circle' implies a shared middle-class respectability. Her claim that she cannot comment with authority on the situation in a previously working-class white group area indirectly suggests working-class white group areas may be more embattled.

Most interviewees do not express concern about the changing demographics of the suburb they live in, provided its class character is maintained. Both Hyslop (2000) and Seekings (2003) argue that the urban white middle class is prepared to share its residential areas and institutions with a black middle class. Interviewee responses raise the question as to whether class becomes the primary articulation of social difference. This implies a realignment from race to class. According to Hyslop (2000), whites were less prepared to defend apartheid from the 1990s onward. In an excerpt above, little sympathy is expressed with 'poor whites', who had 'opportunities' and 'blew it'.

A key concern is maintaining a middle-class lifestyle. All interviewees referred to the trend towards consuming privatised health care, education, and security, even though some could not afford certain services. Gans (1996: 66) argues that 'every group tries to make sure that the institutions and facilities that serve the entire community maintain its own status and culture'. Privatised services play a role in ensuring autonomy, homogeneity, exclusivity, and maintaining privileged access in a context of change. An interviewee commented in this regard:

> Up to '94 I mean the white man actually had it all his way and we've actually, a lot of
> the problems perceived now is, I just want to say, we've been greedy, we don't want to
> share what's been available which is also maybe why we see health care and education
> and so on as not being what it used to be, but maybe that's because it has to cover
> a much broader base now, and if we want it, we're going to have to pay for it, if we
> want it like it used to be ... I would say in many ways its our choice, that we want it a
> particular way, if that's what you want, well, pay for it. [#20]

In the context of consumerism, financial therefore means secure quality of life. Income level determines access to privatised services and institutions. Security services, in particular, reflect a shift towards privatisation and consumerism. This is driven by a perception of high risk, resulting in a significant commitment of resources to safeguard and protect property. Although a process of privatisation of security is not uniquely South African, the deployment of police in townships in the 1980s to deal with the volatile political climate, as well as a more equitable redeployment of public resources after the political transition, served as a catalyst for unprecedented growth in privatised security services. Rapid change heightened a sense of vulnerability and uncertainty felt by middle-class white people. I have pointed out that there was an increase in the incidence of crime in Johannesburg during this period (Davis 1996; Isserow 2001; Parnell & Pirie 1991).

Most interviewees implemented a number of measures to secure their property in accordance with means at their disposal and their assessment of risk. While most had only been victims of petty crime, they were aware of more serious and traumatic incidents that affected relatives, friends, or residents in the neighbourhood. One interviewee living in a security complex noted, in this regard:

> We've got the burglar bars, we've got the alarm, we accept it, uhm we, yes I fear my
> kids walking up to the shops on their own, so it's not something I let them do, so the
> security is an issue in that respect I think that uhm the the lack of effective policing is
> something which uhm is in my opinion quite obvious. So one lives in a constant state
> of, of, of a of a normal apprehension if I put it that way ... [#15]

The conversation in this excerpt suggests 'fear' of crime and increasingly sophisticated security measures to manage the perceived risk that has become part of life. Fortifying homes, residential complexes, or even parts of neighbourhoods by erecting high perimeter fencing and electrified fences and gates, using razor wire, installing closed-circuit cameras, alarms, boom gates, and establishing resident's associations to coordinate initiatives creates a protected private domain insulated from external dangers and threats. A fear of crime is not totally unfounded, even though a perception of risk may be overstated. The level of protective measures is linked to affluence rather than the actual extent of crime. As elsewhere, efforts to address crime take a formally organised, privatised, and commercialised route. Run by competitive for-profit companies, such service is consumer orientated rather than community orientated (Berg 2004; Davis 1996).

The consequence of these protective measures and constant surveillance regulating access is withdrawal to the privatised realm of a self-contained environment isolated from the wider society. Fortification provides a solution to the perceived threat, creating areas where an affluent lifestyle can be lived in privacy without having to confront inequalities in society. Behind the protective barriers of homogeneous gated communities, children can roam around and ride their bicycles in streets. Many interviewees reported spending more leisure time at home and going out less frequently in the evenings, due in part to their fear of crime. Generally, when they went out for entertainment, it was to a shopping mall or themed entertainment complex that had security measures in place. Tomlinson (1990: 5) observes that 'most whites live and work "inside the laager", which means that they seldom feel endangered'.

Current residential and commercial patterns perpetuate the insularity entrenched under apartheid in spite of a willingness to share amenities with the upwardly mobile. In an excerpt cited above, an interviewee refers to black neighbours having the most elaborate security measures because they 'don't trust their own'. The reported actions of black middle-class neighbours justify her own security measures. 'Class' – implied here as level of income – is played off against race. Financial capacity ensures that the right kind of people, who share her material interests, gain access to her neighbourhood. There are clear prescriptions about who qualifies to live in the suburb. She indirectly suggests an association between crime and poverty, and poverty and race. This racialisation of perpetrators of crime raises the question of whether there are other reasons beside the often-cited threat to security for closing off areas.

In his classic study of suburbia, Gans (1996) notes that it provides what residents seek. Gated communities also meet such needs. Within a homogeneous context, residents can organise their lives around their home and family. Several interviewees commented on a withdrawal into their own private space and observed that neighbours were less likely to have sustained friendships with each other than in the past. They compare this trend in their suburbs to their perception of a greater sociability in less affluent black residential areas.

Not all interviewees thought that shared middle-class values ensure commonalities across racial boundaries. Some were more cautious about the impact of a changing demographic composition on their suburb. They referred to the way in which 'cultural' differences might potentially have disruptive consequences. In these instances, the desire for sameness extends to shared cultural practices and hence a shared history. The demographic transition threatens the perceived homogeneity and accepted social practices within the suburb. By raising the issue of changing municipal bylaws and alien cultural practices, an interviewee suggests that some tensions may arise:

> ... and I do not have a problem if here, whatever other-colour guy comes and stays next to me, if he adheres to my norms and the norms of the environment. You know if you go and look at the, at the 'bylaws' ... that changed, if there next to me now is an other-colour guy, whose, whose culture dictates to him, let's say he can slaughter an animal because they have a funeral, they may now slaughter in his backyard. Now I mean, can you think what drama, what, what impact that will have on me and my neighbours and also on children, to see how they slaughter an animal, cut off its throat, and let it bleed like this, and bleed like this, and bleed like this. So that, I see as a future problem, a possible problem. [Translated: #11A] (Excerpts translated by the author from Afrikaans are available on request.)

Concern is voiced about ways in which the quality of life may be adversely affected. Some traditional cultural practices, stereotypically described as a disruptive spectacle threatening privacy, are labelled inappropriate in a suburb. Cultural difference becomes problematic when it is seen as undermining their sense of social order. Amending bylaws to allow traditional practices suggests shifting power to dictate what is deemed appropriate or not. Describing the anticipated impact of transition, an interviewee recalls a conversation with her mother on the threat to their suburb of overcrowding once black people could legally move into a previously white group area:

> Now, we talked about, like, for instance, I stay in this house, and, and say for instance, a black family stays in that house and the two houses cost exactly the same, monthly rental and maintenance and those type of things. But there, here I stay and my family, and there he stays and two, three other families, you know, that doesn't really make it fair in our eyes. Okay. Now, you can say, yes, you could have started a commune and you could also have put more than one family in the house, and then it would have

been financially more fair [sound], but uhm, I don't know, it, I think it is how we have been raised, of uhm, I have my house and my privacy. [Translated: #5]

She suggests that black people typically engage in practices that differ from those of white people. She describes black people as being prepared and often forced, given their class position, to share accommodation. Racial integration raises the perceived threat that white people may be overrun. Both preceding excerpts deal with what the 'right kind of practices' in their suburbs are. One interviewee, in a less exclusive and more racially diverse middle-class suburb, noted:

Well personally, they haven't affected me at all. Uhm, I have for instance, a black neighbour behind me, to the front of me and on one side of me and they are very quiet and, and, and … and we, we get on very well. I would be inclined to say we don't become personal friends, simply because we are different in culture …Um, I would be inclined to say that there has been a deterioration in the actual residential area, because um, a lot of these folks don't do the same type of gardening-cum-housing maintenance that we were used to in the past. In the past it would appear that people were quite proud to have a nice garden and a nice verge. Um, a lot of the people that live here now don't look at the verge on the outside at all. Um, all the swimming pools around us are empty and dirty. Every one. Back, front and both sides. In fact, ours is the only swimming pool that you could swim in. So you can see there's been a deterioration in the actual quality of the resident, residential area. [#16]

The remark at the beginning of this excerpt that 'they haven't affected me at all', followed by 'we get on very well', is comparable to a statement in an excerpt cited earlier by an interviewee that he has no problem with 'other-colour' neighbours. This suggests a tendency to express tolerance even when cultural differences are emphasised as being irreconcilable. Such tolerance is qualified by suggesting that established norms and standards should be maintained. In the excerpt above, the impact of greater heterogeneity in the suburb is described by comparing past practices in maintaining a property to present practices in neglecting it. A deterioration of the suburb is linked to the influx of 'these folks'. While he emphasises getting on well with his neighbours, he also describes cultural difference as a barrier to developing friendship.

The interviewee deflects any charge of racial bias by criticising four neighbours. A distinction between 'we' and 'these folks' is drawn. It becomes clear from an extended passage in the interview that, whereas the white neighbour's lack of attention in maintaining a swimming pool is an individual failure, the three black neighbours' actions reflect a group's way of doing things. A similar shift from the interpersonal to the intergroup context occurs in an excerpt cited above where an interviewee concedes that, although white people may start a commune, it is atypical in comparison to the more common practice amongst black people to share accommodation. Cultural difference is accepted as a fact. Emphasising it deflects attention from race while maintaining a notion of fixed difference.

The desire to express tolerance for diversity and avoid questions of race may be the result of changing socio-political contexts. Race is much less prominent in these recent interviews, whereas Boot-Siertsema and Boot (1982) report a strongly argued taken-for-granted viewpoint justifying segregation on racial grounds among conservative white respondents they interviewed in the 1970s and early 1980s. I do not want to create the impression that such a discourse has vanished completely. Instances occurred in the research where references to racial difference surfaced, often causing some embarrassment to the interviewee, on how what was considered normal and natural in the past may somehow be considered problematic now. One interviewee described what she was taught:

> I think our upbringings are fairly different. Okay, I grew up on a on a farm, so okay, I can't account for a sort of a an upper class black family, but I mean I know the rural blacks and I mean you think, you think differently, you act differently … So for me it's very hard to distinguish what I perceive as a real difference and what is a taught difference, because I was taught a lot of differences, okay. [Q: What differences were they?] They're, they're definitely more stupid, you know, I mean physically, apparently, its been proven that they have thicker skulls so they've got less brain space you see … And they, you know there's all these things that I was taught, I can't distinguish, because I don't have enough to do with them to form a friendship with somebody, with the kind of friendship I have with, with my white friends that I actually know what they think and feel. [#8B]

She initially argues that socialisation of white and black people differs, suggesting cultural difference. The stereotypical images expressed are reinforced by selective observation in a rural context marked by physically close but socially distant asymmetric relationships. Her reference to personal experience excludes 'upper-class', presumably urban, middle- to high-income black people. This protects her from charges of bias. However, she lapses into a highly contentious and offensive claim of biologically determined difference but then recognises that her isolation prevents her from 'testing' the validity of such views.

Opportunities for communication across racial barriers remain limited as a result of continuing patterns of segregation. Spatial patterns of settlement are both a consequence and a determinant of social relations. In general, interviewees repeatedly professed no problem with a changing racial demographic in their suburb. This was often followed by a caveat stressing the need to adhere to middle-class values, or municipal bylaws, or on the impact cultural difference may have. These caveats demonstrate racialised thinking, in a masked form. According to Goldberg (1993) denial of racial prejudice plays a prominent role in its reproduction.

Some reflection is needed on what is seen as middle-class values. In an excerpt above, references to 'the dress of the, the girls, [being] very westernised' and to 'none of us walking around with doeks and things like that' suggest assimilation to a western middle-class lifestyle. Interviewees specify the grounds on which they are happy to associate with black people in spite of an avowed tolerance. This implies that black people should adapt to the way of life and practices to which white people are accustomed. Schutte (1995) suggests the assumption that black people should adapt to a white South African lifestyle demonstrates the exercise of whiteness.

Racial diversity is increasing in schools, residential areas, and malls. To a large extent, racial boundaries prevail in spite of a professed tolerance for diversity and growing mobility which implies that race and class are no longer coterminous. At this stage, the black middle class numerically pose no threat to fundamentally altering the composition of previously white middle-class group areas. Increasing diversity then masks continued exclusion of a majority. Davis (1996) refers to the 'privatisation' of public space in Los Angeles through enclosure and fortification, arguing that, to an extent, such new class divisions mirror old racial divisions. Race and class continue to overlap to a large extent in South Africa, revealing the limits to processes of desegregation. The admission that 'they didn't even really integrate' suggests that race can still divide in spite of a shared middle-class position and professed tolerance.

Change in the inner city

More than half the interviewees described changes in the inner city. The demographic composition of the CBD and high-density inner-city suburbs, formerly white group areas, changed significantly. They described the impact of these changes on the CBD:

> O gosh, many businesses moved out of town. And because theft increased in town, we, for example, seldom go to town. [Translated: 14B]

> Yah town also used to be quite a whitey scene and now I'm one of the few whiteys in town ... Whereas, when I was a kid I remember we would go window shopping in town, we would walk around window shopping uhm now the shop windows look bloody ugly, you know, they're not window-dressed in an artistic way, they're window

dressed in a mass market way 'buy this, cheap this' uhm big signs, loud garish signs you know of that look like everything is perpetually on sale ... And also organisations moving out of town and into Sandton, who would have thought that Sandton would become an, a CBD? [#7]

Uhm, our offices were in town, uhm and if you just think about how town has changed since. I dunno fifteen years ago, uhm it was essentially a white commercial centre ... Anybody who was anybody was situated in town ... there's been massive outflow, you know, and then the influx of black people into into town and and taking up that space and so its like two different forces almost business versus social, uhm competing for space. [#2]

The inner city has changed from being exclusively a domain of 'white' people to increasingly that of 'black' people. They describe a process of invasion and succession, the consequence of competition for space, with black people claiming the streets of the CBD as white people deserted them. These accounts of change in the inner city are not unique to South African cities (Davis 1996).

The importance of the CBD, formerly a focal point of social, cultural, and commercial activity, declined with 'white flight' to gated commercial and business enclaves in suburbs north of the city. Retail in the inner city changed as decentralisation to shopping malls in suburbia occurred. This process began in the 1970s and was consolidated by the 1980s. Decentralisation to office parks fuelled by property speculation characterised the 1990s. Affluent white people centre their social lives on privileged consumption in gated malls with 'themed' entertainment centres and increasingly avoid inner-city areas, generally seen as no-go zones of decay and decline (Mabin 2001). According to Bremner (2000: 88) 'speculation, urbanisation, crime and the growing informalisation of work have altered the city in ways that have superseded and yet reinforced apartheid's patterns'.

Although most interviewees avoided the CBD, some were aware that conditions within it were improving. City improvement district initiatives, in partnership with business, strengthen services in some areas, installing extra measures such as surveillance cameras and providing additional resources for cleansing. This has reduced crime and made these areas more attractive. The CBD is therefore characterised by both decline and regeneration.

The following accounts describe a process of invasion and succession of residents in inner-city suburbs that have become predominantly black and African as a result of 'white flight':

Oh there, yah its definitely, I mean a lot of it has changed. If I think about where I started when I lived in Yeoville and Bellevue, which is basically where I started, it wasn't very diverse, but uhm certainly now if you look about it, look at it, you know basically most of the whites have actually moved out of that area and uh, it's predominantly a black area ... [#9]

and uh those people those people moved out and uhm and were replaced by lower economic group members of, yah maybe they, they became more affluent and could afford to move out and were replaced by a lower incoming group uhm comprised mainly of uhm of coloured, Indian, black. Uhm ... But the problem with high density areas in, in the city is that they they are very embattled uhm ... it's high density and it's rented and it's cheap and people uhm just, there does seem to be a difficulty in maintaining value under those conditions. [#2]

An initial 'greying' of inner-city suburbs results in eventual resegregation. Declining property values were often linked to the change in the racial composition of inner-city suburbs, deteriorating infrastructure, and poor service delivery. Inner-city suburbs were seen as 'embattled', reflected in the dwindling numbers of white residents and plummeting property values. Parnell and Pirie (1991: 142) suggest that lower income whites initially resisted an influx of other groups into their residential areas but that 'lower income whites could escape the ghettoisation of Johannesburg's low rental flatland ... [due to] attractive housing opportunities that existed away from central Johannesburg'.

High-density areas with more reasonable rental are described as vulnerable to such changes. A changing class position is associated with the changing racial composition of these suburbs. For some, the possible knock-on effect of a greying suburb in close proximity to theirs is a concern:

I would say there is a lot of people moving to the areas. If they go, if people have got the money to buy in the area that's fine I have got nothing against that, if you take a look at some of the areas down, down towards Cresta ten years ago it was mainly white areas it has become a mini Hillbrow, now which I don't agree with, because the crime like I have said has shot up there and basically uhm most of them use, most of the peop ... black people used to stick to their townships now they getting out their townships its not that I worry about that but I do worry about uh uh crime going up. [#12]

She describes an influx into a formerly white group area of people who no longer 'stick' to their townships. There is a suggestion that the class status of the area may decline and crime increase as a result of such an influx. Her claim to be concerned about crime rather than objecting to those who could afford to purchase property deflects criticism of racial bias. Yet crime, racialised, becomes a euphemism for race. It indirectly suggests a racial causality to crime. This line of argumentation also surfaced with regard to changes in own suburbs, and it surfaces with regard to concerns about informal settlements.

Interviewees highlight a number of issues with regard to inner-city and high-density areas. A changing demographic composition of inner-city or high-density areas potentially threatens property values and increases the crime risk of established residential suburbs in close proximity.

Informal settlement

A third of the interviewees, commenting on change in the city, referred to the growth of informal settlements. By the 1980s, black townships had a serious housing shortage (Parnell & Pirie 1991). This shortage was exacerbated by abolishing the legislation enforcing influx control in 1986, lifting restrictions on migration to urban areas. The *Group Areas Act* was repealed in 1991. Interviewees observed the impact of a housing backlog and the relaxing of controls:

> The other thing quite honestly is that I don't recall seeing squatter camps and that as a kid, the squatter camps … but now it's in your face. You see poverty far more around you as well. You know so you, to me its almost its becoming not a racial divide but becoming a financial divide in the country. [#8A]

> And of course you know before the, before the, uh the, freedom uh they were very restricted into areas they went into, whereas they're not now, they can now do what they want to. Do you know here in the … road, living in the sewers, were hundreds of them, they got them out last year some time. In uhm, behind [the nursery] there was a village living in those reeds, they've got no homes, they've got, the government as fast as they build their houses they can't cope. [#1]

Encroaching informal settlements implies that the social distance between the affluent and the poor no longer necessarily equates to spatial distance. Poverty is more visible as informal settlements are established in the periphery of the city and on vacant land near a middle-class suburb. The inability of local government to prevent the poor from settling on vacant land suggests disorder and a loss of control.

A white middle class is more accommodating of an emerging black middle class in their midst than of the black poor. A 'financial divide' disqualifies members of informal settlements. The juxtaposition of poverty and affluence is unsettling. Poverty, not affluence or inequality, is the problem. Informal settlement, then, should be managed. The poor bear the brunt of resolving this problem. They should preferably be removed or situated out of sight as is suggested in the excerpt above. One interviewee noted that another potential concern besides her primary concern, crime, was the establishment of an informal settlement in close proximity to her residence:

> I suppose what could be a concern today, although it doesn't affect us directly here, is when there's empty land and you get squatters moving in, that sort of thing, it will be an issue but for me personally here it's not. [#20]

She is aware that close proximity of an informal settlement has an impact, although it is not a direct concern that currently faces her. Vacant land always poses a risk. Informal settlements are a threat because they imply poverty, and poverty is linked to crime. These two concerns are not unrelated. Informal settlements are associated with a failure of authorities to regulate settlement and provide services. An interviewee living in close proximity to one raises the following concerns:

> There's been some dramatic changes just recently, over the last uh eight or nine years, that are very alarming though and I'm inclined to put my money where my mouth is and say that the government has zero zero control over the development of large squatter camps within the area. [Q: Near here?] Very close. Just up the road. You know and these squatter camps are totally and utterly illegal in terms of municipal laws. They're an absolute health hazard to everybody including themselves and they are a very very eyesore to to to the community ... If one had to go back 20 years ago, it would never have been dreamt to be allow ... allowed and now it's just getting bigger and bigger and bigger. It's got to the stage where I believe in my own mind that they have no opportunity of ever changing it. And of course it's full of ... of of uh undesirable people. [Q: Undesirable? Why? Why would you say they are undesirable?] They've got no work, they've got no homes and they've got nothing and therefore they've got nothing to lose. You know when somebody has got nothing, they've got nothing to lose, then they will come and they will break in and rob and steal and do whatever they want ... and now it's right on our doorsteps. [#16]

This conversation describes informal settlements as a problem. Vulnerability is expressed by claiming that authorities have 'zero' control, that the settlement is full of 'undesirable people', and that it is 'on our doorstep'. Undesirability is linked to poverty and poverty to crime. The failure of authorities to exert control over informal settlements and vagrants implies disorder, threatening the suburb in both a material and normative sense. The squalor, disease, and crime associated with informal settlements are perceived as threats to health and safety and raise concerns of decline affecting the quality of life in established suburbs.

Bremner (2000) and Seekings (2003) suggest that the middle class, including upwardly mobile black people having obtained a foothold in the property market, is less enthusiastic about low-income neighbours and uses its organisational capacity and political influence to oppose such housing developments in close proximity to its residential areas. In his classic study of suburbia, Gans (1996) indicates that first-time home owners vigorously protect their property investment against loss of value.

Associated with class position is a set of entitlements and expectations that reinforces the apartheid geography of the city, pushing housing developments for the poor to the periphery in areas where they are currently located. Parnell and Pirie (1991: 144) refer to the strong opposition voiced to a proposed Norweto, with considerably less objection raised against 'a "second Soweto" 50 kilometres south of Johannesburg' in spite of dolomite at that site. As a consequence, the locational disadvantage imposed by apartheid persists, with housing for the urban poor provided in the periphery. In the light of this, there are strong pressures to preserve the class base of residential areas. This social exclusion and consequent segregation marginalises the urban poor and reduces the possibility of broad-scale integration (Bremner 2000; Seekings 2003).

The following comment by an interviewee who voices concerns about informal settlements attributes the undesirability of these settlements to the inhabitants' moral rather than material deficiencies:

at one of the specific squatter camps [a nurse] says to us they had a call from a grandfather that phoned to uhm, to want to hear if they, uh, have birth control medication, for the, for the, for his grandchild, or whatever, then it came out that the grandfather and the father rape the, the daughter. Now I do not need to expand on that. If, you need only to read in the newspapers, and to look at how the people, now okay. It sounds again if a guy is picking the whole time on the other-colours. I know there's of the white people, also that are paedophiles and all those type of things, but, dear God, it was never at such shocking levels as it is now, and then you don't even need to talk about the Cape Flats, of all those numbers of children which are each time shot dead, innocently, and I mean that is coloureds, it's not whites where it is about a white issue for me at all. It is only for me about, about the broader society. Uhm, Jeez, you know if you, just these things, where are we going? … Now how, how, you know, I do not know what you, but it, I only say how do you reconcile these societies, of each other? … Which dif … differs radically of each other. You know I did Anthropology I at Unisa. What I said earlier of these children that are raped, it is so. It is shocking, and ten to one, what [my wife] also said, it already occurs for a long period of time. It is so. In the old days, in the Zulu's days, the, of, of the captains, or whatever, give the king young girls to maintain the peace in certain areas, or so that he would not attack them. What I, and I do not let myself be told that the king left those 14-, 15-year-old girls alone. So maybe it is not, maybe this now is only now in the public domain. It is actually an old tra ... it is, contrarily it is their culture, but in our culture we cannot reconcile ourselves to say we may have sexual intercourse with a girl of 14, 15 years. Good that is now, that is now, but one extreme. [Translated: #11A]

This description is constructed from an anecdote as well as exceptional and sensational cases reported in the media rather than from direct experience. The stereotypical account was offered by an interviewee who emphasised cultural difference as a potential obstacle to integrated middle-class suburbs. The deviance highlighted is attributed to traditional or cultural practices within the community. 'Uncivilised' practices are compared to 'civilised' practices. The 'depravity' of these practices in the informal settlement 'erodes the worthiness' of its residents. To deflect a charge of prejudice against this highly contentious account, he concedes that some white people engage in such deviant practices, but does not suggest this is culturally sanctioned in these instances. Russell (1997), for instance, explores the incidence of incest among white Afrikaner families.

In this account, the interviewee denies an interest, indicating that it is not about a 'white issue and finally calls on the persuasive power of academe to corroborate his claims. Both highly blameworthy behaviour and explanations why it occurs are constructed in the account. This serves the purpose of establishing the factual base of cultural difference while denying prejudice simultaneously.

The implicit discourse in the excerpt reflects rhetoric in the public domain. It suggests a racial other has incommensurate moral standards and unacceptable practices measured against white norms. In this process, culture, reflecting particular practices and values, is reified to provide an acceptable explanation for fixed differences, construed in some respects as being irreconcilable. It is preferable to refer to culture rather than race when describing difference.

For the interviewees, the establishment of informal settlements in the vicinity of middle-income suburbs raises a number of concerns about potential deteriorating health and sanitary conditions as a result of inadequate infrastructure, the strain on service delivery, increasing crime, and the impact on property values. In some instances, besides references to the infrastructural deterioration such settlements bring about, the threat of moral decay is also implied.

8.4 Conclusion

Interviewees reflect on local contexts in describing the change they observe, its impact, and their concerns. This chapter has focused on the representational dimension of discourse. It reveals how interviewees respond to the political, economic, and social dimensions of post-apartheid urban transformation. Such descriptions do not simply reflect reality but the interviewees' own interpretations of it, mediated by their own social context, self-history, and self-identification practices

Societal discourses are linked to changing social relations as a result of political transition. A brief comparison with discourses on the South African society recorded by Boot-Siertsema and Boot (1982) in the 1970s and early 1980s demonstrates the contingent nature of taken-for-granted viewpoints within society. The pervasiveness of race consciousness is demonstrated both directly and indirectly. While the thrust of interviewees' comments suggests crime, or a decline of a suburb is linked to the racial 'other', they qualify their comments to deflect charges of bias. Their caution around issues of race demonstrates their awareness of a wider social taboo in the changing context. Many interviewees went to great lengths to emphasise the contact they had with people of other races, to demonstrate their tolerance, even though such contact remained limited. Shifting attention from race to class is comfortable and attractive. It conceals the past basis of privileging. A few who expressed no desire for social contact justified the maintenance of boundaries by fixing the racial other as having different lifestyles due to their cultural practices. Where a majority of white people expressed overt racism in the past, only a minority do presently. These discourses illustrate how 'whiteness' operates differentially across time and space.

It remains difficult to assess the 'typicality' of the views expressed by interviewees. They repeatedly raise key issues in response to non-directive questions in spite of diverse backgrounds. Interviewees benefited materially from past policies and have shared interests in maintaining a foothold of privilege. Their privileged position is more 'precarious' with the dismantling of racial hegemony, which in the past left their whiteness unmarked as the 'norm'. The concerns they voice cast light on their experience of living in and adapting to a changing context. These accounts of and concerns about a changing urban environment reveal the insecurities of middle-class white residents in more affluent suburbs.

Appendix A: Methodology

This chapter draws on a subset of interviews conducted for a broader research project in which 'discourses of change' amongst people classified white are considered. The category 'white' glosses over many differences eliciting scholarly debate on its analytical usefulness and the danger of reifying race. However, the current situation is best understood by taking the racialisation of South Africa into consideration. Although a small sample is drawn from the northern suburbs of Johannesburg, these suburbs constitute a numerically significant proportion of people classified white in the city.

Three contact persons were approached to suggest potential interviewees for the purposive non-random sample. They were not restricted to people living in their suburb. To ensure diversity, a matrix listing interviewee attributes guided selection, with a bias towards English speakers built in to balance the preponderance of Afrikaans speakers in other areas covered by the broader study.

Twenty semi-structured in-depth interviews were conducted by the author of this chapter with 25 people between July and November 2003. While most interviews were single, in some instances pairs were interviewed. The number in square brackets refers to the interview from which the transcribed excerpt is drawn. An A or B following this number indicates a participant of a paired interview. Q refers to the interviewer. Names are omitted to ensure anonymity.

Aggregated age, sex, language, and occupational characteristics of the interviewees are as follows: Eight (32%) were between 20 and 39, eleven (44%) between 40 and 59, and six (24%) between 60 and 89 years old. Ten were male (40%), and eight Afrikaans speaking (32%). Five were retired, ten were self-employed, and two had been retrenched. Occupations ranged from being housewife, artist, hairdresser, receptionist, executive secretary, administrative official (2), bookkeeper, human resource manager/consultant (3), teacher/lecturer (4), engineer/technician (7), and veterinary surgeon, to serving in religious ministry (2).

Interviewees had lived in the city for periods between four and more than 50 years and in the suburb between one and 38 years. Twenty-one interviewees (84%) had lived for more than 10 years in the city and 13 (52%) for more than 10 years in the suburb. In general, the length of residence in both the city and suburb they were currently living in suggests a high degree of residential stability.

In conducting this research, an attempt was made to encourage a conversational style, using open-ended questions. Interviewees were asked to reflect on the changes they observed in the city, on ways in which these changes impacted on their lives, and on what concerns they had as a result of their experience of these changes. Their responses generated an immense amount of data, which was transcribed verbatim. This provides an indication of the ways in which middle-class whites respond to the changing urban environment they face. Given the limitations in size, composition, and spatial location of the sample, described above, no claim is made of generalisability to the full range of 'white' experience in the city.

I am indebted to the interviewees who were prepared to participate in the study. My analysis is an interpretation of these conversations. Participating in such a study is not without risk to interviewees. In spite of these potential reactive effects, I gained a sense that interviewees were open in their responses and willing to share their experiences.

CHAPTER 9

Class, race and language in Cape Town and Johannesburg

Simon Bekker & Anne Leildé

9.1 Introduction

Over the past decade, cities in South Africa have been deeply influenced by three analytically separate processes: changing economic circumstances due in large part to globalisation, the continuing process of urbanisation and migration – a largely national issue – and, last but not least, a rapidly changing policy environment established after 1994 by the first democratic government elected on the basis of universal adult franchise. Before this date, cities were governed under an apartheid government that structured residential space and economic opportunity unequally along ascribed racial lines.

Post-apartheid national policy aims to correct inequalities flowing from this former national ideology. The urban vision of the new government is succinctly summarised in the following extract from a 1997 policy document:

> Government is … committed to ensure that its policies and programmes support
> the development of urban settlements that will be spatially and socio-economically
> integrated, free of racial and gender discrimination and segregation, enabling people
> to make residential and employment choices to pursue their ideals. (Republic of
> South Africa, 1997)

The aim of this chapter is to identify how collective identities are being constructed in Cape Town and Johannesburg and, since it is generally accepted that the manipulation of residential space and economic opportunity has a direct impact on the way in which people construct their identities, to establish whether new identities are being constructed as a result of this new policy approach (Sharp & Boonzaier, 1995; Houssay-Holschuch, 1999; Martin, 2000; Bekker, Leilde & Puttergill, 2004; Gervais-Lambony, chapter 5 in this book). In particular, since middle- and high-income housing developments seem to be guided by the market and low-income housing developments remain state led (Huchzermeyer 2003; Pottie 2003), it is pertinent to interrogate whether this policy approach has a differential impact on different urban populations.

We will address these aims in three steps. It is apparent that the structures of cities worldwide share an increasing number of common features (Hall & Pfeiffer, 2000). It is appropriate, then, to investigate selected international theories on urban identities to establish theoretical benchmarks against which we are able to assess our evidence. In the second place, we will also identify what South African social scientists have argued are the primary forces shaping South African cities over the past decade. Against this international and national backdrop, we will then provide qualitative data we have assembled from a series of 35 focus groups conducted in Cape Town and Johannesburg over the past five years. A list of these focus groups and details of the way they were organised is provided in appendix A. An interpretation of these research data will suggest which urban identities appear to be emerging in these cities.

At this stage, a brief explanation of the way we conceptualise social identity is useful. According to Castells, 'Identity is people's source of meaning and experience' (Castells 1997: 6). It is neither essential nor immutable but a social construction open to change as circumstances, strategies, and interactions fluctuate. It needs therefore to be situated historically and relationally, since identity is a matter of social context. An identity defines elements of similarity (the 'We') and of difference (the 'They' or the 'Other'). These elements are usually emotionally loaded: they can be based on feelings of pride and 'dignity' or of fear (Taylor, 1994). Identity therefore needs not be conflictual: it can be either open and inclusive or closed and exclusive. It is also generally accepted that individuals construct various identities for themselves. However, 'such a plurality is a source of stress and contradiction in both self-representation and social action', since these identities may be in internal tension with one another (Castells, 1997: 6). Accordingly, under specific circumstances, a primary identity (one 'that frames the others') emerges to prevail over others (Castells, 1997: 7). One way to identify the growing dominance of one identity over others is to detect and describe the identity narratives used by individuals and groups and thereby to infer which is being promoted. Identity narratives contained in the material gathered during focus group sessions have been carefully analysed with this objective in mind.

9.2 Urban identities in the United States

We will study identity construction in selected post-apartheid South African metropolitan areas against the backdrop of two theories on urban identities:

The first one – the *dual city* concept – is formulated by Mollenkopf and Castells (1991) who focus on the socio-economic restructuring that is taking place in American cities. In the case of New York, this concept refers to a changing urban social structure that is progressively polarising, fragmenting, and becoming more exclusionary, due to the restructuring of the labour market. Such a process produces the coexistence in the city of a professional and managerial elite and a growing urban 'underclass'. In addition, this process manifests itself spatially by minimising contact between these two groupings. For the upwardly mobile elite, in fact, home ownership in a middle-class suburb is widely viewed as a stage before selling and buying in a better area. Accordingly, any depreciation in the land market (through low-income housing developments, for instance) is resisted (Huchzermeyer, 2003). In effect, this process embodies the breakdown of what Castells calls the 'urban contract' (Castells, 2002b: 377)

Such a process of social and spatial polarisation has a direct impact on identity construction according to the two authors. Indeed, 'the tendency toward cultural, economic, and political polarisation in New York takes the form of a contrast between a comparatively cohesive core of professionals in the advanced corporate services and a disorganised periphery fragmented by race, ethnicity, gender…' (Mollenkopf & Castells, 1991: 406). On the one hand, economic prosperity leads to social integration promoted by shared values such as individualism, life-style choices and consumption patterns, cosmopolitanism, and increasingly an obsession with security. On the other hand, poverty encourages fragmentation and segmentation, mainly in ethnic terms, of the excluded who build 'defensive communities' that fight and compete against each other for access to work and 'to preserve the territorial basis of their social networks, a major resource for low-income communities' (Castells, 2002a: 310) In the former case, identity expresses itself through individuation, in the latter, through communalism (Castells, 2002c).

The other relevant theoretical input – the *divided city* concept – is used by Nathan Glazer, who conceives of New York as a multicultural city. According to this view, the socio-economic divide developing in this city is insufficient to capture adequately what is of meaning, of interest, and of concern to residents. While dual cities suggest horizontal divisions, divided cities suggest vertical divisions in both society and social space. These divisions, which are mainly ethnic, according to Glazer, 'play an independent role, particularly as carriers of certain values in conflict' (Glazer, 1994: 187). Indeed, divided cities refer to 'cities divided by race, ethnicity, religion rather than by economic fortune, income, wealth, even though the latter divisions are real enough … Divided cities refer to divisions that we sense to be of kind, rather than quantity … Sometimes, as we know, this kind of division is marked by a real wall, but generally the invisible wall is good enough to keep groups apart' (Glazer, 1994: 178).

These two conceptions of New York City – the one founded on elite class group solidarity and 'underclass' fragmentation, the other on cultural diversity – will guide our analysis of emergent urban identities in Cape Town and Johannesburg. First, however, we will show that, despite numerous public efforts to the contrary, most current analysts view Cape Town and Johannesburg as fast becoming dual cities. (It is appropriate to note here that Johannesburg refers to the Johannesburg Metro, excluding the Ekurhuleni Metro).

9.3 Cape Town and Johannesburg

Both metropolitan areas share a certain number of characteristics, among which a past of racial segregation imposed by former apartheid policies. Racial segregation divided Cape Town spatially between the City Bowl and two developed north-south and east-west urban spines, on the one hand, and coloured and black townships (generally known as the Cape Flats), located on the south-eastern periphery of the city, on the other. Similarly, according to Beall et al., 'during the growth decades of the 1950s and 1960s, the spatial pattern of a middle-class northern half of Johannesburg and a working-class southern half of the city was reinforced by state-imposed racial segregation and suburban expansion for the white middle class in the north' (Beall et al., 2002: 49).

Both metropolitan areas also inherited large free-standing informal settlements that grew rapidly after 1990 as African families from disadvantaged rural areas flocked to the cities. Setting itself the goal of building one million houses during its first term, the new National Government in 1994 developed a government housing subsidy for households qualifying in terms of income as the main policy instrument to achieve this ambitious goal. Consequently, large RDP housing schemes were built in the 1990s, overwhelmingly in the peripheral areas of the two metropoles (Pottie, 2003).

Profiles of Cape Town and Johannesburg

The thumbnail demographic profiles offered here are intended to highlight certain similarities and differences between the two cities. With similar population sizes in 2001 (2.9 million in Cape Town and 3.2 million in Johannesburg Metro), both cities are multicultural and multilingual as well as religiously diverse. In these terms, Johannesburg is probably the more diverse of the two. More detailed information is given in the profiles of Cape Town and Johannesburg in chapter 3. Employing South African ethnic classification, Cape Town's largest group is coloured (48%) followed by 32% black, and 19% white, while Johannesburg's majoritarian group is black (74%) followed by 16% white, 6% coloured, and 4% Indian. Furthermore, Cape Town is dominated by three home languages which represent the three provincial official languages: Afrikaans (41%), English (28%), and isiXhosa (29%). This city, moreover, continues to reflect a strong coincidence of race and language – the black community, in particular, is 90% isiXhosa speaking. Johannesburg reflects a greater diversity of languages. African languages predominate (isiZulu, 26%, Sesotho, 11%, Setswana, 9%, and Sepedi and isiXhosa, both 8%) while English is the mother tongue of 19% of the population and Afrikaans of 8%. While the vehicular language of Johannesburg is increasingly becoming English, Afrikaans retains its position 'as medium for primary and secondary communication' in Cape Town (see chapter 10 on language identities). In addition, Cape Town and Johannesburg differ in terms of recent urbanisation flows. Internal migration toward Johannesburg is more diverse than toward Cape Town since it comprises a plurality of sending areas from both contiguous provinces as well as neighbouring and other African countries. Finally, Cape Town contains the largest Muslim community in South Africa (Mandivenga, 2000).

Policy aimed at one city, a compact city

Substantial institutional reform and policy changes have taken place in Cape Town and Johannesburg since 1994. The primary underlying aims of these changes were to integrate the city spatially and to reduce inherited inequalities. To this end, both cities now have a single-tier metropolitan authority with a single tax base. Parallel to these structural and financial changes to city government, planning strategies have been designed and implemented to foster residential densification and promote urban sustainability (known as the Metropolitan Spatial Development Framework in Cape Town and the Strategic Metropolitan Development Framework in Johannesburg).

What appears to be happening in South African cities

Despite such policy and structural changes, most analysts believe that the 'market' has replaced the 'state' as primary urban development driver in South Africa. Their views may be summarised by identifying three market-driven processes that are believed to lead toward continuing social and spatial polarisation. The first process is located within the labour market: traditional manufacturing sectors in these cities have been shrinking as the service and financial sectors strengthen. This encourages an expansion of a highly skilled labour force, while employment for blue-collar workers diminishes. As a consequence, wage differentials rise. The second process is located within the land market. The state appears unable or unwilling to intervene in the process of land acquisition. Rising land prices in middle-class residential areas are accompanied by well-orchestrated middle-class opposition to state interference in their land market. As a consequence, most low-income housing development continues to be located in the periphery of cities where land is cheapest (Turok, 2000; Bremner, 2000). As Pottie (2003) puts it, 'In the end, the market sanctions inequality, and, as market rationality has structured housing policy in South Africa since 1994, this rationality has generated important limits to the transformative potentials of political and economic restructuring of South Africa' (Pottie, 2003: 141). The third process is 'the suburbanisation ... of new economic activity' (Mabin, 2001: 10), leading to the location of private sector investment in the northern sectors of both Cape Town (Blaauwberg, as an example) and Johannesburg (the edge cities of Sandton and Midrand, for example), thereby sidestepping employment demand in the populous but poorer Cape Flats and Soweto areas of these cities. This general pattern of spatial development in these cities fuels the process of polarisation both within the labour market as well as regarding residential segregation. It is far removed from the policy ideal of the 'compact' city and signals rather the emergence of a 'dual' city. To quote Saff, 'racial segregation has been replaced by social segregation, in effect by "deracialised apartheid"' (Saff, 1998: xvii–xxii).

This identification of Cape Town and Johannesburg as dual cities has led analysts to distinguish sharply between processes of identity construction among the middle- to high-income groups and among the poor. In the former case, identities are conceptualised as deracialised where residents join together around economic interests and tend to adhere to middle-class values (Robins, 1998) and 'international norms of urban consumption and culture' (Beall et al. 2002: 7), processes that Hyslop (2000) argues began in the 1970s, from which time

> whites were willing to accept residential and school desegregation, but only if it did
> not involve a change in the class identity of their neighbourhood. (Hyslop, 2000: 40)

For the poor on the other hand, at least in the case of Cape Town, increased polarisation along racial and ethnic lines takes place in low-income areas. One reason given is competition over scarce resources between black and coloured communities (Maré, 1997), leading to the reproduction of racially based socialisation (Sharp, 1997). For instance, according to Lohnert, Oldfield, and Parnell (1998),

> the minimal impact of desegregation, plus the relative failure of state initiatives
> to ameliorate racialised poverty draws our attention to the coping strategies of
> the urban poor of Retreat and Imizamo Yethu ... Many aspects of urban life have

become so racialised that the once pejorative label coloured is now seen by some as a legitimate primary identity … The overall picture that emerges is one of increasing social polarisation within racially homogenous settlements, a vision far removed from the lofty ideals of equity and non-racialism. (Lohnert, Oldfield & Parnell, 1998: 86–92)

At a more general level, in the words of Marks and Bezzoli (2001),

released from the grip of state control, our cities are now at the mercy of that most nebulous of conceits (*sic*) – the free market … Released from the grips of the Apartheid State, the 'free market' has been set loose on existing inequitable urban conditions, consolidating our cities into evermore divided and segregated spaces. No longer only along race but along class lines as well. (Marks & Bezzoli, 2001: 27–29)

In short, according to these analysts, middle-class identities constructed in middle-class suburbs converge around shared middle-class values; the identities of the poor constructed in segregated townships continue to fragment along inherited racial and ethnic lines.

9.4 The construction of urban identities in Cape Town and Johannesburg

Our interpretations of qualitative focus-group (FG) data have been guided by two principles: the extent to which FG narratives appear to accord with identities influenced either by the 'dual city' or by the 'divided city' concepts, and the extent to which such identities appear to emerge from the narratives as primary identities, as identities that 'frame' others. After a preliminary scan of these data, moreover, we decided to classify narratives into an 'urban middle class' and an 'urban poor' category and to analyse data in these two categories separately. This decision was based on results of the scan that revealed a wide range of similarities in both cities of narratives falling within each category and clear variance in both cities of narratives across categories. The urban middle class category is defined as comprising respondents in FGs that fall within a middle and higher income range within which residents live in suburbs and are formally employed in white collar (or established blue collar) positions; and the urban poor category is defined as comprising residents in FGs that fall within the ranks of the poor and unemployed and who reside in informal or low-cost formal accommodation. It is relevant to point out that the class categorisation of focus groups was not part of the original research design but flowed from the decision to set up focus groups on the basis of shared residence in an urban neighbourhood.

The SA urban middle class
Similarities between Johannesburg and Cape Town
The issue of racial mixing in residential areas – such as in former white and coloured middle-class areas – was raised a number of times. Typically, the issue was discussed in terms of racial stereotypes, although sometimes stated in covert terms:

> Another thing is that you've got a lot of coloured people moving into this area ... I mean, your more affluent coloured group [and therefore] you're in a ... diverse set-up ... too diverse. (Panorama, white Afrikaans-speaking middle income, Cape Town)

> But even [the town of] Paarl is getting blackish, you know. If you drive through it ... (Linden, white Afrikaans-speaking middle income, Johannesburg)

Nonetheless, racial issues were rarely raised as reasons to move into a neighbourhood. Rather, residential choice among middle-class residents appears to be motivated by the socio-economic status of the neighbourhood:

> I don't mind if my neighbour is black or coloured as long as we live in harmony, with the same standard. [That] I [may not] have decent people next to me, that [is] what bothers me. The colour doesn't bother me. (Oranjezicht, German-speaking middle income, Cape Town)

> Why are we all migrating to Pinelands? Investment purposes, what feels good. You have to think of a place where your children grow up ... and it's sort of, how can you say, up-market. It's nothing to do with whites, [rather] something that is more up-market that you can afford ... You know, we are actually moving towards class distinction whereby whatever you earn ... pretty much dictates where you stay ... You are starting to think along class lines, not racialistic lines anymore. (Pinelands, coloured middle income, Cape Town)

> I also think that anybody of a different colour moving into our area have uplifted themselves so therefore, you're socially able to communicate with them ... there's a vast difference between him and the man who collects the rubbish. (Roodepoort 1, white English middle income, Johannesburg)

> It would be nice to live [in Bosmont] for the sense of community, but not from a

personal living point of view ... [I want to live] where I can have a pool, and a nice house, and I won't have people breaking in and I can drive my car, which is a bit of a yuppie car, without somebody discriminating against you because you progress, you understand. So you actually move out of there so that you can live with people who have the same status as you ... (Florida, coloured middle income, Johannesburg)

One exception pointing to residential choice being influenced by multicultural considerations was found in the new 'greenfields' residential area of Summergreens (SG):

In our environment, I never grew up with the black or white kids, I never experienced it. Like my daughter, today kids grow up with a multiracial, a multiplicity of cultures. ... I call SG the new South Africa. It's the only area where there is no racial tension. We live in total harmony. SG to me is a melting pot of people ... I didn't know who I was going to live next to. I didn't care who I was going to live next to ... You don't want to run around [with] this business of 'whities', of coloureds anymore. This is old stuff. To me that is pre-94 stuff ... Here, people choose SG for that specific reason, because we have been denied [it] as kids ... we would be willing to allow our kids to grow up with all races, creeds, colours and I think people make a conscious choice. I made a conscious choice that I'm going to stay here. (Summergreens, coloured middle income, Cape Town)

These class identities appear to be constructed around shared values, a shared 'way of life' and common interests and concerns such as crime, property values, and neighbourhood tidiness. Contrary to what is often claimed regarding 'middle-class' individualism, a close-knit community or a sense of 'neighbourliness' is actively sought out by middle-class residents. These class identities also seem to accord with Castells and Molenkopf's conceptualisation of the dual city. In particular, they point to the mental map that middle-class residents carry of spatial distinctions, of places one visits and places one avoids, in their cities:

But then, Jo'burg's structure is such that you don't need to go to those [dangerous] places. It is just like any other city, it's like New York, and Cape Town, you live there but you don't need to go to Khayelitsha or Mitchell's Plain ... you can bypass them ... What I am trying to say is that you don't need to go and do your Saturday morning shopping in downtown Johannesburg at the moment if you don't want to. (Fleurhof, coloured middle income, Johannesburg)

If I remember Cape Town when I was a child, [i]t was a pretty picture in your mind but it's just gone. The streets are filthy, the drivers ... they ride you off the street if they can. The only nice place to go to in town is the Waterfront now. You know, when you want to say you are going to shop and you want to shop nicely and you can find underground parking. (Punts Estate, coloured middle income, Cape Town)

Differences between Cape Town and Johannesburg
While class appears to play a major role in the choice that middle-class residents are able to make regarding residence, in the case of Cape Town, choice of residential area appears also to be based on shared cultural traits.

I think the other thing [about] moving to Pinelands was that, we've lived in other areas … we found it's a safer area. Safe but not behind the [Afrikaans-speaking] 'sausage curtain' [*boereworsgordyn*] … in Pinelands, it is cosmopolitan and it's more English as well, and you see more colours. We relate more to English style than to Afrikaans style. (Pinelands, coloured middle income, Cape Town)

In the Cape Town middle-class FG narratives, there are also numerous examples of sentiments of pride and self-esteem, rooted in language, religion, and traditional practices that appear to be shared at a residential neighbourhood level. The first example is drawn from an Afrikaans-speaking FG:

A good thing about our area is the schools that are here because the Christian element is very much alive and that is very important for us. There are a lot of Christian elements. There is more [here] than in lots of other places and for us it is very important. So that is very good. (Panorama, white Afrikaans-speaking middle income, Cape Town)

In the formal area of a former black township:

I've long been wanting to move to Rondebosch but my wife wouldn't agree because in those areas, there is a lot of crime, house-breaking, people break into people's houses. Here, I know, when I'm at work, my neighbour is looking after my house. Other than the neighbours' watch (*sic*), here we have *Ubuntu*. Another reason [not to move] is that here in townships, in the Khayelitsha area, we love one another but … maybe because I'm black, the people in Rondebosch will have attitudes towards me and I will also have attitudes towards them because our cultures are not the same and I won't be able to do what I do here in Khayelitsha. As an example, Christmas time or New Year's time, I slaughter a sheep, now coming to Rondebosch, people would start looking at me. Because this is our culture, during Christmas, I have to slaughter a sheep … Here, I easily do that but there, people would stare at you. (Khayelitsha 1, African middle income, Cape Town)

In the 'Malay' quarter of Cape Town, religion rather than income status is expressed as the criterion of selection of place of residence:

> We have people who, even though they can afford to go and stay between people who are not Muslims, prefer to stay in a Muslim area. This preference is not because they are anti-white or anti-black, it is simply because they feel that the environment in which they are living is conducive to religious culture. They prefer to stay where there is a Mosque nearby and they will look for that. ... In so far as residential integration is concerned, I think a lot of it is because of established customs and culture within an area and then moving [from] that, perhaps into a much more sophisticated or grander house doesn't compensate for the loss of ... community spirit so you are staying in a very beautiful palace up in Constantia but you've lost track of your roots, of who your neighbour is, who was a Muslim, the Madressah down the road where the children go to school, the Mosque which you can walk to, you know those kinds of things we cherish. That just reflects our prioritisation of us being Muslims and that we are not that class conscious. (Bo-Kaap 1, Muslim middle income, Cape Town)

These preferences for cultural homogeneity at neighbourhood level in Cape Town appear to lead in some cases to claims rooted in shared language and religious belief that transcend neighbourhood boundaries and flow into the public domain at city and even at national levels.

> If you think [about] politicians trying to put their pen down [to suppress] Afrikaans as a language, I know, and I think 99% of Afrikaners know, nothing will get the Afrikaans language down. That's to say it doesn't matter what they are trying to implement or whatever law they will try and [pass], it is not going to get us down ... Even if we are forced to speak English or whatever language, but we will still be Afrikaners, nothing will take that away from us. (Panorama, Afrikaans-speaking middle income, Cape Town)

> If you look at the demographics of the Cape Peninsula, I mean the Muslim community make up 23% of that total community ... 23% is a quarter of the population in Cape Town and yet we don't exert the clout which a quarter of a population should be able to ... Our strength is not at national level. I mean we represent what population? 1.5% of the national population, so there's going to be no impact. But we can create a situation where [we could have] a sizable impact upon city council decisions ... (Bo-Kaap 1, Muslim middle income, Cape Town)

These narratives conform to Glazer's conceptualisation of the divided city since they reflect both strong cultural as well as class features. Such cultural features may lead, as Martin (1999) has argued, to identity narratives reflecting peaceful interaction between groups thought to be different, as well as to narratives as sources of potential conflict between such groups. Examples of each type of narrative were found in the Cape Town FG material:

> One of the major changes since 1994, which I think most of us wrestle with, is the sudden emergence of a third language as a requirement for business to function ... That is a major shift. And the problem is that it is not simply a matter about learning a language, it is a whole cultural thing you have to learn for which there is rather less tolerance than there should be. The fact is that Xhosa culture is different, there is a general perception that it's wrong and there is very little understanding. (Business, middle income, Cape Town)

At neighbourhood level, on the other hand, cultural heterogeneity – at least in the three examples cited – appeared to imply a degree of potential conflict:

> [This neighbourhood] is predominantly Afrikaans ... there is definitely prejudice, I mean we get called 'Soutie' and ... 'Laaitie' and 'rooinek' ... Yes, there is definite animosity from neighbours, and purely based on the fact that we speak English ... It is not like we are exactly socialising ... Due to the fact that we're English in an Afrikaans suburb ... you don't socialise that much with your neighbours, really. (Kraaifontein, white English-speaking lower middle income, Cape Town)

> There is a piece of land next to the tennis court. It was bought by the Muslim community and they are going to build a Mosque on it, which means that we are going to have lots of traffic in and out, which we never really had before. And they will park up (sic) all the streets, because they have wedding[s] or whatever ... And then of course, when they call people to prayer, that would be a big thing, the noise. And the school as well. So we signed a petition against it. (Punts Estate, coloured middle income, Cape Town)

> Because Long Street was Bo-Kaap, the Waterkant [neighbourhood] has become [an] affluent white yuppie area and that was where the residents of Bo-Kaap have been pushed out. They are becoming smaller and smaller because of where we are situated, this is just prime land for those people but it's not just all about the nice view and prime land, it's also for us about a way of life and a culture. This is the main problem here, people moving in and not respecting other people's ways and religion. They must respect our religion and culture, it's in our constitution. That respect is just breaking down and it shows the big differences between our community and the rest throughout Cape Town. Here we believe in our morals and values and we are trying

to maintain that. And with these outside influences coming in, it's just not on. (Bo-Kaap 2, Muslim middle income, Cape Town)

The sense of cultural 'compartmentalisation' captured in these narratives was succinctly stated in the following FG:

Cape Town appears to be very white, that's what I think. And that's why they say we are very racist. We are very European-centric (sic). It's very white, unfortunately. It's so Euro-centric, it's almost like it's a separate place from South Africa in terms of its cultural mixing. Over and above race, I think it's colour, creed and religion. I think we are also very intolerant about other races as well as religions. We are very polarised here, even within our inter-denominational [congregations], we tend to be very intolerant. (Pinelands, coloured middle income, Cape Town)

In Johannesburg, in contradistinction to Cape Town, narratives about community at neighbourhood level appear to be based more on a 'shared lifestyle' than on common cultural features:

About 50 years ago, Linden was the heartland of the old *Broederbond*. It used to be called the Afrikaner Houghton but now, it's not that, it's more a middle class type of thing. (Linden, Afrikaans-speaking middle income, Johannesburg)

I wouldn't go for a [Bo-Kaap area in Johannesburg] like there's this [exclusive] Muslim camp. My religious beliefs don't allow me to have that … We actually thrive living amongst other races, cultures, creeds. I think that is also important, otherwise you are very one-track minded. (Bosmont, Muslim middle income, Johannesburg)

I like Johannesburg for one thing because it is more at the centre of South Africa, it gives you the opportunity to meet other people from different provinces and that makes a city-type dynamic. (Dube, Soweto, African middle income, Johannesburg)

Cultural ties that remain important appear in Johannesburg to have been domesticated, practised by family and friends in private and not playing an important role in the choice of residential neighbourhood.

I am definitely living here because it is central … central in relation to shops, in relation to schools, churches, petrol stations, it is just very central. And it is an established area. It is very peaceful, and it is very beautiful here. Language was not a consideration when we bought the house. Because a guy's friends come and visit you at your place, I mean your neighbours are … hallo and how is it going, and what are you doing, are you working in the garden, yes, no, and what/what/what but one's friends do come through, I mean all our friends don't live in this area ... our friends come from different neighbourhoods and areas, that come and visit us. (Roodepoort, Afrikaans-speaking middle income, Johannesburg)

Simultaneously, English appears to have been accepted as *lingua franca* in Johannesburg:

Johannesburg is a more relaxed city than Pretoria. I know about language, for instance, people don't tend to make such an issue about language [here] as they do in Pretoria. [There] you go to a shop and you speak Afrikaans, and you insist in being answered in Afrikaans. Otherwise you get upset. Whereas in Jo'burg, I tend to immediately speak English and then after five minutes I realise I'm actually speaking English to somebody who's Afrikaans speaking. You know, we switch and then eventually we don't even know what language we're speaking. (Linden, Afrikaans-speaking middle income, Johannesburg)

The SA urban poor
As in the case of middle-income FG narratives, the combined FG narratives of the poor in Johannesburg and Cape Town also appear to reveal both similarities and differences.

Similarities between Cape Town and Johannesburg
While issues relating to pride and satisfaction with selection of residential neighbourhood made up an important part of middle-income FG narratives, those of the poor in contradistinction focused on access to jobs and to housing. Selection of residential neighbourhood appears to be of little importance, possibly because the poor are able to exercise little choice over what area to live in.

I'd go anywhere else so long as it's in South Africa and there is everything you need. There's nothing here but we are compelled to stay because that's the place we got (Tembisa, African poor, Johannesburg)

When living area is in fact raised, the narratives tended to point to spatial exclusion rather than neighbourliness:

Khayelitsha is one of the townships which is not close to Cape Town. Cape Town is the nearest city but it is not so close and we have to spend a lot of money on transport to go to Cape Town. (Khayelitsha 2, African poor, Cape Town)

In addition, struggle over residential turf within a living area reflects the fragmented nature of the 'underclass':

> The community didn't come together and stand together as one ... they won't stand close to fight these gangs, now the community looks and stands when they shoot, they rejoice in it ... Here we don't want to support one another. If I get evicted we laugh about it, our water gets cut, the one laughs with the other, they rejoice. ... It's this one block of flats, and these people will stand together. Then you will go to the next block of flats, and then instead of people [sharing] community, it differs from one block to another block. (Lavender Hill, coloured poor, Cape Town)

The dual city concept characterised the urban underclass as a set of communities competing with one another over both employment as well as over accommodation 'turf'. Lines of cleavage dividing these communities are said typically to be ethno-racial. In both Cape Town and Johannesburg, competition over jobs and scarce resources appears to have led the poor to widespread stigmatisation and scapegoating of African immigrants. They are considered to be responsible for a wide range of harmful and negative practices:

> An alien comes tomorrow from wherever he is from, this afternoon he's got a cell-phone, tonight he's got a flat, tomorrow he goes with a box of chips he will sell. Where did he [get it] ... You just walk around and you see all the aliens have got cell-phones and they have got a flat. They are all over town. (Lavender Hill, coloured poor, Cape Town)

> The people from Zaire ... that is the main problem, because it causes us to not get better jobs. These people occupy spaces [of] our people by selling things in Cape Town. But our people are not having a chance to sell, because Cape Town is full of these people, they are everywhere. (Khayelitsha 1, African poor, Cape Town)

> Another point to show how bad these people are, they brought fake money into South Africa. Drugs as well were brought by them into this land. Before these people arrived our life was all right. We respected each other and whenever you did something wrong we were able to reprimand you. Today we cannot [reproach them] because you are controlled by drugs and guns. Guns enter the country because of them. (Tsakane, African poor, Johannesburg)

> Foreigners come from Maputo, the Maputos are the most and also Malawi, Zimbabwe. These people accept any offer like, for example, if I am looking for a job, and the employer is offering to pay R500 and I refuse it, the foreign people, they

accept it no matter what and they work non-stop, Monday to Monday. And that way, the employers prefer these people because they are cheap. Even R10 per day is fine for them so we South Africans can't work. (Tembisa, African poor, Johannesburg)

Differences between Cape Town and Johannesburg
The primary differences in narratives among the poor in Cape Town and Johannesburg relate to the importance of a racial divide among the underclass. In Cape Town, social exclusion appears to be experienced, in both coloured and black townships, on the basis of race:

> Before, they said that you don't have to pay [rent] because the government said you can have a house free because the native people in Khayelitsha, and those places there, live for free. What they pay is maybe next to nothing for the house they've got … So then all the other communities tried to live free and then they found out that it doesn't work like that. (Lavender Hill, coloured poor, Cape Town)

> Look how children are struggling to get work and they have matric … For me basically, this is now precisely the opposite of what happened in the white man's time … now the black man is trying to fix what the white man did wrong. But now they are attacking each other … I have a question, we coloured, where are we? … still in the middle? (Eersterivier, coloured poor, Cape Town)

> There are a lot of places where I would not go in Cape Town, because apartheid is still around. Africans who live in Cape Town don't get jobs. Our people in our society are isolated. This province is different to other provinces. Our people come from other provinces where apartheid is gone … Gauteng is better. Here African people have problems. Here in Cape Town, only coloureds and whites get better jobs. But if you are African, it's like in apartheid a long time ago. (Khayelitsha 1, African poor, Cape Town)

> There are grades in Cape Town. Colours have grades. 1st grade, 2nd grade, 3rd grade. Blacks are regarded as 3rd grade in Cape Town. [I]n work places … people who discriminate the most are coloureds. Coloured people of Cape Town are discriminating, especially compared to coloured people in places such as Uitenhage and Ibhayi [Port Elizabeth] … Coloured people, if you work with them, will always look at a black man as down (*sic*). They will always think they are better than you … (Joe Slovo Park 1, African poor, Cape Town)

Though race appears to be an important line of cleavage, an important boundary between 'us' and 'them' among Cape Town's underclass, there appears to be little pride or self-esteem in this ethnic or racial identity. Rather, it is carried as an imposed identity.

> There is a problem about speaking isiXhosa in Cape Town because nothing has changed, the Boers are still in control and they speak in Afrikaans. And people who get opportunities are coloureds. So if you want a job it can happen that you [do not get it] even if you qualify for that job ... because of your inability to speak Afrikaans. So those of us who come from the Eastern Cape ... become disadvantaged here. So that is one of the problems that we get, that of not being able to speak Afrikaans. They say that isiXhosa speakers like to *toyi toyi*. They say we are difficult. (Joe Slovo Park 2, African poor, Cape Town)

> ... but go to Nyanga, Khayelitsha, the [blacks) support one another, they support one another. Here we don't want to support one another. If I get evicted we laugh about it, our water gets cut, the one laughs with the other, they rejoice. It's not a nice thing. I never thought that one day I would suffer [like this]. (Lavender Hill, coloured poor, Cape Town)

In Johannesburg, issues of access to jobs and housing also figure prominently in most narratives of the poor but sentiments of exclusion – economic, social, and political exclusion – are interpreted in class rather than in race terms.

> Life here in Johannesburg is not so easy. The crime is too high and there are no jobs. There are too many people looking for a job ... The problem of Johannesburg is because [for] everybody in the rural areas, when you need a job, you think of coming to Johannesburg but it's terrible these days because there are not those kind of jobs. ... In the old days, the apartheid era, there was too much jobs (*sic*). Never mind [that] the income was less, you get little money but you have a job, you get some bread on the table at the end of the day. ... For the [loss of] jobs, I blame the government of today ... they do little for the people. All they do is corruption. They spend a lot of money on things that are not needed. ... The government now ... only hires ... people who earn a lot of money ... the people who are educated. We are not rich enough to go and further our education because you have to pay a lot of money for university ... They don't worry about us on the ground. (Brixton, African poor, Johannesburg)

> The people we have voted into power are turning [out] to be our enemies. Someone who loves you will not make your wife and children to suffer. You know I am working but this man is my best friend and he is not working. And I don't like it if I have R10.00 in my pocket [when] he does not have it. And so [for everything to] be wonderful, let everybody get equal opportunities. Let there be work. Let them not

sing us a song that there will be jobs. And they … lie to us saying we got democracy. What is democracy if you are unemployed? What democracy do you enjoy if you are hungry? (Tsakane, African poor, Johannesburg)

The person who placed us here is a person called Vusi but he's passed away now. He was trying [to do] something good for us because he saw that we were suffering without jobs … He was a comrade, he was against government … The government has given people RDP houses, why is it taking them back saying they don't pay? Government builds houses for people who earn very little money, but yet, it turns around to take them, saying they don't pay. (Tembisa, African poor, Johannesburg)

That's one of our problems in this country, not necessarily in Alexandra alone. You see, a person will come here telling you that 'whenever you need me, I'll be there, I'll serve the community'. Immediately you give him that position and that's the start of the problem. You're no longer going to see that person. Most of our leaders, especially municipal leaders, they're operating things unprofessionally. You find some of them, they are in the shebeens and you start to ask yourself 'how can this person be like that? … he doesn't look like a person committed to my community'. (Alexandra, African poor, Johannesburg)

Even though Johannesburg is multilingual, language discrimination similar to that expressed in Cape Town's poor narratives did not figure in equivalent narratives in Johannesburg. Rather, the use of various languages and frequent code switching was noted:

We feel free here in Johannesburg, you can see it's many languages you can speak in Johannesburg … we have to learn each other's language, like it or not. The first time, it's not so easy. Most of the blacks, we sometimes use English, Afrikaans, Zulu and Sotho … (Brixton, African poor, Johannesburg)

In short, the narratives of the poor in Johannesburg appear to express widespread exclusion and put this down to an increasing divide in access to education, to the labour market, and to political influence between haves and have-nots – between classes – rather than between ethnic or racial groups.

9.5 Conclusion

Both Cape Town and Johannesburg exhibit characteristics of the 'dual city'. It is apparent from the narratives we have considered that polarisation between the middle classes and the underclass, both in terms of labour market access and in terms of residential space, is something residents worry about. Sentiments expressing social distance and the need for residential separation between these classes suggest strongly that living in these cities – thinking of oneself as a Capetonian or a Johannesburg resident – carries very different meanings for middle class and poor residents. These meanings that range from pride in neighbourhood and self-esteem in career achievement to frustration about exclusion and anger about stigmatisation appear to be at odds with the lofty post-apartheid ideals of 'one city for all'.

Urban middle-class identities in both cities appear to be constructed around shared middle-class values that in turn are significantly related to living in neighbourhoods where notions of a close-knit community and of neighbourliness ought to be shared. In contradistinction, though the poor in both cities are trapped in racially homogeneous low-cost formal and informal residential areas, it is not the nature of this residential space but rather economic and social exclusion as well as fierce competition over local resources that shape the identities of the urban poor.

Simultaneously, significant differences emerge between such urban identities in Cape Town and in Johannesburg. In the first place, where choice of residence in better-off neighbourhoods is available, shared culture, language, and religion appear to play a significant role in the decision-making process in Cape Town. This in turn suggests that residents in middle and higher income neighbourhoods perceive themselves *at both neighbourhood and city level* to be culturally and linguistically diverse and at times deeply divided along cultural lines of cleavage. Residents of these neighbourhoods express pride and derive substantial self-esteem not only from their class positions but also from their linguistic and religious affiliations, revealing a degree of conformity with Glazer's model of a 'divided city'. Such a trend appears to be much less pronounced in Johannesburg where cultural identities are domesticated and accordingly lived out in the private domain. This divergence between the two cities, expressed in a middle-class Johannesburg narrative, is interpreted in race terms:

> It's too white, Cape Town. You're so used to seeing black people over here so … Imagine staying over there and seeing white people as your neighbours. You know, all the areas have a certain type of culture … Like if I am in Cape Town, say after six o'clock, you don't see black people, you [can] count them actually. Here in Johannesburg even [at] 10 o'clock, you still see black people. Cape Town has its own culture and Johannesburg has its own culture and you know that people with money like to cluster [by] themselves. (Soweto, African middle income, Johannesburg).

In the second place, while bonds of solidarity and of community among the urban poor appear to fragment as residents compete over access to scarce resources, the lines of fragmentation are not always the same in Cape Town and in Johannesburg. Xenophobia and stigmatisation of the foreign African is a shared narrative among the urban poor in both cities. In Johannesburg, it appears that shared sentiments of suffering at the hands of employers and of the new political elite, as well as emotionally loaded responses to competition and conflict over local turf, fashion the identities of the underclass. It is the shared experience of the divide between the haves and the have-nots that appears to be most significant in this city. In Cape Town, on the other hand, the perception – shared by different groupings of the urban poor – that there is racialised privileged access to resources such as jobs, services, and housing adds race to the dominant underclass identity in this city. This racial label, moreover, appears to be experienced more as imposed – as a stigma – than as a badge of pride.

In conclusion, race remains part and parcel of the way urban residents speak of themselves and those around them. To infer from the continuation of this racialised discourse that racial boundaries in these cities will take on more meaning among more residents may well prove to be wrong. Among the middle-class, social networks appear to be established on the basis of shared class and cultural values rather than on the basis of shared racial classification. Among the poor, though racial identification persists where access to privilege is perceived as racialised, social networks reflect fragmentation not only within racial groups but also within neighbourhoods. As Salo (2004) put it recently in reference to an underclass neighbourhood in Cape Town:

> For the outsider Manenberg appears to be a homogenous racial township, a single geographic and social unit. However, for the residents of Manenberg, socio-spatial boundaries criss-cross the apparently continuous geographic unit, dividing it into multiple small communities ... Local communities may be limited to a single street, or cover a number of courts. ... Eleven male gangs exist in Manenberg, each associated with its own particular turf. ... [The] turf boundaries represent the physical, social and moral limitations of the local community. (Salo, 2004: 7)

In short, urban middle-class identities in Cape Town and Johannesburg reflect pride and self-esteem drawn from what was called social integration and lifestyle choices in the 'dual city' model. The underclass in these two cities, on the other hand, faced with exclusion and competition over local turf, fall back on local institutions for shared strategies for survival. These institutions, which are typically micro in scale and small in number of members, lead to identities that are rooted in local organisations rather than in racial or ethnic loyalties (Bekker

& Leidé, 2004). We conclude, then, that both cities reflect a mixture of dual and divided city attributes, that choice over residential space plays an important role in the construction of urban identities, and that the divided city attributes appear significantly stronger in Cape Town than in Johannesburg. That this may imply that race is a more salient sentiment in Cape Town than in Johannesburg, we leave to the reader to decide.

What influence have new urban policies had on the construction of these urban identities? Succinctly, it appears that those who were excluded under apartheid legislation from exercising choice over where to live and with whom to live today fall into two categories. One of these consists of upwardly mobile groups with sufficient resources now to exercise choice over where to live and with whom they prefer to live; the other grouping is the poor, who continue to experience exclusion in both a spatial as well as a class sense, and, in the case of Cape Town, in ethnic terms.

Appendix A: Focus group data

Research involved discussions with rank-and-file groupings selected on a wide range of criteria: residential area, religious affiliation, language, age, and domain of work activity. Each focus group was requested to discuss how they 'felt' about living in their local residential area – in Cape Town/Johannesburg and in South Africa. Discussions were conducted in the preferred language of each group and transcriptions were subsequently translated into English for analysis. The three research prompts and subsequent non-directive facilitation of discussion were deliberately chosen to enable groups freely to probe areas of shared interest, concern, and meaning. Since focus groups were not asked to debate specific issues, identification and discussion of themes produced evidence of shared sentiments regarding their importance.

Choice of non-directive focus group methodology was based on the hypothesis that identity is a process rather than a property. Accordingly, people's narratives, which issues they chose to discuss, and in what way, played a role in the construction of their collective identities. Furthermore, FG discussions revealed collective social representations that wouldn't have been accessible to us by using quantitative research methods such as surveys. The disadvantage of such methodology, however, revolves around issues of representivity and potential generalisation.

Research took place between 1999 and 2004. The constitution of the focus group began with the identification of a coordinator within the milieu of the focus group. This milieu coordinator was requested to approach between six and ten potential adult participants from the milieu. The coordinator was also requested to select participants with varying ages, as well as approximately equal numbers of women and men. The focus group venue was selected on the basis of a location known to the participants. Discussions ranged from 40 to 90 minutes in duration and were, in some cases, followed by face-to-face discussions with a few individual participants. Though three prompts were used, participants were not discouraged from pursuing a particular theme. Accordingly, few focus groups allocated equal discussion time to each theme.

Sketch of focus groups from which data have been drawn

Table 9.1: *Focus groups in Cape Town*

Business Focus group with a group of business people	06/08/1999
Oranjezicht (former white area) Focus group with a middle-income German-speaking community	12/08/2001
Panorama (Former white area) Focus group with a middle-income Afrikaans-speaking community	22/08/2001
Kraaifontein (Former white area) Focus group with a lower income English-speaking white group	21/04/2004
Durbanville (Former white area) Focus group with a middle-income English-speaking white group	27/04/2004
Ruyterwacht (Former white area) Focus group with a lower income Afrikaans-speaking community	06/08/2003
Pinelands (Former white area) Focus group with a middle-income coloured community	25/08/2001
Summergreens (New middle-income area) Focus group with a low- to middle-income coloured community	21/09/1999
Punts Estate (Former coloured middle-income area) Focus group with a middle-income coloured community	31/08/2001
Westridge (Mitchell's Plain) (Former coloured township) Focus group with a low- to middle-income coloured community	02/05/2003
Lavender Hill (Former coloured township) Focus group with a poor coloured community	18/08/2001
Tafelsig (Mitchell's Plain) (Former coloured township) Focus group with a poor coloured community	27/05/2003
Eerstrivier (Former coloured township) Focus group with a lower income coloured community	03/03/2004
Bo-Kaap 1 (Former Muslim area) Focus group with a middle-income Muslim community	12/09/2001
Bo-Kaap 2 (Former Muslim area) Focus group with a middle-income Muslim community	16/04/2003
Gugulethu (Former African township) Focus group with a middle-income Xhosa community	13/07/2003
Khayelitsha 1 (Former African township) Focus group with a middle-income Xhosa community	12/08/1999
Khayelitsha 2 (Former African township) Focus group with a poor Xhosa community	01/08/1999
Joe Slovo Park 1 (New low-income area) Focus group with a lower middle income Xhosa community	03/11/2001
Joe Slovo Park 2 (New low-income area) Focus group with a poor Xhosa community	04/12/2003
African foreigners CT Focus group with French-speaking African foreigners living in Cape Town	21/09/2001

Table 9.2: *Focus groups in Johannesburg*

Linden (Former white area) Focus group with a middle-income Afrikaans-speaking community	28/03/2002
Roodepoort 1 (Former white area) Focus group with a middle-income English-speaking white community	18/03/2002
Roodepoort 2 (Former white area) Focus group with a middle-income Afrikaans-speaking community	29/06/2004
North Riding (New cluster development) Focus group with a young middle-income white community (mixed languages)	11/03/2002
Fleurhof (Former coloured middle-income area) Focus group with a middle-income coloured community	24/03/2002
Bosmont (Former Muslim area) Focus group with a Muslim middle-income community	20/03/2002
Florida (Former white area) Focus group with a Muslim middle-income community	20/ 03/2002
Mayfair (Former Indian area) Focus group with a middle-income Indian community	17/03/2002
Brixton (Former white area) Focus group with African domestic workers	03/03/2002
Dube (Soweto) (Former African township) Focus group with an African middle-income community	12/03/2002
Alexandra (Former African township) Focus group with a poor African community	10/03/2002
Tembisa (Former African township) Focus group with a poor African Community	10/03/2002
Tsakane (Former African township) Focus group with a poor African Community	11/01/04
African foreigners JHB Focus group with French-speaking African foreigners living in Braamfontein	21/03/2002

Table 9.3: *Classification of focus groups according to 'race', income,* and city*

	Cape Town			Johannesburg			
	White	Coloured	Black	White	Coloured	Black	
High income*	1. Business 2. Oranjezicht 3. Panorama 4. Durbanville	1. Pinelands 2. Punts Estate 3. Bo-Kaap1 4. Bo-Kaap2	1. Khayelitsha1	1. Linden 2. Roodepoort1 3. Roodeport2 4. North Riding	1. Fleurhof 2. Florida		15
Middle income*	1. Ruyterwacht 2. Kraaifontein	1. Summergreens 2. Westridge	1. Joe Slovo Pk1 2. Gugulethu		1. Bosmont 2. Mayfair	1. Dube 2. African foreigners JHB	10
Low income*		1. Lavender Hill 2. Tafelsig 3. Eersterivier	1. Joe Slovo Pk2 2. Khayelitsha2 3. African foreigners CT			1. Brixton 2. Alexandra 3. Tembisa 4. Tsakane	10
	6	9	6	4	4	6	35
		21			14		

* Income has been inferred from profession and type of housing.

CHAPTER 10

The importance of language identities to black residents of Cape Town and Johannesburg

Robert Mongwe

10.1 Introduction

From colonial times until 1994, South Africa had two official languages, namely English and Afrikaans. These two languages were used in government communication, commerce, science, and technology. The democratisation of South African society in 1994 has led to the official recognition of eleven most-spoken languages, nine of which are African. Despite their claim to official status, communication in the African languages is virtually limited to private or informal domains. This raises the question whether this state of affairs will lead to the emergence of a politics of identity based on language in black communities of South Africa. I argue in this chapter that due to factors such as the widespread use of African languages in informal and private contexts, the official and constitutional recognition of the African languages serves to instil amongst the black masses a view of post-apartheid South Africa as a multilingual society. This state of affairs prevents the development of language-based identity politics in black communities.

> [L]anguage is … important in the construction of individual and social identities. It can also be a powerful means for exercising social control. Identifying yourself as belonging to a particular group or community often means adopting the linguistic conventions of that group, and this is not just in relation to the words you use, but also in the way that you say them. (Thornborrow, 1999: 136)

Language is important as a means of transmitting meaning as well as for marking cultural belonging for individuals and groups. The language used in communication and the manner of speech also tell observers about what is being said, and they tell about the social backgrounds of those involved in the communication. By communicating in a particular language, social norms and values are being transferred between the groups in question. Language is, in other words, an important cultural attribute through which social boundaries are drawn between different groups in the society.

However, it is the powerful groups in the society that determine which languages or varieties become standard forms in order to achieve socially sanctioned goals (Rahman, 2001; Anderson, 1983). In other words, languages do not become dominant in the societies because of their superior linguistic structures but rather due to the political, economic, and cultural power of respective speech communities. Therefore, non-standard language varieties are low in social prestige not because of their inherent inferiority, but due to the economic, social, and political power of the groups who speak the languages in question. The status of languages mirrors the balance of economic, political, and cultural power in the society. Language in this sense symbolises social power. This point is succinctly expressed by Prah (1995):

> The subcultures of the leading social classes and groups serve as reference categories for the less endowed elements of the society; they serve as cultural pacemakers and claim supremacy in the hierarchies of subcultures. (Prah, 1995: 12)

Individuals from lower level social strata who desire to enhance their chances of access to opportunities such as higher education and employment are compelled to acquire dominant languages (Boughey, 2002; Arua & Magocha, 2002; Rahman, 2001). The status of languages in the society is not only the function of individual factors such as motivation, attitudes, and perceptions, but is also influenced by structural-historical factors (Tollefson, 1991).

The aim of this chapter is to discuss the importance of language in identity formation amongst black South Africans living in two cities, namely Johannesburg and Cape Town. The chapter is guided by two hypotheses. In the first place, I hypothesise that if residents who speak the same language live together in a monolingual community they will use their common language as cultural resource to build and maintain social capital, and to protect the community in question against what they perceive to be negative external influences. In the second place, language identity may be of lesser significance as a means for political and economic mobilisation in communities where people from diverse cultural and linguistic backgrounds live together in the same neighbourhood. Cape Town and Johannesburg represent two appropriate cases in which the above hypotheses can be tested. The differences in the social histories and demographic profiles of the two cities are some of the factors that make the study interesting. Before proceeding with interrogating the hypotheses, I first turn to discussing the methodology used in this study.

10.2 Research sites and methodology

Focus group discussions were conducted in Johannesburg and Cape Town. The Johannesburg focus group discussions took place in five sites, Alexandra, Brixton, Soweto, Tembisa, and Tsakane (a residential area in the East Rand and accordingly not strictly within the Johannesburg metropolitan area). The Cape Town focus groups took place in two sites, Joe Slovo Park and Khayelitsha. The sites selected vary in terms of settlement type and class affiliation. Three of the sites studied in Johannesburg are formal, namely Soweto, Tsakane, and Brixton. The Tembisa and Alexandra focus groups were conducted in informal areas. The participants of the Soweto focus group can be described as middle class since all held professional jobs. The participants of the Brixton focus group in contradistinction were female domestic workers. Participants in the Tsakane focus group may be classified into two categories: people who were in some form of semi-skilled employment and those who were self-employed (in the formal economy). I now turn to the Cape Town focus groups.

Five focus groups were conducted in Cape Town. Two of these focus groups were conducted in Khayelitsha, a sprawling township that came into being in the 1980s following the political violence that took place in Crossroads (Cole, 1987). Of the two focus groups conducted in Khayelitsha, one took place in a formal settlement, with middle-class residents. The second Khayelitsha focus group was conducted in an informal settlement, with residents who were either unemployed or employed with low pay. The three other Cape Town focus groups took place in Joe Slovo Park, a new public housing settlement in northern Cape Town. One focus group was conducted with middle-class participants who were all in formal employment. The two other focus groups were conducted with young men and women who were either unemployed, underemployed, or in full-time employment with low wages.

Focus group participants' narratives were guided by the following three prompts: How do you feel about living in your local area? How do you feel about living in this city and this province? How do you feel about living in South Africa? Subsequently, discussion continued in a non-directive manner. The facilitator consented fully to participants taking charge of conversations and only intervened in order to stimulate further discussion and to ensure that everyone had a fair chance of making a contribution. These discussions took place in the preferred language of the participants. They were recorded and subsequently translated into

English and transcribed so as to render them available in written form.

The next section will focus briefly on the social and economic histories of Johannesburg and Cape Town since colonial times. This is done in order to situate the debates on language in a broader societal context.

10.3 A social history of languages in South Africa since colonial times

Writing a detailed social history of South African languages since the beginning of the colonial era would be a daunting task. What I therefore present here is an incomplete but sufficient account of the social history of language to allow one to have a broad picture of the language policies and practices of successive colonial and apartheid regimes. When the representatives of the Dutch East India Company arrived at the Cape in the 1600s, they proclaimed Dutch as the official language of communication in matters of governance and commerce.

Similarly, when the British gained control of the Cape in 1806, they replaced Dutch with English as a medium of official communication. When the *Act of Union* was passed in 1909, Dutch (which later evolved into Afrikaans) and English became the two official languages of communication (Alexander & Heugh, 2001: 17). This state of affairs remained until the end of the apartheid period. In the first four years of schooling, black children were taught in their mother tongue. However, successive colonial regimes did not develop these languages sufficiently to be used in high-order functions such as in the areas of science, politics, and economics. In 1976, the state tried to impose Afrikaans as a medium of instruction in all black state schools. That act led to the Soweto Uprising. In the confrontation that followed between learners and the police, approximately 700 learners were killed and several thousand others were injured.

A consequence of the June 1976 political drama was the political rejection of the Afrikaans language and the increased legitimation of English as the preferred language of formal communication. Although Afrikaans was not entirely abolished in black schools as a consequence of the Soweto Uprising in 1976, the language became deeply stigmatised. Earlier, generations of black learners had studied Afrikaans in order to fulfil a curriculum requirement. Today, some thirty years after the Soweto Uprising, the Afrikaans language is yet to recover fully from this political stigmatisation.

Following the 1994 political dispensation, eleven major languages of South Africa were given official recognition. Of the eleven official languages, nine of them are spoken in black communities. In order to realise the political goals of the new state, a team of language experts was appointed to look into language issues, and to recommend institutional reforms that could facilitate a process towards a practical implementation of the language policies of the new order. Consequently, the Pan South African Language Board (PANSALB) was established. The mandate of PANSALB is, among others, to look at ways to develop languages that were neglected as a result of apartheid policies. (Alexander, 2001: 31–33; Mkhulisi, 2000: 121; Marivate, 2000, 131–133). The next section will present an overview focusing on the economic and political histories of Johannesburg and Cape Town. First, such an overview will help us to understand the economic and political development of the two cities over time, and how these affected the black population in each case. Second, the overview will help us account for demographic differences between the two cities.

10.4 The social and political histories of two South African cities

This section commences with a table comprising the relative proportions that speech communities make up of the populations of Cape Town and Johannesburg. These proportions are first presented within the black populations of each city and subsequently within their populations as a whole. Data are based on mother tongue identification during the 2001 census. Second, I will discuss the social and political histories of languages in the two cities.

Table 10.1: *Relative sizes of speech communities in Cape Town and Johannesburg: Percentages in black and total metropolitan populations, 2001*

Language	Cape Town		Johannesburg	
	Black	Total in metro	Black	Total in metro
Afrikaans	3	41	1	8
English	2	28	2	19
isiNdebele	-	-	1	1
isiXhosa	92	29	10	8
isiZulu	1	-	35	25
Sepedi	-	-	10	8
Sesotho	2	1	15	11
Setswana	-	-	12	9
Siswati	-	-	1	1
Tshivenda	-	-	3	3
Xitsonga	-	-	8	6
Other	-	1	1	1
Total	100	100	100	100

Source: Statistics South Africa, 2003

Johannesburg

Johannesburg was established as a mining town in 1886. From the small one-product town it then was, its economy diversified into manufacturing, heavy industry, and commerce. Today Johannesburg is the economic hub of the continent. Although Johannesburg's labour force was mainly drawn from South Africa's rural areas, some of the labourers came from other countries of the Southern African region (Moodie & Ndatshe, 1999; Harries, 1994).

From the early period of the twentieth century, the state recognised the need to balance its economic interests on the one hand with political goals on the other. Thus, in 1923, the *Black Urban Areas Act* was passed in order to regulate the presence and movement of blacks in the cities. In 1950, the *Group Areas Act* followed. The *Group Areas Act* gave the state powers to plan cities along ethnic and racial lines. Moreover, suburbs that were multicultural in nature such as Sophiatown and District Six were demolished. In line with the political goals of apartheid, the *Prohibition of Mixed Marriages Act* of 1952 was passed. The *Prohibition of Mixed Marriages Act* prevented people from different cultural backgrounds from intermarrying. The parliament of the time also passed the *Separate Amenities Act* in order to confirm its commitment to a racial and ethnically divided society.

Although it can be argued that the aforesaid laws had little to do with language, I will argue these statutes criminalised intercultural mixing and legalised the racialisation and ethnicisation of South African society. One of the social consequences of these laws was social polarisation, especially between blacks and whites. Thus, South Africans were denied the opportunity to develop as a fully-fledged multilingual society in which the various linguistic groups could co-exist with a degree of equality. Nowhere can the effects of these policies and laws be seen more clearly than in the sphere of languages.

On the one hand, the majority of white South Africans speak only English and Afrikaans. On the other, the majority of uneducated blacks speak African languages, with inadequate command of Afrikaans and English. I say inadequate because the black majority can hardly use English and Afrikaans for high-order functions. According to a recent study (MarkData, 2000), just over one-tenth of the South African population speak English adequately. On the other hand, it would seem that the proportion of white South Africans who can lay claim to command of an African language hardly exists. It appears that, since they speak two of the dominant languages, they see no need to study or learn African languages especially since they probably are of the view that African languages have no economic value. In other words, command of English and Afrikaans correlates strongly with race and class. For blacks, it is both poor schooling and isolation from the speakers of dominant languages that lead to these differences in language skills.

In the absence of adequate housing, migrants from the rural areas and elsewhere in the Southern African region were housed in single-sex hostels. The state did everything to recruit from certain ethnic groups. Moreover, migrants were accommodated according to their ethnic groups (Mamdani, 1996; Themba, 1985). The worsening housing crisis in Johannesburg's black areas, together with forced removals, led to state housing programmes south west of Johannesburg (Masekela, 1993). The state attempted with limited success to order the black townships along ethnic and linguistic lines. Thus, places such as Mapetla and Moletsane were meant for Sesotho or Setswana speaking blacks, while Chiawelo and Meadowlands were meant for Batsonga and Bavenda. There were also residential areas such as Zondi and Mndeni designated for Zulus. This policy failed in Johannesburg's black townships because of the high degree of cross-cultural friendships, marriages, and the work of the liberation movements.

By the mid 1980s, when influx control was abolished, black migrants who entered the city from the rural areas found that Johannesburg was already home to millions of blacks who had lived there for generations. This black population was diverse in its ethnic and linguistic character. To this present day, Johannesburg is a multilingual city in which all the nine official African languages are spoken. However, languages such as isiZulu, Sesotho, and Setswana predominate. Others, such as Xitsonga, Siswati, isiNdebele, and Tshivenda, are minority languages. The next sections will focus on Cape Town's social and political history.

Cape Town

The settlement at the Cape of Good Hope, the origin of the city of Cape Town, was established in the 1600s by representatives of the Dutch East India Company to create a replenishment station for the company's shipping. From early colonial times, Cape Town developed both as a political capital and a trading centre. By the 1700s, this city was inhabited by people from various cultural backgrounds including European colonialists, slaves of Malaysian descent, the Khoi, and other local African groups. Dutch was the medium of communication. When the British took over the Cape in 1806, English was introduced as medium of official communication. This state of affairs continued until the time of the Union Government when English and Afrikaans were made official languages of communication. This policy of colonial bilingualism (Alexander & Heugh, 2001) was maintained until the end of apartheid in the 1990s.

By the 1920s, the city of Cape Town was already attracting black migrants who then played a role in the seaport economy. One of the first black settlements was Ndabeni; the residents were later moved to Langa. There were other blacks who spread throughout the city, including places such as District Six. Gugulethu was established in 1958 to cater for the growing black population. In the 1960s,

Cape Town was declared a 'Coloured Preferential Area'. The aim of this policy was to encourage coloured in-migration into Cape Town while expunging black presence (Goldin, 1984). This policy resulted in the stringent monitoring of black migration, the freezing of housing and other social amenities, and job reservations for the Coloured population. Although laws such as the *Group Areas Act*, the *Immorality Act*, and the *Black Urban Areas Act* applied in all South Africa cities, some commentators believe that these laws were more strictly enforced in Cape Town than anywhere else in the country (Lemon, 1976). Political changes in the 1980s led to the abolition of influx control and other restrictive regulations.

Democratic rule followed in 1994. Given the new political context and the deterioration of economic conditions in the rural areas, rural-to-urban migration ensued. The Eastern Cape became Cape Town's new hinterland. The majority of the migrants, however, encountered an environment that was somewhat culturally hostile. First, since most of the isiXhosa-speaking migrants were under-resourced, they were compelled to find housing with kin in the informal settlements (Mongwe, forthcoming; Yose, 1999). Second, most migrants originated in the Eastern Cape, a province in which 83 per cent of the population speak isiXhosa as a first language. A negligible minority of Eastern Cape citizens speak English and Afrikaans as home languages (Barkhuizen & De Klerk, 2002). That minority consists of people who come from Afrikaans-speaking regions such as the Karoo and the Northern Cape towns of Upington, Prieska, and Kimberley. Another category of isiXhosa-speaking migrants had learnt Afrikaans at school.

Yet the city of Cape Town is predominantly Afrikaans speaking. One of the reasons for the dominance of Afrikaans in the city of Cape Town is that the majority of Cape Town's members of the coloured population are Afrikaans speaking. Since command of English in South Africa is linked largely to the period and quality of formal education received, coloureds of Cape Town origin are at an advantage compared to their isiXhosa-speaking migrant counterparts. The advantage of the Cape Town coloured population stems from the better quality of education offered in the Western Cape province. The migrant isiXhosa-speakers are poorly educated and have little command of the languages of power. Research conducted recently into the state of state education in the Eastern Cape and the Western Cape provinces confirms the acute educational challenges in the former, and the healthy state of affairs in the latter. In turn, the socio-economic challenges faced in the Eastern Cape contribute to poor teaching, learning, and performance (Bekker, Mongwe, Muller & Myburgh, 2003; Van der Berg & Acheterbosch, 2001).

The lack of linguistic proficiency in Afrikaans amongst isiXhosa-speaking migrants constitutes one of the greatest hurdles to economic opportunities and to the optimum utilisation of government services such as municipal offices, health centres, and so on. The importance of Afrikaans as medium for primary and secondary communication in the Western Cape has been confirmed by recent research (Du Plessis, 2000: 102). This claim is also confirmed by a study (2000) commissioned by PANSALB investigating the distribution and use of languages in South Africa. In the sections that follow, I turn to a discussion on language and identity politics in South Africa's urban areas.

10.5 Urban blacks, language, and the politics of identity in South Africa

This section focuses on the politics of identity making amongst black South Africans living in some of the selected sites in the cities concerned.

Language and the politics of identity in Johannesburg
In his recollection of life in Alexandra in the 1940s, South African jazz legend Hugh Masekela wrote,

> when I was about 8, we moved to the 'free hold' African settlement of Alexandra Township … Alexandra better known as 'Toneship' or 'Dark City' [because of its lack of electricity and sewage system] … with a populace of 100 000 made of Ndebeles, Zulus, Basothos, Shangaans, Vendas, Chopis, Swazis, Xhosas, Bapedi, Karangas, Coloureds [people of mixed race] … (Masekela, 1993: 6)

For Masekela and other like-minded people, Alexandra was given its identity as a place by the structural conditions that obtained at the time. These included a lack of basic services such as electricity and proper sanitation. The residents of Alexandra and other similar settlements drew meaning from their daily struggles as they tried to make the best of a difficult situation. In order to demonstrate their claim to Alexandra, they named it 'Toneship' and 'Dark City'.

A second factor from which the residents of Alexandra drew meaning for themselves was the multicultural character of their neighbourhood. It was a neighbourhood characterised by people from various linguistic and cultural backgrounds. This multicultural nature of Alexandra gave it sparkle and vibrancy. It was also one of the places from which South African jazz, fashion, art, and soccer emanated. Therefore, Alexandra was the vanguard of black urban cultural life. In addition, Alexandra is known for its long history of resistance to apartheid.

Regarding Alexandra, it can be said that the more things change, the more they stay the same. When one researcher visited Alexandra for the purposes of conducting research in March 2002, she encountered informal settlements without adequate social services. Although these residents reported that some parts of Alexandra were rehabilitated, some sections of it were yet to be developed. Second, this researcher found that Alexandra continues to retain its multilingual character. People from various ethnic and linguistic backgrounds live together. When asked about the nature of social relations in a multicultural context and its implications for language use, one of the respondents present answered:

> We live like one nation. As we are, we have Xhosa, we've got Pedi, we've got Shangaan, all of us are the same. If I am sitting at a place with Pedis, I feel free. If I sit at a place with Xhosa, I also feel free. We just live together peacefully. (Focus group participant, Alexandra, March 2002)

The multilingual character of Alexandra and the everyday objective circumstances that the residents face on an everyday basis are important factors for meaning and identity making. Yet both multilingualism and challenging objective circumstances are features common in Johannesburg's black communities. Despite the difficult living conditions, Johannesburg's black urban areas are eulogised for being hubs of black cultural life and political resistance (Masekela, 1993; Themba, 1985).

Even the media have taken note of Johannesburg's multilingual character. Take the case of Community Radio, a Gauteng-based radio station that broadcasts to railway commuters throughout the country. Although the messages are almost entirely in English, Commuter Radio's music slots are dominated by South African recordings in English and South African vernacular languages. Black Johannesburgers in general and Sowetans in particular hold the view that the cultural diversity of their city is an important identity marker that distinguishes it from other places. A black resident of Soweto testified as follows:

> I love staying in Soweto more than all the other areas because here, I've learnt many things especially when it comes to language. I've learnt plenty of languages. If I was in the rural areas, I was not going to learn all these ... (Focus group participant, Soweto, March 2002)

A black resident of Brixton endorsed the words of the speaker mentioned above:

> We feel free here in Johannesburg ... you ... see it's many languages [that] you can speak ... but we have to learn each other's language, like it or not. And for the first time, it's not so easy ... (Focus group participant, Brixton, March 2002)

Black Johannesburgers, both native and migrant, are continuously challenged to expand their linguistic repertoires by learning more languages. According to black Johannesburgers, other places – especially the rural areas – are bereft of such an opportunity. They compare township life to that of the former white suburbs and the rural areas. They believe that Johannesburg's former white suburbs are culturally alienating. As an example, black urban residents living in the townships point out that social interaction in the former white neighbourhoods is orientated towards the family, at the expense of the neighbours. This is a far cry from township life where physical proximity between people's homes is also assumed to signify intimate social interaction. In the next section, in line with anthropological research traditions, I will share my own views and observations on the question of language and identity formation.

Personal observations

It is October 2003, early morning, and we are preparing to board a flight to Libreville, en route to Togo. I am sitting at a table with one of the members of the research team. Suddenly I realise that one of the music recordings they are playing is by a black South African musician. The song is sung in isiZulu, mixed with Sesotho and the township lingo (often called 'Tsotsi Taal'). The disk jockey at the Johannesburg International Airport then plays two other songs by artists of South African origin. I remark on this to my colleague, who nods, saying 'it must be a good feeling for you'. Later on, as I prepare for boarding, the officer across the desk speaks to me in Sesotho. I realise that the officer has just used English in communicating with her colleague. I am struck by the comfortable manner in which she switches between English and Sesotho.

I have yet to make a similar observation regarding a linguistic interaction at the Cape Town International Airport.

As my own observations indicate, black Johannesburgers, wherever they are, espouse a tolerant attitude towards multilingualism. This is even clear in a place such as the Johannesburg International Airport. Black staff who work at the airport switch between English and the African languages in front of customers. In so doing, they advertise the scope of their linguistic repertoires and thus encourage those who can speak any of these African languages to use them in conducting their business.

By communicating in the African languages, black Johannesburgers assert and declare their cultural identities to the rest of the world. By so doing, they are able to reclaim their cultural heritages that were denigrated over many years of apartheid and colonialism. Nonetheless, this is not to dispute English's hegemonic position, particularly in a setting such as that of the Johannesburg International Airport. Furthermore, black Johannesburgers waste no time in making their views known concerning other cities. Of Cape Town, a black Johannesburger living in Soweto remarked:

> Living in Soweto is quite an experience because of different cultures, different people ... I have been to ... Cape Town. [It] is nice to visit or anything like that but to stay, I still think that Soweto is much better. (Focus group participant, Soweto, March, 2002)

The speaker continued as follows:

> It's too white, Cape Town. You're so used to seeing black people over here so ... Imagine staying over there and seeing white people as your neighbours. You know, all the areas have a certain type of culture. (Focus group participant, Soweto, March, 2002)

In the context of the same discussion, another Soweto resident stated:

> [A]fter six o'clock in the city of Cape Town, you don't see black people, you count them actually. Here in Johannesburg, even [at] ten o'clock, you still see black people. Cape Town has its own culture and Johannesburg has its own culture and you know that people with money like to cluster themselves. (Focus group participant, Soweto, March 2002)

Black Johannesburgers acknowledge Cape Town's stunning beauty and its cosmopolitan shopping malls. For that reason, they admit that Cape Town is an excellent tourist destination. However, black Johannesburgers (especially Sowetans) perceive Cape Town as a city inhabited by the rich whites who are also culturally distinct from them. It is in these circumstances that they experience a city like Cape Town as culturally alienating.

An interesting finding of the Johannesburg research is the relaxed attitude that blacks are exhibiting towards Afrikaans. In one focus group, a respondent complained of the use of Afrikaans in the courts. This respondent argued that Afrikaans usage was common amongst legal professions, irrespective of their ethnic or racial background. In the courts, those who do not speak Afrikaans must depend on court interpreters. He complained that the impact of such a practice was exclusion, especially of the accused, from full participation in legal processes. In another Johannesburg focus group, a respondent living in the inner city of Johannesburg reported a language shift towards Afrikaans especially amongst children:

> [T]he children ... speak English at school and some of them use Afrikaans and [isi]Zulu because the government says you must use eleven languages. (Focus group participant, Brixton, March 2002)

There are two explanations for the practice of code switching. First, code switching is inevitable, given the ethnic and linguistic composition of Johannesburg's black population. Second, children of school-going age are encouraged by parents to learn dominant languages. Parents encourage their children to acquire dominant languages (in this case English and Afrikaans) because they want to enhance their children's opportunities in life. In the case of children who live in a cosmopolitan context such as that of Johannesburg, they also learn to speak Afrikaans from their friends. Furthermore, parents do not mind that their children are speaking Afrikaans and other languages since multilingualism is considered a constitutional and societal virtue. In a recent study commissioned by PANSALB (2000: 12), questions were asked to determine the language-use patterns and preferences of respondents. Table 10.2 presents findings on the prevalence of code-switching behaviour in the various provinces of South Africa.

Table 10.2: *Code-switching behaviour in South African provinces*

Province	Proportion in percentages
Gauteng	25
Western Cape	15
Mpumalanga	11
KwaZulu-Natal	11
Other	-

Source: PANSALB, 2000

If the findings of the above research are anything to go by, code-switching behaviour is most prevalent in Gauteng. Gauteng is followed by the Western Cape, with Mpumalanga and KwaZulu-Natal occupying the third place.

According to the study, code-switching behaviour hardly occurs in the other provinces of South Africa. For that reason, these provinces are lumped together in the category of 'other'. One of the conclusions to be drawn from the above findings is that code-switching behaviour is a feature that characterises metropolitan and immediate surrounding regions. This is understandable, given that structural factors in South Africa compel people from various cultural and linguistic backgrounds to congregate in and around the metropolitan centres. The section that follows will focus on language and identity formation in Cape Town.

Language and the politics of identity in Cape Town

Although in both Cape Town and Johannesburg the African languages are dominated by Afrikaans and English in high-order functions, Cape Town's blacks admire the tolerant attitude towards multilingualism that exists in Johannesburg. Cape Town's black people argue that speakers of African languages are able to communicate optimally in Johannesburg. In turn, this tolerant attitude towards multilingualism removes the stigma attached to the African languages. A native speaker of isiXhosa who migrated to Cape Town a decade ago remarked that, 'in Jo'burg … one speaks in Sepedi, isiXhosa, Sesotho, isiZulu, different languages' (Focus group participant, Joe Slovo Park, October, 2003).

Another migrant, a native isiZulu speaker now living and working in Cape Town, concurred:

> In those places [Johannesburg] if you speak in isiXhosa you are also understood by another person who speaks isiZulu because the languages are similar. And if you speak in Setswana a person who speaks Sepedi will understand you. So if you speak to one another in English and one is struggling it is easy if there is another language that you both understand. (Focus group participant, Joe Slovo Park, October 2003)

Cape Town blacks without sufficient command of Afrikaans point out that the hegemonic position of Afrikaans in public and commercial affairs impacts negatively on their ability to take advantage of labour market opportunities. In a focus group discussion held in October 2003 in Joe Slovo Park, one of the participants contended:

> [T]here is a problem about speaking isiXhosa in Cape Town because nothing has changed, the Boers are still in control and they speak in Afrikaans. And people who get opportunities are Coloureds. So if you want a job it can happens that you may not get it even if you qualify because of your inability to speak Afrikaans. (Focus group participant, Joe Slovo Park, October 2003)

Blacks who live in Cape Town believe the more things have changed, the more they have stayed the same: According to them, in the last 10 years language has taken over from race as a criterion of exclusion. In a focus group discussion, one of the participants expressed this point as follows: '[I]f you are African, it is like in apartheid time, long time ago.'

The exclusion from economic opportunities of isiXhosa-speaking migrants makes them feel unwelcome. Some Xhosa migrants believe that 10 years after the transition to democratic rule they continue to suffer the indignities associated with the apartheid era. Disaffected Xhosa migrants hold the view that, although in general terms South African society has moved on, Cape Town and more generally the Western Cape have lagged behind. According to isiXhosa-speaking migrants, Cape Town is a city that is still mean towards black South Africans. As shown earlier, language is the new vehicle of social injustice. Today, just as in the past, whites and coloureds claim the lion's share of the social resources. Just as in the past, blacks are left out. As isiXhosa speakers, they feel like outsiders:

> I feel that Cape Town is a place that was meant for whites and coloureds. As a black person you are expected to be Afrikaans speaking, you understand. Even if you are proud, you will do so in the township. (Focus group participant, Joe Slovo Park, December 2003)

In an endeavour to escape the language-based economic exclusion and cultural stigmatisation, some isiXhosa-speaking migrants contemplate switching their identities from Xhosa to coloured:

> I cannot even say I am proud of being Xhosa, because sometimes I wish to be coloured. I say that if I were coloured in the Western Cape my life could have changed, but I am Xhosa. (Focus group participant, Joe Slovo Park, October 2003)

Xhosa middle-income migrants also find that, besides English, Afrikaans is a prerequisite in certain jobs. Hence, as a pre-condition for accepting certain jobs, they are duty-bound to enrol in Afrikaans-language courses:

> [M]y friend will lecture at Stellenbosch; they are giving him the job but he is supposed to attend classes for a year for this Afrikaans in order to qualify for the job. He is supposed to know Afrikaans before he can enter. You can know English but if you do not know Afrikaans there is nothing you can do, you see. (Focus group participant, Joe Slovo Park, October 2003)

The above excerpts attest to the following claim by Neville Alexander:

> It is axiomatic that the dominant languages or language in the economy of any society is or are the language(s) of power. This power derives from the fact that in the economic domain, language is a necessary condition for production by virtue of its crucial function as an instrument of communication. Hence, citizens and others who have to engage in economic activities in the country concerned are empowered to the extent that they know the standard form of the language(s) of power. (Alexander, 2001: 16)

Although, objectively speaking, Afrikaans and English occupy a similar position in relation to the African languages, blacks in Cape Town and throughout South Africa seem to be more tolerant of the latter's hegemonic position than the former. There is some evidence to suggest that black South Africans across classes regard English as the legitimate medium for linguistic communication in formal contexts. If anything, this evidence suggests that urban blacks across societal levels prefer a further Anglicisation of society rather than a revolutionary elevation in the status of the African languages. For that reason, black parents send their children to schools in which they can acquire the standardised form of English. The black middle-level groupings also encourage the other groupings to learn English rather than the African languages.

In a contribution concerning the language question published in a daily newspaper, the *Cape Times*, one black resident wrote:

> My mother tongue is [isi]Xhosa and yet I choose to speak English most of the time … The reason people like me choose English is very simple. There is an entire world of knowledge, skills, jobs, power, and influence which is totally closed to us if we can only speak an indigenous language. How many books are there in [isi]Xhosa on physics, mathematics, or history of art? What does a [Se]sotho speaker do if they want to improve themselves and gain knowledge? How many encyclopaedias are written in [isi]Zulu? (cited in Moodley, 2000: 110)

In a focus-group discussion held in Joe Slovo Park, an unemployed participant with seven years of schooling justified his preference for English over Afrikaans thus:

> You know the language that combines different nations is English. It is a language of the world. All other nationalities from other countries that enter South Africa enter through English. (Focus group participant, Joe Slovo Park, December 2003)

In the context of globalisation, whereby black elites need to interact with their foreign counterparts in an attempt to claim resources for their societies or for reasons of self-advancement, the position of the English language is enhanced. For these reasons, black South Africans, just like any other formerly colonised people, invest time and resources in learning English (Arua & Magocha, 2002; Nair-Venugopal, 2001; Bilaniuk, 2003). Black South Africans opt to learn English in order to avoid complete cultural and economic isolation. English hegemony is not limited to the Third World nations alone. Even in a country as economically resourced and culturally diverse as the United States of America, government policy seems to encourage Anglicisation at the expense of the heritage languages of immigrant minorities (Suarez, 2002: 516).

In the South African context English has gained new ground, becoming the *lingua franca* in the government service since 1994 (Barkhuizen & De Klerk, 2002: 162, 167–169; Republic of South Africa, 2001: 5). Furthermore, politicians also use English as a *lingua franca* when disseminating important information on television and radio. This practice, however, ignores the findings of a recent study that suggests that English is a minority language. This is shown by the fact that an overwhelming majority of South Africans do not speak English in their homes (see table 10.3).

Table 10.3: *Patterns of language use in South Africa*

Language	Proportion in percentages
Home language + English	11.52
Home language + Afrikaans	4.6
Home language + isiZulu	3.6
Home language + Sesotho	3.24

Source: PANSALB, 2000

Interestingly, the PANSALB (2000: 13) study found that the majority of black South Africans understand and fluently speak the following languages in descending order: isiZulu, isiXhosa, Afrikaans, and Setswana. The study also suggests that these languages must be given due recognition by planning institutions of the state. This view concurs with that of Prah (1995), who argues that the participation of the black masses in the areas of science, technology, and economic affairs can only be enhanced if the African languages were developed to the same level as the European languages.

Despite the dominated position of their languages, black South Africans are proud people. They draw their sense of meaning and identity from the long struggle they waged against the apartheid order. Their collective experience of humiliation as a race group has resulted in their constructing their identity on grounds other than ethnicity or a particular language. Today, black South Africans attach significance to the democratic institutions that have come into being since the 1994 elections. They pride themselves for being the people who, in contemporary times, have successfully fought for and established democratic rule. Even though the African languages are still subordinate to the formerly colonial languages, black South Africans hold that, given the democratic nature of the society, they will be able to use state institutions in order to enhance the social standing of the African languages.

10.7 Conclusion

The democratisation of South African society in the 1990s has led to the official recognition of the 11 most-spoken languages. The official recognition of 11 languages was a radical step, compared to the bilingual policy that was followed during the periods of early colonialism and apartheid. The constitutional status of the African languages notwithstanding, English and Afrikaans continue to be dominant languages in the government services, commerce, science, and technology.

As far as Cape Town is concerned, Xhosa migrants live in predominantly isiXhosa-speaking neighbourhoods, in a city in which Afrikaans is the dominant language of communication at high-order functions. The effect of this language policy is that isiXhosa speakers are barred from effectively participating in the economic, cultural, and government affairs of the city. Paradoxically, instead of Xhosa migrants campaigning for an isiXhosa language movement, they call for the substitution of Afrikaans with English (yet another dominant ex-colonial language) in high-order communication, and a more liberal attitude towards the African languages.

Unlike Cape Town, Johannesburg's black urban communities are multi-ethnic in character, as well as exhibiting a tolerant attitude towards multilingualism. Black Johannesburgers take pride in the multi-ethnic character of their neighbourhoods. Despite the dominated position of their languages, they draw their sense of meaning and identity from the long struggle they waged against the apartheid order, the multi-ethnic nature of their communities, and their experiences as residents of neighbourhoods that have been neglected over many years of apartheid rule. For these reasons, Johannesburg's black communities are eulogised even by blacks living in such distant cities as Cape Town.

Finally, although the African languages have been officially recognised, English and Afrikaans continue to dominate in the spheres of business, politics, science, and technology. Nonetheless, factors such as the widespread use of African languages in informal and private contexts, the official recognition of the African languages, and their protection in the Constitution suggest to some extent that the state acknowledges that South Africa is a multilingual society. This state of affairs constitutes a sufficient condition to prevent the emergence of a language-based politics of identity in the black community.

CHAPTER 11

The importance of language identities in Lomé and Libreville

Simon Bekker & Anne Leildé

11.1 Introduction

This chapter aims to establish how important language identities are to residents of the multilingual capital cities of Togo in West Africa and Gabon in Central Africa. This will be done by analysing the relationship between language identity construction 'from above' and 'from below' – by establishing state language policy in each city and subsequently by focusing on people's narratives regarding language in each city. How these narratives were obtained is discussed in appendix A (see also chapter 2 on qualitative research methodology). Both countries within which this research was carried out are former French colonies, although Togo was a German Protectorate from 1884 until the First World War (see chapter 4).

By language identity construction 'from above', we mean the process of state policy formulation typically aimed at building a shared national language community and at facilitating commercial exchanges both within the country as well as with external partners through the use of a vehicular language. A national language serves the purpose of state nation-building whereas a vehicular language serves as an 'instrument of communication within and beyond the territorial limits and the socio-cultural borders of [the] national community of origin' (Sow, 1977: 20). In both Togo and Gabon, French was adopted as the official national language at independence in 1960. Two kinds of explanation have been offered for this choice in the two countries. In the first place, it is argued that neither country has a vernacular language widely enough spoken and understood to be able to act as *lingua franca*, as is the case with Swahili in Tanzania or Lingala in both the Congos (Brazzaville and Kinshasa). Accordingly, the selection of one indigenous language above others as official national language could easily have led to shared sentiments of exclusion among, and conflict between, sub-national linguistic groups. In the second place, elite attitudes of prejudice toward local languages, together with elite sentiments of cultural alienation from indigenous cultures, led to the selection of the former colonial language as the only official national language. In the words of Moodley (2002), 'the mental colonisation of the post-colonial elites led to a perception of non-English [speaking], non-French-speaking rural compatriots as uneducated and backward, thereby devaluing indigenous languages, while equating foreign language fluency with modernity' (2002: 108).

It is therefore apparent that collective identities are fashioned by such dominant institutions which 'extend and rationalise their domination vis-à-vis social actors' through such identity construction (Castells, 1997: 8). On the other hand, they become identities only if and when social actors internalise them – only if and when they are experienced as meaningful by these actors themselves. Our aim here is to establish the extent to which the institutionalisation of French as official language has been accepted by residents in these two cities or, inversely, the extent to which this policy is resisted by residents who may feel deeply about the loss of their indigenous languages or who believe these vernacular languages ought to be used more frequently in the public sphere.

There is a prevalent conviction that vernacular languages are globally threatened and marginalised by dominant – mainly Western – languages and that minority languages ought to be protected, particularly through promoting their use in the public sphere and through their allocation of 'high-status' functions. The United Nations 1993 declaration on minority rights is an apt example. Similarly, the South African linguist Neville Alexander recently proposed a declaration of 'The Decade of the Indigenous Languages of Africa', 'whose task must be the efficient and effective promotion of the development of the languages of the African people for use in high-status functions locally, nationally, regionally and – where appropriate – internationally' (Alexander, reported in Moodley, 2002: 114). Similar concerns have been expressed by linguists in both Gabon and Togo. In Gabon, Idiata (2002: 76, our translation) argues that 'the use of Gabonese languages is decreasing due mainly to the fact that French occupies all the prestigious functions and that the use of Gabonese languages is normally reserved for a few family, religious, interpersonal activities within the community'. In Togo, according to Lebikaza (1999: 5), 'the imposition of a European language as the official language and the only language of work poses the risk that indigenous languages lose progressively all their importance'. Calls to protect such vernacular languages are often accompanied by a conception that 'languages are in some sense natural and primordial' (Kriel, 2003: 163) and that people are forced against their will to give up their languages in order to adopt the socially dominant language, thereby forfeiting a critical element of their identity.

In our conception of language identity, however, shared meanings around language are neither essential nor immutable but social constructions open to change as circumstances, strategies, and interactions change. Identity, in short, is a matter of social context. Furthermore, while it is clear that each identity defines elements of similarity (the 'We') and of difference (the 'They' or the 'Other') (see Martin, 1995), this need not necessarily lead to conflict. Where an identity leads to experiences of stigmatisation and exclusion, the 'Other' may well be rejected, but where an identity leads to experiencing pride and growing self-esteem, the 'Other' may well be viewed in inclusive terms (Martin, 1999). Language identities, accordingly, may be of more or less meaning to urban residents and may be more or less inclusive (or exclusive) of other urban residents.

11.2 Lomé and Libreville: Language demographics and official language policy

Situated between Anglophone Ghana to the west and Francophone Benin and Burkina Faso to the north and east, Togo had an estimated population of 5.2 million inhabitants in 2001. Its territory covers some 57 000 square kilometres. Lomé itself has a population of one million inhabitants (Danioue, 2004). There are 37 ethnic groups, speaking about 30 languages in the country (Lebikaza, 1997). These language groups may be categorised into two main families, the Gur group in the north and the Kwa group in the south (Takassi, 1983). The major ethnic groups are the Ewe (23.19%) (a southern ethnic group), the Kabiye (13.79%) (the President's ethnic group from the north), the Ouatchi (10.30%), and the Tem (5.75%) (1981 Census). Lomé, which is located on the coast, includes a population made up of 70% of the ethnic group Adja-Ewe (Danioue, 2004). As a consequence, Ewe-Mina (Mina being a form of Ewe) is 'the commercial language of South Togo' and of Lomé (Lebikaza, 1997: 157).

Situated between Spanish-speaking Equatorial Guinea and bilingual Cameroon to the north and Francophone Congo-Brazzaville to the east and south, Gabon has a population of 1.2 million inhabitants (Census 1993), including 200 000 foreign migrants (mostly migrants from neighbouring African countries and about 15 000 French expatriates). Its territory covers some 268 000 square kilometres (Idiata, 2002). There are 62 'linguistic entities' (*parlers*) in Gabon (Kwenzi Mikala, 1998), most of which include fewer than 10 000 members and which can be regrouped in ten bigger groups due to mutual understanding. The vast majority of these languages belong to the Bantu linguistic family. Fang forms the largest language community and is spoken by 30% of the population. Ipunu and Inzebi are the two next largest language communities in the country (Idiata, 2002). Libreville itself has a population of 420 000 inhabitants, representing some 40% of the country's total population. In contradistinction to Lomé, there is no city vernacular language in Libreville. The Fang form the largest minority language community (38%), followed by the Shira Punu (28%) and the Nzebi (12%). It is worth noting that 24% of Libreville's population is of foreign origin, thereby increasing the likely use of French as a vehicular language in Libreville.

It is difficult to assess accurately the number of people who are able to speak French in Togo and in Gabon. While the French colonial power favoured a policy of cultural assimilation in its colonies (Sow, 1977), no more than a small local colonial elite was encouraged to learn its language. In both countries, the use of French as a vehicular language only spread after independence when access to education was democratised by new national governments (François, 1993) and when the process of urbanisation which had been fuelled by economic activities (phosphate and petroleum exploitation in particular) created a burgeoning urban population in the two capital cities. However, both countries have high rates of school attendance (reaching more than 90% in the capital cities). In addition, non-literate urban residents acquire French through contact rather than through schooling (Lafage) and speak what is called 'Ivorian French' or 'Moussa French', a pidgin mixing French words and grammatical structures with those of vernacular languages.

Language policy

Neither Lomé nor Libreville has a municipal language policy that applies at city level. Rather, urban dwellers, together with their rural counterparts, are party to national language policy. While differing on paper, in practice they are very similar in Togo and in Gabon. Both countries adopted French as their official language after independence. However, in Togo, two additional languages, Ewe-Mina and Kabiye, were declared national languages in terms of the 'authenticity policy' advocated by the government in the 1970s. This addition was intended to 'revalorise' Togolese cultures and languages. This was to be done by using these two languages as medium of instruction in state schools while French was intended to become a taught subject. The lack of implementation of such a policy was put down to material difficulties (e.g., teacher training and writing of adequate material) and to 'a lack of political will' from the elite. This policy has thus remained 'virtual', and these languages 'are taught (as subjects) in state schools, have access to half a page in the governmental newspaper, to 15 minutes a day on TV and a time share superior to the one allocated to the other Togolese languages on the radio. Not more' (Lebikaza, 1997: 159).

Similarly, in Gabon, while the inclusion of Gabonese languages in the education system has been on the government's agenda since 1983, to date this has not come about and these languages are taught only in a few private – mostly confessional – institutions, (Idiata, 2002). State actions have not moved beyond the inclusion of an article in the 1994 constitution recognising the need to promote vernacular languages (1994 Constitution, Article 2, section 8), the creation of a Department of National Languages in the education ministry, a few state radio programmes in vernacular languages, and their occasional use during electoral and health campaigns (Idiata, 2002).

In both countries, accordingly, French is the language of the public service, of schooling and of the formal economy – in short, French is used for all 'high-status' functions – while vernacular languages are left for the private domain. Two qualifications need to be made, however. First, in practice, the main impact of this national policy is felt in urban rather than in rural areas since urban areas are *de facto* multilingual and multi-ethnic environments lacking a vernacular *lingua franca* and since their residents enjoy high literacy rates. Rural areas in both countries remain largely monolingual and the use of indigenous languages remains widespread. Since Gabon has an urbanisation rate of 73%, significantly higher than that of Togo (35%), the impact of the national language policy in that country is probably more invasive. In the second place, commercial activities for rank-and-file residents in both cities are largely informal and take place in a series of open marketplaces (*les marchés*). Languages that tend to be used here are indigenous rather than French.

11.3 Language identity 'from below': Analysing the narratives of members of the language communities resident in Lomé and Libreville

Before turning to our research data, we identify three hypotheses that will be used to analyse the narratives collected. We have constructed these hypotheses from a literature focused on the role of language as capital and as an important element in social reproduction (Bourdieu, 1991; Alexander, 1999; Moodley, 2000; Prah, 2002). The first hypothesises that French as the official language in a multilingual population may be experienced as imposed and may lead to resentment since it is a foreign language – the language of the former coloniser – mainly acquired through the formal education system. Accordingly, particularly among poorer urban residents, this imposition may lead to sentiments of exclusion. The second hypothesises that the use of French as *lingua franca* is bound to diminish the use of vernacular languages and that this may lead to fears of the undermining of traditional cultural practices, especially in capital cities where foreign and western influences are widespread. In reaction, a cultural backlash rooted in linguistic community may take place and be especially strong where residents tend to live in ethnically homogeneous neighbourhoods. In the third place, we hypothesise that such linguistic tensions might be felt more strongly among minority language communities since majority vernacular languages may be perceived to maintain a strong presence not only in the private sphere but also in the informal sector of the urban economy. The fact that Ewe-Mina in Lomé, for example, plays this role of a vehicular language at the biggest market (*le Grand Marché*) of the city is a test case in point.

To test such hypotheses, however, is no simple matter. Our use of focus groups to gather appropriate data was not only guided by the virtual absence of any relevant published work in these cities but also by the need to establish residents' views of how language and linguistic issues inform their everyday lives in general. Accordingly, the analysis of their focus group narratives addresses not only these narrower hypotheses but also seeks to tease out those more general shared social representations of residents that relate linguistic issues to their residential neighbourhoods, to the job market, and to their cities. It is perhaps appropriate at this point to introduce the dimension of language and state power in multilingual societies. As Crawford Young puts it,

> reason of state beckons to the choice of a single medium for the conduct of public business; thus language becomes tied to hierarchies of power and privilege. If access and exclusion are measured by mastery of the language of the state, then the stage is set for conflict. (Young, 1994: 21)

Results

In both cities, for different income levels and ethnic groups alike, residents remain attached to their specific ethnic and linguistic community. This attachment is found most clearly in patterns of residential settlement and appears to hold as much for established residents as for new urban migrants. In effect, a preference to live in a neighbourhood where the majority language is one's own, as well as a preference to shop at a market place where one's language is dominant, is widely expressed. The outcome seems to be circular in its logic: Residents use ethnic and linguistic social networks to find accommodation and the resultant largely linguistically homogeneous neighbourhood in turn conditions socialisation and linguistic practice in that neighbourhood.

In Lomé, for instance,

> [t]he North of the Laguna is the 'first neighbourhood' of Lomé so it's inhabited by indigenous people as we call them. Those who come from Kpalimé prefer to buy

land towards Kpalimé. Those who come from the North are going to buy towards the North. It makes it easier for us regarding certain things … like social life, community life, people are attached to community life. When they meet each other, they are used to certain things, they organise themselves, they get on well with each other, they practice their traditions, their ancestral culture. When they are together, they practice it, they feel at ease living in community. It's a kind of cultural attraction. People are attracted to each other. (Kabiye, middle income)

I live in Amoutive. That's where I grew up and that's where I still live and it's a big joy to stay next to people who saw me growing up. (Ewe-Mina, middle income)

As noted earlier, ethno-regionalist tensions experienced in Lomé during the political crisis of the 1990s have accentuated such a situation:

Before we didn't really have this [ethnic] problem but since 1990 … now people often say 'ah, this neighbourhood is inhabited by this ethnic group, they live there, it can create problems, etc …' but it's a problem we tried to overcome. (Kabiye, middle income)

Similar preference for homogeneous neighbourhoods was asserted in Libreville:

In Libreville, people live in neighbourhoods according to their ethnic group, each ethnic group has a specific neighbourhood. You'll see that in Nkembo, they are Fang … In Pont-Akebe over there, it's people from the Haut-Ogooué … So people settle where their elders are, the first to arrive settled there and then others followed. (Fang III, low income)

In daily life, the Fang person will go to a specific market place, he won't go to all the markets of the city so by definition when he arrives at a market, he knows he can discuss prices in Fang. (Fang I, middle income)

You have for instance Akebe Plaine which has 'a connotation' Obamba/Teke, you have Akebe … which is majority Kota, you have 'the five' which is majority Nzebi, you have Nkembo, Cocotie 'derriere la prison' which have a Fang connotation … It's due to the arrival of the parents, there is a parent who arrives and settles somewhere. If you are at the village and you arrive here, you will be told 'listen, don't go far, X is in such neighbourhood', when you arrive X gives you a room today, tomorrow, you have a small job, what do you do? X tells you 'listen, the house is a bit small, you should take next door's plot' and if I myself come, it would be the same thing and so on. So you'll see after five or 10 years, it's almost a small neighbourhood which has 'a family connotation' and with weddings and so on, you have a Fang or Nzebi community which is settled. (Nzebi, low income)

Such a preference for living in ethnically and linguistically homogeneous neighbourhoods does not appear to prevent harmonious interaction with people from other ethnic groups or with foreigners. Nor, in fact, does it appear to lead to a rejection of French as the official language of these two cities. Rather, it seems that each language is regarded as having a specific generally accepted function. Vernacular languages are used in the private sphere with family, friends, and within community:

> I don't have any trouble speaking Nzebi in my neighbourhood because most residents are Nzebi, we all come from the same area so I don't have any difficulties speaking Nzebi, my father speaks Nzebi, my mother speaks Nzebi. (Nzebi, low income)

> Us Kabiye, we're all the same. Kabiye is important for us because it's our language. When we're at home, we speak our language. (Kabiye, low income)

French, on the other hand, is used as a vehicular language with people of other groups, particularly when residents have not mastered the others' languages. This point was made by several focus groups both in Lomé and Libreville. The following is an illustration:

> We meet together in the neighbourhood … If I am with my brother, I am at ease speaking my mother tongue with him but if I am with an Ewe friend, I speak Ewe or if I can't speak Ewe, I'll speak French. (Kabiye, middle income)

A similar relaxed attitude toward other languages was expressed in Libreville by the Nzebi focus group where French appears to be accepted (and re-appropriated) as the national language:

> If I speak Nzebi and the person in front of me can understand, that's fine but if he speaks Fang, and I haven't been into contact with Fangs, I won't be able to speak, I won't be able to understand, so we speak our national language, French. (Nzebi, low income)

French is also considered to be the language of the public domain, especially in the educational sphere:

> French should be the vehicular language between teachers and children, it would be more rational because outside of school, at home, when they come back, they are

in contact with their mother tongues. At home, we are the teachers of the mother tongue so at school, we need the teachers to speak in French and they must not speak the mother tongues. (Kabiye, low income)

Accordingly, people seem to develop a form of comfortable code-switching, using one language or another according to the demands of the situation. The need for such multilingualism is stated as a fact of life, without resentment regarding the role of French or of a regional vehicular language (Ewe-Mina in Lomé and to a lesser extent Fang in Libreville):

> The dominant language is Lomé's language, Ewe. Everybody speak Ewe because the indigenous people don't understand our language, so we must learn their language … because we are in their home. But if there are Ewe in the North, they learn Kabiye when they arrive in the North. (Kabiye, low income)

> French really remains a dominant language but one must also say that beside French, the second language is Mina. Mina is also necessary especially when you go to the 'Grand Marché' … If you don't speak Mina, they are going to cheat you, if you speak French, they're going to say 'here comes the foreigner'. Whatever they sell for CFA500, they're going to sell to you for CFA2 500 now. (Kabiye, low income)

> At the market, some Fang people, I don't know why, they would speak to you in Fang but if you have been in the North, where they come from, you can speak Fang. (Nzebi, low income)

One language group, however, the Fang language community, developed a significantly different narrative about language identity. This shared difference, moreover, was found in different income classes. In the first place, sentiments of language discrimination were distinctly expressed in all Fang focus groups:

> It's a general trend, it's not recent that more than 80% of the administration is from the Haut-Ogooué [a province which is in majority Mbede-Teke]. If you arrive and speak Obamba or whatever, it isn't abrasive but if you speak Fang, they look at you badly and you can be sure that you won't be able to advance in your investigations the way a person from the Haut-Ogooué would. (Fang I, middle income)

Such sentiments appear to lead to perceived difficulties regarding sharing neighbourhoods with non-Fang speakers:

This neighbourhood is originally Fang, but unfortunately there's a fact that is happening: people who come here don't want to consider Fangs as autochthonous [i.e., indigenous], they see them as human targets and don't want to see them as simple cohabitants. (Fang I, middle income)

There is a mix here because in my neighbourhood around here, I cohabit with people from Togo, from Nigeria and a few Cameroonians. The mixing between these residents and us is a bit difficult ... There is a big linguistic problem, it's people who refuse to speak others' language ... (Fang III, low income)

These sentiments and fears are accompanied by expressions of concern regarding the loss of Fang as a mother tongue:

I speak French despite myself because it became more or less a national language here. It's the national language but a national language which is imposed on us while making sure that we ignore our own languages. (Fang I, middle income)

In contradistinction to the narratives of other language communities, the Fang appear uncomfortable with regular code-switching as an acceptable way of urban life:

Can the Fang accept it if the authorities suggest a language which is not Fang as a national language? It would be very difficult. The Fang man is very proud, I stayed in four provinces, I can't even make three sentences in another language so we don't really like speaking another language, we'd rather see somebody speaking our language. (Fang III, low income)

As a consequence of these strongly held sentiments and attitudes, Fang narratives move toward demands for the recognition of their language in the public domain:

'Francophonie' doesn't bring anything to Africa ... Is it specific to Gabon? Yes, because next door in Congo, Punu is spoken and Punu is taught at school ... On the side of East Africa, from Congo downward, I'd say even from Congo-Brazzaville, in Central Africa, the Sango and Lingala are spoken and it goes down until Rwanda even, so it's a question of political will. If one day a specific vernacular language was chosen to be a national language that one could learn at school in Gabon, everybody would adapt to it in the same way as we learn French but it's a question of political will. It's a problem of inferiority feeling if I may say. Why not choose the Fang language, I am Fang, but since everybody already learn our language in private in any case ... because every migrant decides to learn how to speak Fang in the first place ... (Fang I, middle income)

And this sense of linguistic discrimination against the Fang language appears to be linked to a sense of wider ethnic discrimination regarding access to jobs, to promotion, to bursaries, to plots of land, and so on:

Today, there are ethnic groups where you simply have to be from this ethnic group to know that tomorrow you'll get a job that's waiting for you, whether you work for it or not. There are even study bursaries which are ethnically given ... (Fang I, middle income)

One mustn't hide it, we endure a lot of things in our [public] services because we are Fang, you can't be as easily promoted as others. (Fang II, middle income)

The Fang and the Punu live together, we've cohabited without problems, we are brothers but when one knows how the distribution of positions takes place in this country, even if we want to live with the Punu, we are not able to do it, why? Because we'll see that today the Punu has a position that he doesn't deserve and myself, the Fang, I deserve that position and I don't have it. What does it bring about? Simply conflicts. Outwardly we just pretend to accept each other but in the heart, we have this fear. (Fang III, low income)

If you take the case of state-allocated leases, 80% of these are used by people who are today in power but the rest of us don't have access to them. We don't have access to state subsidised housing we must go and manage for ourselves in the periphery, in the Savannah. (Fang I, middle income)

These shared perceptions of discrimination on the basis of ethnicity and language are not found in the narratives of the Nzebi group in Libreville or of residents in Lomé:

There are sectors which at the beginning had been reserved [to certain ethnic groups] a long time ago. I remember, when we were in our villages, we were told that to go into the presidential guard, you had to be Obamba or Teke ... but after a while, it changed, they had to take a Nzebi and so on ... In the hospitals, it was a connotation for instance Fang. In the education system, it was a connotation Punu/Nzebi and the industrial sector was dominated by Fangs, especially in the Estuary. But at a certain time, with the evolution ... everybody made his position somewhere and that's how the other ethnic groups came in and people with degrees also made an impact, one can't prevent someone with a degree ... if for instance Sobraga needs an engineer ... whether he is Fang or Nzebi or Punu, we can't prevent him from working ... (Nzebi, low income)

In Lomé, in fact, though complaints of a socio-economic and state service-delivery nature were frequent, they were not linked in the narratives to ethnic or linguistic discrimination. Rather, respondents perceived themselves as urban citizens, and ethnic tensions were explained as the product of political manipulation. The example below is drawn from a focus group of the state president's ethnic group:

> Those [ethnic] problems in fact didn't use to exist but it's our political problems which entail these types of antagonism. Politicians, for them, it's a question of 'divide and rule'. That's their philosophy ... to want to oppose community groups ... the one says this community group is mine, the other one says that one is mine, I come from this and that, I am the leader, etc. and at the end of the day, community groups who used to live in peace and good understanding end up having bad relationships. That's what we experienced especially those last 10 years, we saw situations where people from the South said they didn't want people from the North and ... vice versa and it created tensions but it is because of politicians. It is not because of individuals themselves, they don't have this kind of spirit. (Kabiye, middle income).

11.4 Conclusion

The research conducted among residents in Libreville and Lomé is exploratory. As such, the interpretations above need to be treated as suggestive of results rather than as definite conclusions. The three hypotheses have guided these interpretations. Simultaneously, more general shared representations within focus groups have been teased out.

In both cities, official language policy appears largely to have been accepted: French is perceived to be, and is used as, the vehicular language. No difficulties with speaking French were expressed, not even by urban residents with lower educational and socio-economic backgrounds. While in both countries anti-French sentiments were expressed, this did not extend to language, which seems to have been accepted as a national asset. Simultaneously, with one exception, few sentiments of anxiety and fear regarding the loss of vernacular languages were expressed. These languages appear to be widely used in neighbourhood interaction as well as in private. This appears as true in minority as in majority language settings – that is, groups other than the Fang in Libreville or the Ewe-Mina in Lomé. Residents from these groupings appear to have developed high levels of individual situational multilingualism (or code-switching), which entails speaking their mother tongue, the local *lingua franca*, and the official language according to the demands of the urban situation in which they find themselves. This finding does seem to question at least the main thrust of the argument that continued language use depends on the maintenance of 'high-status' functions of that language in the public domain.

Linguistic resentments were expressed by one group only, the Fang community in Libreville, and these resentments appeared to translate into exclusive feelings towards other linguistic groups – into a rejection of French as official national language, and into claims for the recognition and use of Fang in the public sphere. These sentiments also appeared to be rooted in shared ethnic representations beyond language. Narratives pointed to common sentiments of multiple exclusion, often in the socio-economic domain.

In conclusion, then, it may be that language-based identity politics is better seen as a symptom of other resistance identities rather than as a sense of discrimination and exclusion in itself. This appears to be the case with the Fang in Libreville and with isiXhosa-speakers in Cape Town (see also chapter 9 in this book). As Kriel has pointed out, 'the problem is that language struggles are hardly ever about language alone; they have been and continue to be nationalist struggles (and as such power struggles) at heart' (Kriel, 2003: 164) and accordingly, 'language differences are not responsible for important conflicts, they simply serve to identify enemy groups' (Lebikaza, 1999: 6).

Appendix A: Focus group data and how they have been used

Research involved discussions with rank-and-file groupings selected either on the basis of living together in a neighbourhood or on the basis of sharing a common home language (or both). Each focus group was requested to discuss how they 'felt' as members of their linguistic community about living in their local residential area, in Lomé or in Libreville and in Togo or Gabon. Discussions were conducted in the preferred language of each group (French, except in part of one focus group discussion – Fang I) and transcriptions were subsequently translated into English for analysis. Choice of non-directive focus group methodology was based on the hypothesis that people, through collective discussions or narratives, construct social representations that would not have been accessible to us by using quantitative research methods such as surveys. The disadvantage of such methodology, however, revolves around issues of representivity and potential generalisation. Given the number of languages in both countries (between 30 and 40), it was difficult to be representative in terms of language groups. Focus group discussions were organised with the largest linguistic groups country-wise (Ewe-Mina and Kabiye in Togo; Fang and Nzebi in Gabon). Table 11.1 summarises the make-up of the focus groups in Lomé, Togo and Libreville, Gabon.

Table 11.1: *Sketch of focus groups from which data have been drawn*

Lomé	
Kabiye I Low income Kabiye-speakers, Agbalopédogan, Lomé	14/11/2003
Kabiye II Middle-income Kabiye-speakers, Agbalopédogan, Lomé	15/11/2003
Mixed languages (Losso, Anan, Kabiye, Ewe-Mina) Low-income residents, 'quartier administrative', Lomé	21/11/2003
Ewe-Mina Middle-income Ewe-speakers, Amoutive, Lomé	21/11/2003
Libreville	
Fang I Mixed-income Fangs, Nzong-Ayong, Libreville	23/06/2004
Fang II Middle-income/upper-middle income Fangs, near Lycée Léon Mba, Libreville	23/06/2004
Fang III Focus group with low-income Fangs, Nkembo (Deux Rivières), Libreville	25/06/2004
Nzebi Focus group with low-income Nzebi, Ancienne Sobraga, Libreville	29/06/2004

Research took place in Lomé in November 2003 and in Libreville in June 2004. The constitution of the focus group began with the identification of a coordinator within the milieu of the focus group. This milieu coordinator was requested to approach between six and 10 potential adult participants from the milieu. The coordinator was also requested to select participants with varying ages as well as approximately equal numbers of women and men. The focus group venue was selected on the basis of a location known to the participants. Discussions ranged from 40 to 90 minutes and were, in some cases, followed by face-to-face discussions with a few individual participants. Though three prompts were used, participants were not discouraged from pursuing a particular theme. Accordingly, few focus groups allocated equal discussion time to each theme. While all groups allowed recording, confidentiality was an important issue.

PART 5: THE AFRICAN CONTINENT

CHAPTER 12

What is an African?

Narratives from urban South Africa, Gabon and Togo

Anne Leildé

12.1 Introduction: The debate over an African identity

While Western media and popular culture continue to represent Africa and its people 'in tantalising tarzanic and essentialist terms' (Nyamnjoh, 2000: 9), constantly reasserting the 'fevered imaginings' that underpinned the so-called civilising mission of colonial powers, as Pottier (2003) puts it, the notion of an African identity has initiated vigorous debate among African scholars over the past decade.

Most critical debate comes from a 'a younger generation of "postmodern" scholars' (Robins, 1994: 18) who contend that the idea of an overarching and unproblematicised African identity is simply a discursive strategy, an 'empty myth' initiated by post-independence elites in their search for a unified approach to the struggle against colonialism and for African development. What those Africanist intellectuals loyal to this struggle fail to represent is the multiplicity and hybridity of identities constructed by those who live on the continent. According to Sewpaul, such a discourse constitutes 'the substitution of one hegemonic discourse, that of Eurocentrism, with another hegemonic discourse, Afrocentrism', which 'continues modernism's binary classifications' (2004: 1–2). For Mbembe, this representation of Africa and its inhabitants is advanced by two narratives that are implicitly rooted in the ideologies of Marxism and of nationalism in Africa during the last century. The first, *nativism*, emerges from 'the malaise resulting from the encounter between the West and the indigenous worlds' and 'proposes a return to an ontological and mythical "Africanness" in which the African subject might once again say "I" and express him- or herself in his or her own name' (Mbembe, 2002b: 629). This narrative of cultural uniqueness serves to legitimise policies of 'authenticity' in various African countries and to promote the search for an endogenous knowledge, 'an African interpretation of things'. The second of these two narratives, that of *afro-radicalism*, stems from a 'reified vision of history' whereby 'the present destiny of the continent is supposed to proceed not from free and autonomous choices but from the legacy (both) of a history imposed upon the Africans and of [current] economic conditionalities' (Mbembe, 2002a: 243). Mbembe argues that both narratives ignore African agency and require 'a profound investment in the idea of race' since they are 'discourses of inversion', drawing 'their fundamental categories from the myths they claim to oppose', in particular 'the very conviction that race exists and is at the foundation of morality and nationality' (2002a: 257).

The main criticism directed at this notion of an homogeneous African identity is accordingly that it is conceived in primordial and essentialist terms, leading scholars to ignore 'the enormous differences within Africa and amongst Africans that inhabit the continent; differences that express themselves along the lines of gender, sexuality, class, ethnicity, religion, language, region, nationality, and so on' (Robins, 2004: 24). 'Postmodern' scholars call for a re-evaluation of theories based on economic dependence and cultural determinism and for a recognition of African individuality and agency as Africans express themselves differently in various post-colonial societies. These scholars draw attention to the 'contemporary everyday practices through which Africans manage to recognize and maintain with the world an unprecedented familiarity' (Mbembe, 2002a: 258).

Notions of subjectivity, autonomy, and agency are at the core of social science debates on identity formation in late modernity. However, this conception of identity as the product of free will and individual choice remains contested. While the primordial and essentialist approach to the study of identities has generally been discarded, many scholars highlight the structural-material determinants within which identity choices are made. In the African context, Nyamnjoh argues that

> the causes of Africa's problems are neither simply external, nor exclusively internal, but a combination of both. Africans have been, and still are, both dependent and autonomous agents in relation to the historical forces that have impinged, and are impinging, upon them and their continent. While it would be too simplistic to see Africans entirely as zombies totally overwhelmed by external forces, one must also be careful not to credit them with utopian agency, which is certainly not feasible within the current structures and relations of unequal exchange championed by the giant compressors of the West. (Nyamnjoh, 2000: 18)

Sindjoun highlights broader cultural discourses within which identity formation takes place. He argues that popular narratives often parallel those of the elite, in a process of the internalisation of official narratives:

> By focusing exclusively on the fluidity of identities and on popular (urban) practices, the post-modern discourse partially ignores official narratives … The 'official' nature of these narratives should not lead to their disposal as if popular narratives and practices had a monopoly of legitimacy … The myth of a united Africa is not only an issue for elites. A Pan-African identity manifests itself in the daily lives of Africans through music, sport and beauty pageants … (Sindjoun, 2002: 16–19, my translation)

Finally, Sichone points out that recognition of the multiplicity of identities that Africans create for themselves in their daily lives does not preclude the emergence of a common 'Africanness'. '(A)fricanisation is something that happens to everyone at some time … In identity politics, the question who is an African is clearly incomplete (even meaningless) unless one also asks: when is one an African? Why and How?' (2004: 15). Sichone argues that such an identity emerges primarily in connection with Europe: 'One is never actually African but becomes Africanised under specific circumstances … Being African is … rarely a term of local value but is rather best understood as a global term that exists in juxtaposition to Europe' (Sichone, 2004: 1).

12.2 The debate within South Africa

Over the past decade in South Africa, the notion of an African identity has also been vigorously debated. The debate moreover has been indelibly coloured by the idea of South African exceptionalism. Mamdani, when at the University of Cape Town in the late 1990s, launched a debate on the teaching of African history at South African universities. A dominant narrative, Mamdani claimed, is that Africa is not defined as the whole continent – North Africa is depicted as part of the Middle East, and South Africa as an island of civilisation, as an exception.

> [We] have to take head-on the notion of South African exceptionalism and the widely shared prejudice that while South Africa is a part of Africa geographically, it is not quite culturally and politically, and certainly not economically. It is a point of view that I have found to be a hallmark of much of the South African intelligentsia, shared across divides: white or black, left or right, male or female. (Mamdani, 1998)

This exceptionalism undoubtedly echoes the apartheid myth that 'white South Africa was a big Orania built in isolation without any contribution from the rest of the continent … [that] even though the majority of South Africans are black Africans, the country itself was not part of Black (sub-Saharan) Africa' (Sichone, 2004: 9).

Simultaneously, after apartheid, as South Africa emerged as a legitimate actor on both African and international fora, the 'Africanisation' of the country became a fundamental element in the South African state's policy and projected foreign image. This underpins both Mandela's declaration in 1993 that South Africa 'could not escape its African destiny' (Hendricks & Whiteman, 2004) and Mbeki's well-known 1996 'I am an African' speech at the adoption by the Constitutional Assembly of the new South African Constitution. This is also the cornerstone of the African Renaissance project initiated by Mbeki, a project aimed at political, economic, and cultural renewal of the continent as it enters the twenty-first century.

These two narratives of exceptionalism and of an African renaissance have fuelled the identity debate in South Africa. Some view the debate as emancipatory since it will launch a process of re-appropriation by Africans of self-authorship after centuries of imposed representation, as well as the promotion of an Afrocentric scholarship. These views, in turn, have elicited the criticism that the debate introduces a new form of essentialism and accordingly that this has not transcended the hoary issue of race, thereby reasserting patterns of inclusion and exclusion in post-apartheid South Africa that are antithetical to the democratic ideal (Sewpaul, 2004). Further criticism holds that the debate is confined to the elite and is a strategy aimed at deflecting attention from prominent cleavages in social grouping and gender. It has also been described as a state-legitimising discourse and a political strategy aimed at attracting 'the Africanist' section of South African voters (Crouzel, 2000). The African Renaissance concept, moreover, has been interpreted as a strategy to promote South Africa's national interests (rather than those of the African continent) and to legitimise South Africa's claims to continental leadership.

The notion of African identity – both within South Africa and elsewhere on the continent – is contested since it comprises different, and sometimes contradictory, definitions. It is clear that more is at stake than mere theoretical lucidity. The notion is caught between 'the desire to know and to think and the urge to act' to quote Mbembe (2002b: 636) as much analysis struggles to differentiate between what the identities of Africans *are* and what they *should be* for action and redress to take place. Further difficulties stem from the paucity of empirical evidence to back up theoretical analysis.

12.3 How do urban residents in South Africa, in Gabon, and in Togo construct 'Africa'?

This section presents qualitative evidence gathered in three African countries, South Africa, Gabon, and Togo – countries that arguably belong to different 'Africas'.

South Africa is widely accepted as the regional hegemon of Southern Africa and as a key economic, demographic, and military power on the continent. It represents 25 per cent of African GNP and 40 per cent of continental industrial output. Gabon and Togo are two small Francophone countries, located geographically in Central Africa and in West Africa respectively. Exploitation of oil reserves in Gabon guarantees interest in the country both internationally and by France, whereas Togo is one of Africa's poorer countries.

The qualitative evidence was assembled by convening focus groups in a series of residential neighbourhoods in the cities of Cape Town, Johannesburg, Libreville, and Lomé. Each focus group was requested to discuss how they 'felt' about their own country, about South Africa (or in the cases of Cape Town and Johannesburg, about Francophone Africa) and about the African continent. Discussions were conducted in the preferred language of each group and transcriptions were subsequently translated into English for analysis. The three research prompts and subsequent non-directive facilitation of discussion were deliberately chosen to enable groups freely to probe areas of shared meaning. Since focus groups were not asked to debate issues directly related to a specific topic, identification and discussion of narratives produced evidence of shared sentiments regarding their importance. While recognising that the researcher influences focus group narratives, they take place in a socio-cultural context that is at least partly revealed through their content. This work is accordingly synchronic rather than historical, and is exploratory rather than quantifiable and generalisable. In short, this chapter merely hopes to shed some light on the various ways in which Africa is conceptualised and given meaning in very different African urban contexts. (References for quotes in the text follow the convention used in chapters 8 and 9 in this book. More information on the focus groups is given in tabular form in appendix A to this chapter).

Narratives from South Africa (Cape Town and Johannesburg)

The president of South Africa, Thabo Mbeki, once made the statement that 'South Africans (are) ignorant of the continent's great civilisations and reputable centres of learning ... and (have) an unwarranted superiority complex with regard to their peers' (2003). Narratives gathered during this research seem to confirm that South Africans from all economic and ethno-racial backgrounds display scant knowledge of Africa. Francophone Africa in particular appears in the minds of South Africans either as a nonentity or as something still 'under construction'. Unsurprisingly, narratives on Africa focus on contiguous countries and especially on Zimbabwe, a country that has figured at the forefront of news reports in South Africa recently. Very often, representations of Africa in the minds of South Africans are deeply negative and expressed in a derogatory manner. Perceptions are based on a number of prejudices and stereotypes that seem to echo Conrad's 'Heart of Darkness'. Images of a continent in disarray dominate, and key words in these narratives are 'diseases', 'uneducated', 'hunger and starvation', 'unsafe', 'corruption and political instability', and 'natural problems'. 'Africa' in sum often emerges as the polar opposite of what South Africa should be striving for both politically and economically. Such negative perceptions are captured in the following extract:

> All you see is what you get through the television in the newspapers, and it is wars and crime and poverty; disease and money laundering. And dirty. So my perception is Africa ... they are the rest of the continent. I don't want to be part of that. I am not really interested. (Strand, Cape Town)

Sentiments of separation and of distance from 'Africa' were both widespread and openly expressed by all South Africans represented in focus groups, irrespective of class or colour. Being part of the continent is conceived as a geographical accident, and lends credence to Sewpaul's findings among students at the University of KwaZulu-Natal:

> Africa, from the students' responses, emerges as two worlds juxtaposed – one that they hold in their heads, an Africa with all its archetypal representations, and an Africa that they actually inhabit ... a world of denim jeans, cellphones, TV, computers and concrete buildings. (Sepaul, 2004: 8)

It is apparent that narratives on Africa are deeply influenced by a shared belief in South African exceptionalism. This belief is rooted in South Africa's perceived economic and political advantages in Africa, in the conviction that 'South Africa is hope for Africa' in the words of a Kayamandi resident in Stellenbosch. This belief often translates into a conviction that 'what is good for South Africa is good for the rest of Africa', thereby revealing paternalism and sometimes condescension:

> I have read in Sunday newspapers that there is a huge expansion going on from South Africa in Tanzania. For example, Game has opened there, and Telkom is there, and we deliver electricity and stuff like that. So I don't feel threatened by Africa, because I feel that if it was not for us, then nothing will go on in Africa. (Roodeport 2, Johannesburg)

Conversely, South Africa's location in Southern Africa is seen, particularly by middle-income focus group respondents, as disadvantageous to the economy of the country. Proximity to countries that are politically unstable is said to discourage foreign investments. Implicitly, this view proposes a policy of isolationism:

> Look for instance at the service delivery; it's very bad compared to other countries. We are not progressing fast enough. It's because we are part of the SADC region and we are dependent on what's happening there. We are part of a contingent group. If something is happening in Zimbabwe, we have a problem here. We have to become more independent … (Mayfair, Johannesburg)

> Yes, we want to see our country succeed with people coming here with a degree of confidence, and saying this is a good pick. But there is always this negative perception which is blown up. Why when something happens in Zimbabwe, or Nigeria which is far away from us, do we get affected? That is the worrying thing about the international community, the way they perceive South Africa or don't know South Africa. We're always portrayed as this banana republic, you know. It's a misrepresentation of our country. (Fleurhof, Johannesburg)

A belief in exceptionalism and an evasion of identification with Africa are rationalised through two narratives, both clearly instrumental in nature: the first focuses on the government's policy towards Africa and the second on South Africa's immigration policy. Though aware of government's 'African Renaissance' concept, of its economic initiatives on the continent such as NEPAD (New Partnership for Africa's Development), and of its military involvement, South African respondents were generally not supportive, for a variety of reasons. South Africa's role tends to be perceived in an altruistic light, as provider of finances and support (rather than as investor) and as costly for the South African taxpayer. Accordingly, there is a widespread belief that state resources for South African backlogs to combat inequalities ought to be given priority over external demands:

> Our president is taking the lead in this Africa initiative [NEPAD] … It's like Europe and the European Union … the difference is that Europe has money, it's rich countries. (Soweto, Johannesburg)

> The Sub-Saharan continent … I'm just afraid that they will become more and more dependent on South Africa … And us guys who pay tax. We will be helping Africa more, instead of our own people here. And when I'm saying, our own people, I don't mean only us whites, I also mean blacks. I think charity should begin at home. (Roodeport 2, Johannesburg)

> The government wants a relationship with the rest of the African countries. We should first look at our own people. You know, most of our people are still struggling;

the struggle is not over yet ... struggle against poverty and discrimination which is still big. And the sad part is that the people who really fought for the struggle is not really benefiting now. (Atlantis, Cape Town)

A belief in exceptionalism and an evasion of identification with Africa are also clearly expressed through narratives on African immigration to South Africa. Perceptions of South Africa as a 'land of milk and honey' contribute toward the image of African migrants as economic migrants, rather than political refugees – of people who entered illegally in search of a better life or of an 'easy buck' and who benefit immensely from their stay in South Africa:

> They come because they see us as prosperous. South Africa – compared to their countries – our streets are paved, we are light-years in advance ... We are an organised society; even in our squatter camps we are actually better-off ... Six Nigerians can live in my flat, pay me two thousand a month, that to them is first class accommodation ... they can go down, get a job at the Waterfront, get a job as a parking attendant. What they earn, coupled with the weather, coupled with relative law and order ... living in a nice flat at a reasonable rate, is better than being in a township in Sierra Leone. (Durbanville, Cape Town)

This image of the foreign migrant undermines what remains of the belief that South Africa ought to remain mindful of past support by African countries for the ANC in exile:

> In the apartheid years, there was what they called exile and a lot of people used that, and there was a lot of sympathy for certain groups in those days, and there were a lot of those people there that side wanting to help this people over here. I see nothing wrong with that, but I'm saying now that everything's changed ... don't come in and don't try and take over, I mean they know the situation, 35 million blacks and there is X amount percentage of them without work. They've been there to help. Why do they want to take it away? (Kraaifontein 2, Cape Town)

> We did not go to their countries to look for jobs. And we did not leave because of corruption. People who left for outside countries went there for military training, so that they could attack the apartheid government, not to seek jobs. But they are coming to snatch bread from us. And then they capitalise on this matter. (Tsakane 1, Johannesburg)

In short, xenophobia appears to be widespread in South Africa, and openly expressed. Narratives regarding immigrants, Nigerians in particular, are infused with stereotypes and prejudices. African immigrants are accused of a variety of social ills and criminal activities – drug dealing, arms trafficking, contract killings, and prostitution. Such sentiments have been expressed by South Africans from all socio-economic and ethno-racial backgrounds – by respondents living in Johannesburg and in Cape Town, in metropolitan areas and in rural Western Cape, in townships, in suburbs, and in informal settlements:

> They just sell drugs … and another thing they are also used by some of us to destroy our community. They tell a foreigner that 'we give you R400.00, remove this person'. The foreigners will kill that person because it will be an unknown; these people do not have an identity. We can see that this one is a foreigner but home affairs do not have these people's identity. So it is easier for us to be arrested in such cases. But it is not easy for them to be arrested. (Tsakane 1, Johannesburg)

African migrants are largely conceived as a burden upon South Africa's scarce economic resources. Middle-income respondents focus their narratives on the impact of immigration on basic infrastructure, on public housing, and on the unskilled and semi-skilled job market:

> I spoke to [a government official] this afternoon about the housing, this is my area of business, we were speaking about the housing [development] which is taking place … like all this RDP housing taking place and the question I posed him is what guarantee has he got for me that all these houses that the government is building, which is our tax-payers' money, [are] going to South Africans and he could not give me an affirmative answer. Foreigners … (Bosmont, Johannesburg)

> I'm just looking at the percentage of people [who are] without jobs and I think you have all these guys coming in and taking all the work that could have been given to or done by our local boys … I don't mind hearing a French-speaking guy in the parking area, but then again that could have been one of our blacks doing the job, especially on the different flea markets. (Kraaifontein 2, Cape Town)

Among the poor, resentment about migrants was openly expressed regarding competition over scarce job opportunities. Foreigners represent cheap labour, and are believed to benefit from their illegal status in the country since they thereby evade taxes.

> If you go to buildings especially Wimpy actually Rivonia consists of shopping centres that are full of places which sell food, Spar and so on. Ninety per cent of those who work in Rivonia are foreigners and the reason it is done that way is because

they exploit them. And we the children of this side, the people who have voted the government into power are the ones who are starving because jobs opportunities are filled by those ones. (Tsakane 1, Johannesburg)

This is the problem, because these people occupy spaces for our people to sell things in Cape Town. But our people are not having a chance to sell, because Cape Town is full of these people, they are everywhere. So maybe if the government can do something about these people, maybe it can give us a chance to find jobs. (Khayelitsha, Cape Town)

Discourse on immigration clearly revolves around notions of rights and obligations that respondents perceive to be attached to citizenship. By failing to implement stricter immigration policies, government is seen by many respondents to be reneging in its obligations towards citizens and voters:

The responsibility of our government is to see to it that the citizens of this country are protected … How do you expect a person who is untraceable, a foreigner for that matter, who has done something wrong to taste the cost of justice? It is very true that as a continent, Africa is a whole, we are Africans, but there is a need of this government of ours to have some regulations and rules which will be able to regulate the movements of the Africans in their own continent. We're not saying they are the only people who are doing crime but at least if I am a SA citizen, I know if I am doing crime out there, one day I am going to be traced and I'll have to face the law. The problem with these people is that they are doing crime knowing very well that nothing is going to happen to them. (Alexandra, Johannesburg)

As already pointed out, these narratives are shared by South Africans drawn from all ethnic, racial, and class or economic level backgrounds in focus group narratives. This suggests that they are based on instrumental (rather than aesthetic or symbolic) factors that derive from a definition of the continent in economic rather than racial terms. This is not to say that discourses on Africa and its inhabitants are devoid of any essentialist references. The vocabulary used by some white South African respondents differs from that of other South Africans in that social distance often takes on clear racial overtones:

That scares me, if you look at Africa, if you look the whole of Africa is black … and we are this fistful of whites here on the bottom, then it sometimes worries you. (Roodeport 2, Johannesburg)

In a few cases, narratives reveal a positive identification with the continent and express frustrations with neo-colonial practices and of Western portrayals of Africa's failures rather than praise of its successes:

> I think there are possibilities on getting people to come and invest in different countries in Africa. There's a lot more emphasis on getting the message out, especially to European businesses, that Africa is a wealth of talent and resources but I think there's a long way to go. I think people's perception of Africa is that it's still primitive, very backward and that perception needs to change. (Rondebosch, Cape Town)

> We've got a lot to offer, more than the gold and the silver and the diamonds that have been taken from this continent to build Europe, because Europe has been built with riches from here ... In Europe, they still don't want Africa to be part of the world ... and [this] is not fair ... But this generation is going to make it work because we've got a heart. There's a desire to make this country and this continent a place to be. (Kayamandi, Western Cape)

To an extent, these views of Africa and of an African identity correspond with Sichone's claim that one becomes 'Africanised' in relation to Europe.

Narratives from Gabon (Libreville) and Togo (Lomé)

Narratives from Gabon and Togo share a number of characteristics. Knowledge of South Africa is often sketchy, something often put down to distance: 'South Africa is far away; we can't really talk about it'. First-hand acquaintance of South Africa is rare, though a few Gabonese respondents had visited the country. Information is largely obtained from news reports, TV documentaries, magazines, and newspapers articles and therefore tends to conform to views of South Africa found in Western media. In particular, stereotypes and prejudices regarding levels of crime in South African cities, sexual violence, and HIV infections, which were said to 'create fears' among respondents, were common themes in narratives. In both cities, a degree of exoticism regarding 'Zulus' as custodians of a South African culture was mentioned.

> South Africans keep their traditions intact ... They are keeping their culture, if you look at their dances ... their Zulu dances, they're beautiful. Us as Kabiyé, we find ourselves through their dances, their movements, and their traditional dress. (Mixed languages, Lomé)

The fact that English rather than French is South Africa's international language is well known to respondents. Though it has often been argued that language 'is a determinant factor in shared cultural identities' on the continent (Sindjoun, 2000: 13), both Togolese and Gabonese respondents point to differences in colonial experience. These differences are perceived to reach beyond language. Anglophones are said to be more entrepreneurial, more 'street-wise', and less public-sphere oriented – 'they have a leadership spirit', a 'business ethos':

> Most Anglophone countries are rich and South Africa is too. Anglophone countries seem to have a good mind to work with … They are more creative than us, they do things better than us. It seems like they are more educated, more advanced. I think it's a question of colonisation … I think the French only taught us how to say intelligent things, how to speak and that's it, whereas, the Anglophones, they have a know-how. (Kabiye II, Lomé)

> The Anglophone and Francophone colonial powers didn't have the same view on colonisation. You'll agree with me that Francophone countries are less developed than Anglophone countries and I think that is what we regret the most from the French colonisation. The examples are obvious, today South Africa is here, Nigeria is another example … a country from 'Black' Africa, a country which has been colonised by Britain, is more advanced, more developed than most Francophone countries so it's a pity that French colonisation acted in that way. (Fang I, Libreville)

In contradistinction to the South African narrative that NEPAD is 'South Africa's brainchild', respondents in Libreville and Lomé locate the initiative in Anglophone Africa:

> The role that SA is playing today, others had the same opportunity before to play this role and what did they do in terms of development? Nothing. If you look at the NEPAD's people today, who thought about it? Anglophones, to whom you can add one single Francophone, A. Wade. The rest of them (Francophone leaders) just follow. (Fang I, Libreville)

Simultaneously, narratives express beliefs in a South African exceptionalism that sets it apart from other African countries. The 'new' South Africa is presented as a model 'African' country, a 'window' for Africa, a 'dream' country. It inspires pride for the continent as a whole and is used to refute common 'Afro-pessimist' representations. In political terms, it is represented as a model of peaceful transition, of 'effective and representative democracy', and of accommodation of various groups' interests. The iconic role that Nelson Mandela plays in this narrative is significant:

Mandela is a myth to whom we owe respect. He is an emblem and could have acted like other Africans and stayed in power for a second, third or fourth mandate as is the case in Africa ... But he only had one mandate in SA. It's this myth of Mandela which has allowed whites and blacks to accept each other. You can even look at some symbols ... the different colours (of the national flag) ... These are symbols which explain why SA has gone back so quickly to occupy an important position on the African international scene. (Fang I, Libreville)

It seems that the relationship between blacks and whites in South Africa is working well and if that is the case, then it ... gives us some reassurance that one day, we'll be there too. We know that things are slow to change because people were used to certain ways for a long time but they are changing in South Africa ... We are all black here but there have been ethnic wars so we hope that what happened in South Africa can happen here. (Ewe, Lomé)

In economic terms, the country is seen to be a 'driving force' in terms of industrial development and medical research in Africa, and its infrastructure is described as very advanced.

South Africa is a model for us because the European countries tend to say that, in Africa, there isn't much good, but when one looks at it today, it's really a country of which Africa is proud ... It is almost the United States of Africa ... it's a model for African countries because it has achieved development compared to the rest of Africa and it's our model in comparison to Europe ... It's the only country which can measure with big powers, economically, demographically and culturally, it's an African power. (Fang III, Libreville)

Accordingly, expectations regarding South Africa taking the lead on the continent are common. The idea that South Africa's and the continent's economic interests coincide – an idea expressed by a number of South African focus group respondents – is echoed by respondents in Gabon and Togo. In Gabon, such calls are often concretised since cooperative ventures in the fields of health services and universities are known to many Libreville respondents.

I wish for SA to bring us its technological knowledge. If SA is what it is today, it is because South Africans have taken into their hands the future of their country. If they can teach us this way of doing things, we would appreciate it. (Fang I, Libreville)

I think that South Africa is going forward and when they do so, for instance in the research field, what is certain is that we also are going to benefit from it. Yes, SA can help the African continent to go forward. In Africa, SA is a power in many fields, industrial and otherwise, it is a power. (Mixed languages, Lomé)

The need for South Africa to take the lead in continental institutions was also raised in a number of focus groups. South Africa is seen to have emerged as a credible political leader and model on the continent after its successful struggle against apartheid.

SA must play a leadership role. I think that as a people that has suffered as much as they did ... I can remember seeing the Soweto events, the 16th of June ... I was hurt in my soul. And as people that have the means and the freedom to choose their leaders today, SA will have a leadership role. Our eyes are turned toward this country. (Fang II, Libreville)

In Gabon, moreover, where the French presence is experienced as pervasive, South Africa is portrayed as a potential countervailing presence:

I'd like for South Africa to do what Asians do. The Chinese are present in Gabon at commercial and financial levels. SA should also come here without minding 'our colonials' because they have this worrying attitude ... As soon as they saw the Chinese coming in, the French had a problem with it and tried stop our cooperation with China. We need a country that can act as a policeman, even one without uniform ... SA could play this role. (Fang III, Libreville)

These narratives on South Africa's potential role on the continent express an instrumental rather than essentialist image of South Africa in the sense that they associate the country and its government with economic and political characteristics rather than with ascribed characteristics of its population. On the other hand, there were notions related to more essentialist features in certain narratives, though these were clearly exceptions. These tended to be expressed in terms of black racial solidarity:

South Africa is a country that shows that the black man can do something, that the black man has a place somewhere. We admired the courage of Nelson Mandela who showed us, as black people, that we all have this courage and that there is some hope for our country as well. (Ewe, Lomé)

We understand that South Africans won't like it if foreigners go there and receive the fruits of their struggle, of their suffering while they themselves are still living in poverty ... but whatever small finances blacks have, especially the black middle class, they have to invest it in other countries, they must come and cooperate with other African countries. (Fang II, Libreville)

Simultaneously, in the case of one focus group, South Africa's racial mix was found both to be puzzling and to detract from the otherwise progressive image of South Africa on the continent:

> South Africa ... we don't understand ... We know Nelson Mandela ... but is it Africans who are over there or whites? We don't know. We know there were problems but we still don't understand what is happening over there. It's an African country but we don't understand why there is a dominance of whites, we really don't understand this racism. Those whites, are they Africans or are they foreigners? What is South Africa really, to which continent does it belong? (Kabiye II, Lomé)

12.4 Conclusion

South African narratives about the African continent reveal an evasion of identification with Africa by most respondents. These narratives, shared by black and white, poor and rich, seem to suggest that Africa is rarely perceived in essentialist terms, as a black continent, but in instrumental terms, as a continent in disarray which in turn impacts negatively on the national economy and labour market. Though it is often stated that 'many South Africans [are] still largely ignorant about other African countries and this has fuelled the current xenophobia in the country' (Hendricks & Whiteman, 2004: 8), these narratives suggest that an evasion of identification with Africa is due less to ignorance than to rational choice, a choice based 'on a fair assessment of the cost of being African' (Sichone, 2004). These representations of other African countries moreover 'matter because they are used to articulate expressions of personal and national identity and are a reflection of the local political context' (Nyamnjoh, 2002: 632). These narratives, accordingly, shared as they appear to be by many South Africans, probably point to an equally shared, significant identification with South Africa and with rights derived from its citizenship. It would seem then that the multiple identities South Africans construct for themselves extend beyond the popular singular paradigm of race and class.

Gabonese and Togolese Francophone narratives distinguish between Francophone and Anglophone Africa and their divergent colonial histories and experiences. In so doing, they locate the meaning of Africa in a European–African context. The image of the 'new' South Africa as a credible leader and model on the continent, in both the political and economic spheres, is widely stated and accepted. In this sense, South Africa is presented as an African country that could help to reverse Western afro-pessimist representations of the continent. At least among members of the urban focus groups analysed in this chapter, this mentor image of South Africa appears to supersede any concerns that South Africa as continental hegemon may misuse its power. In their narratives, South Africa is squarely located on the African continent and plays the role of 'an important locus in the post-colonial imagery of Africa' (Sindjoun, 1999: 41). This image contrasts with those of European countries and of neo-colonial practices.

Respondents in Libreville, Lomé, Cape Town, and Johannesburg construct images of various Africas. The main cleavage within these images (beyond regional, linguistic, or ethnic divides) is between a rich and a poor Africa. While South Africa is seen beyond its borders as a potential motor of development in Africa, in the country itself, Africa is seen as a limitation. These images are also sometimes racialised. In Gabon and Togo, this serves to legitimise expectations that brothers and sisters from the South will offer support and protection to those in need. Curiously, in South Africa, where race remains part and parcel of the way residents talk about themselves (Bekker & Leildé, 2000), images of Africa are rarely racialised. This finding underlines the situational nature of racial discourse and racial identifications.

Finally, what of South African exceptionalism? As Mamdani (1998) puts it, 'a hallmark of much of the South African intelligentsia [is that] ... while South Africa is a part of Africa geographically, it is not quite culturally and politically, and certainly not economically.' While South African respondents' narratives appear to conform to this hallmark, it is equally apparent to them that South Africa is actively engaging in continental activities as an African member. Though they may not support this new role, they cannot but be aware of it, not least since other Africans in their narratives appear to be embracing South Africa as an African mentor. One clear implication is that the images of Africa that will be constructed in the future by residents within South Africa as well as without will be influenced by these changing circumstances and narratives.

Appendix A: Details of focus groups participating in the study

Table 11.1: *Focus groups, South Africa, by city, neighbourhood, income level, and ethno-linguistic affiliation*

	Cape Town				Johannesburg				
	White	Black	Coloured/Moslem/Indian		White	Black	Coloured/Moslem/Indian		
Poor		Jo Slovo Park 1 (X) Jo Slovo Park 2 (X) Khayelitsha (X)	Eersterivier (A) Lavender Hill (A)			Tsakane 1 (M) Tsakane 2 (M) Alexandra (M) Tembisa (M)			9
Middle income	Strand (A) Panorama (A) Durbanville (E) Kraaifontein 1 (E)	Kayamandi (X)	Summergreens (M) Atlantis (A) Kraaifontein 2 (E) Rondebosch (E)		Roodeport 1 (A) Roodeport 2 (A) Krugersdorp (E) Randburg (E)	Soweto (Z)	Mayfair (E) Fleurhof (M) Bosmont (E)		17
	4	4	6	14	4	5	3	12	26

A: Afrikaans speaking E: English speaking X: Xhosa speaking M: Mixed languages Z: Zulu speaking

Table 11.2: *Focus groups, Togo and Gabon, by city, income level, and ethno-linguistic affiliation*

	Lomé	Libreville
Poor	Kabiye I Mixed languages	Nzebi (Ancienne Sobraga) Fang III (Nkembo)
Middle income	Ewe Kabiye II	Fang I (Nzong-Ayong) Fang II (Mixed areas)
	4	4

References

Abrams, M. 1988. Ikitchini: The hidden side of women's labour. Unpublished master's thesis, University of Cape Town.

Adegbija, E. 2000. Language attitudes in West Africa. *International Journal of the Sociology of Language* 141: 75–100.

Agger, B. 1998. *Critical social theories: An introduction.* Boulder, CO: Westview Press.

Alasuutari, P. 1998. *An invitation to social research.* London: Sage.

Alexander, N. 1997a. Language policy and planning in the new South Africa. *African Sociological Review* 1(1): 82–92.

Alexander, N. 1997b. Language politics in South Africa. Unpublished paper.

Alexander, N. 1998. Multiculturalism in the rainbow nation: Policy and practice. Unpublished paper.

Alexander, N. 1999. Language and the national question. In G. Maharaj (ed.), *Between unity and diversity: Essays on nation-building in post-apartheid South Africa.* Cape Town: Idasa & David Philip.

Alexander, N. 2000. Why the Nguni and Sotho languages in South Africa should be harmonised. In K. Deprez & T. Du Plesssis (eds.), *Multilingualism and government in Belgium, Luxembourg, former Yugoslavia, South Africa.* Pretoria: Van Schaik.

Alexander, N. & Heugh, K. 2001. Language policy in the new South Africa. In R. Kriger & A. Zageye, (eds.), *Culture in the New South Africa.* Cape Town: Kwela Books & South African History Online.

Ameganvi, C. 1998. *Pour l'avenir du Togo.* Lomé: Nyawo.

Amin, S. 1973. *Neo-colonialism in West Africa.* Harmondsworth: Penguin African Library.

Anderson, B. 1983. *Imagined communities: Reflections on the origin and spread of nationalism.* London: Verso.

Arua, A.E. & Mogocha, K. 2002. Patterns of language use and language preference of some children and their parents in Botswana. *Journal of Multilingual and Multicultural Development* 23(6): 512–530.

Attisso, F. S. 2001. *La problématique de l'alternance politique au Togo.* Paris: L'Harmattan.

Baker, B. 2004. Multi-choice policing in Africa: Is the continent following the South African pattern? *Society in transition* 35(2):204–223.

Bamgbose, A. 1994. Pride and prejudice in multilingualism. In R. Fardon & G. Furniss (eds.), *African languages, development and the state.* London: Routledge.

Barkhuizen, G.P. & De Klerk, V. 2002. The role of Xhosa in South African prisons: 'The situation is leading you'. *Journal of Multilingual and Multicultural Development,* 23(3): 161–174.

Bauer, M.W. & Aarts, B. 2000. Corpus construction: A principle for qualitative data collection. In W.W. Bauer & G. Gaskell (eds.), *Qualitative researching with text, image and sound: A practical handbook* (pp. 19–37). London: Sage.

Bauman, Z. 1996. Morality in the age of contingency. In P. Heelas, S. Lash, & P. Morris (eds.), *Detraditionalization: Critical reflections on authority and identity.* Oxford: Blackwell.

Beall, J., Crankshaw, O., & Parnell, S. 2000. Victims, villains and fixers: The urban environment and Johannesburg's poor. *Journal of Southern African Studies* 26(4): 833–855.

Beall, J., Crankshaw, O., & Parnell, S. 2002. Uniting a divided city: Governance and social exclusion in Johannesburg. London: Earthscan.

Beavon, K.S.O. 1997. Johannesburg: A city and metropolitan area in transformation. In C Rakodi (ed.), *The urban challenge in Africa: Growth and management of its large cities.* Tokyo: United Nations University.

Becker, H.S. 1998. *Tricks of the trade: How to think about your research while you're doing it.* Chicago: University of Chicago Press.

Bekker, S. 1996. Conflict, ethnicity and democratisation in contemporary South Africa. In S. Bekker & D. Carlton (eds.) *Racism, xenophobia and ethnic conflict.* Durban: Indicator SA.

Bekker, S. 2003. Identity and ethnicity. In S. Bekker, M. Dodds, & M. Khosa (eds.), *Shifting African identities.* Pretoria: HSRC.

Bekker, S., Dodds, M., & Khosa, M. (eds.). 2001. *Shifting African Identities.* Volume 2. Pretoria: Human Sciences Research Council.

Bekker, S & Leildé, A. 2000. The emergence of new identities in the Western Cape. *Politikon,* 27(2): 221–237.

Bekker, S. & Leildé, A. 2003. Residents' perceptions of developmental local government: Exit, voice and loyalty in South African towns. *Politeia* 22(1): 144–165.

Bekker, S. & Leildé, A. 2004. Is multiculturalism a workable policy in South Africa? In J. Rex. & G. Singh (eds.), *Governance in multicultural societies* (pp. 157–171). Aldershot: Ashgate.

Bekker, S., Mongwe, R., Muller, G., & Myburgh, K. 2003. *History text books and learning support materials at South African state secondary schools: An analysis.* Pretoria: Department of National Education.

Bekker, S. & Prinsloo, R. (eds.) 1999. *Identity? Theory, politics, history* (Vol. 1). Pretoria: Human Sciences Research Council.

Bemba, S. & Fletcher, J. 1998. Why do we write in French? *Diogenes* 46(4): 105–110.

Bénit, C. 2001. La fragmentation urbaine à Johannesburg: Recomposition des pouvoirs locaux, mobilités de travail et dynamiques résidentielles dans la ville post-apartheid. Unpublished doctoral thesis, Université de Poitiers.

Bénit, C. & Morange, M. 2004. Les domestiques, la ville et l'accès à l'emploi au Cap et à Johannesburg: Logiques de proximité et logiques de réseau. *Revue Tiers Monde,* Varia, 179(XLV), July – September: 539–565.

Berg, B.L. 1995. *Qualitative research methods for the social sciences.* Boston, MA: Allyn & Bacon.

Berg, J. 2004. Challenges to formal private security industry–SAPS partnership: Lessons from the Western Cape. *Society in Transition* 35(1):105–124.

Berger, P.L. 1963. *Invitation to sociology: A humanistic perspective.* Harmondsworth: Penguin.

Berque, A. 1993. *Du geste à la cité: Formes urbaines et lien social au Japon.* Paris: Gallimard.

Bhorat, H. 2000. Are wages adjustments an effective mechanism for poverty alleviation? Some simulations for domestic and farm workers. Working Paper No. 00/41, Development Policy Research Unit, University of Cape Town.

Bilaniuk, A. 2003. Gender, language attitudes, and language status in Ukraine. *Language in Society* 32(1): 47–78.

Bissielo, A. 2001. The urban space as field of analysis of poverty: The case of Libreville. Paper presented at the Congress of the South African Association of Sociology, University of Pretoria, 3–6 July 2001.

Bloch, R. & Wilkinson, P. 1982. Urban control and popular struggle. *Africa Perspective* 20: 2–40.

Bonner, P, 1994. *African politics on the East Rand: 1900–1980*. Johannesburg: Centre for Development and Enterprise.

Boot-Siertsema, B. & Boot, J.J.G. 1982. *Praatboek uit Zuid-Afrika*. Amsterdam: Buijten & Schipperheijn.

Boucher, K. n.d. Approche des répresentations sociolinguistiques dans un groupe de jeunes Librevillois. Online at www.unice.fr/ILF-CNRS/ofcaf/13/boucher.html

Boughey, C. 1998. Language and 'disadvantage' in South African institutions of higher education: Implications of critical challenges to second language acquisition: Discourses for academic development practitioners. *South African Journal of Higher Education*, 12(1): 167–171.

Boughey, C. 2002. 'Naming' students' problems: An analysis of language-based discourses at a South African university. *Teaching in Higher Education*, 7(3): 295–307.

Bourdieu, P. 1993. Effets de lieu. In P. Bourdieu, *La misère du monde*. Paris: Éditions du Seuil.

Bourdieu, P. & Thompson, J.B. 1991. *Language and symbolic power*. Cambridge, MA: Harvard University Press.

Breitenbach, M.C. & Peta, R.N. 2001. The effects of a minimum wage on the demand for labour in the domestic service networks: Preliminary findings from the Phillip Nel Park area. *South African Journal of Labour Relations* 2001: 22–35.

Bremner, L. 2000. Reinventing the Johannesburg inner city. *Cities* 17: 185–93.

Bremner, L.J. 2000. Post-apartheid urban geography: A case study of greater Johannesburg's rapid land development programme. *Development Southern Africa* 17(1): 87–104.

Calhoun, C. (ed.). 1994. *Social theory and the politics of identity*. Cambridge, MA & Oxford: Blackwell.

Cape Argus. 2003. Domestic workers angry at 'dompas' plans. (5 March 2003, p. 7).

Cape Labour and Industrial Consultants. 2002. *You, Your Domestic Worker and the New Laws* (Updated September 2002). Cape Town: Straight Talk, in association with Cape Labour and Industrial Consultants.

Cape Times. 2002a. Tax deduction for employers better than minimum wages for domestics, says DA. (16 August 2002, p. 5).

Cape Times. 2002b. Domestic workers survive by borrowing. (19 August 2002, p. 3).

Cape Times. 2003a. Domestics forced to have HIV tests, claims trade union. (14 March 2003).

Cape Times. 2003b. Register domestic workers. (31 March 2003.).

Cassell, P. 1993b. Introduction. In P. Cassell (ed.), *The Giddens reader*. Houndmills: Macmillan.

Castells, M. 1997. *The information age: Economy, society and culture* (Vol. 2: The power of identity). Malden, MA & Oxford: Blackwell.

Castells, M. 2002a. Information technology, the restructuring of capital: Labor relationships, and the rise of the dual city. In I. Susser (ed.), *The Castells reader on cities and social theory*. Malden, MA & Oxford: Blackwell.

Castells, M. 2002b. The culture of cities in the information age. In I. Susser (ed.), *The Castells reader on cities and social theory*. Malden, MA & Oxford: Blackwell.

Central Statistical Services 2001. *91 Census CD database: 2001 Census*. Online at www.statssa.gov.za//SpecialProjects/Census2001

Champion, J. 1974. *Les langues Africaines et la Francophonie*. Paris: Mouton.

228 REFERENCES

Chase, S.E. 1995. Taking narrative seriously: Consequences for method and theory in interview studies. In R. Josselson & A. Lieblich (eds.), *Interpreting experience: The narrative study of lives* (pp. 1–26). Thousand Oaks, CA: Sage.

Chipkin, C. 1993. *Johannesburg style, architecture and society*, 1880s – 1960s. Cape Town: David Philip.

Christopher, A.J. 2001. Urban segregation in post-apartheid South Africa. *Urban Studies* 38(3): 449–466.

Christopher, A J. 2004. Slow progress in desegregation of South African cities, 1996–2001. Paper presented at the International Geographical Congress, Glasgow, 2004.

Cicourel, A.V. 1964. *Method and measurement in sociology*. New York: Free Press.

City of Johannesburg. n.d. Official website, online at www.joburg.org.za

Cock, J. 1980. *Maids and madam: A study in the politics of exploitation*. Johannesburg: Ravan Press.

Cole, J. 1987. *Crossroads: The politics of reform and repression, 1976–1986*. Johannesburg: Ravan Press.

Collins, P. 1998. Negotiating selves: Reflections on 'unstructured' interviewing. *Sociological Research Online* 3(3). Online at www.socresonline.org.uk/socresonline/3/32.html

Comaroff, J. & Comaroff, J. 1991. *Of Revelation and Revolution*. Chicago: University of Chicago Press.

Cornevin, R. 1988. *Le Togo: Des origines à nos jours*. 4th edition. Paris: Académie des Sciences d'outre-mer.

Cox, W. 2002. Land use and public transport in low income urban areas. Paper presented at Codatu X Training Programme, Lomé, Togo, 16 November 2002.

Cross, C., Bekker, S., & Eva, G. 1999. En waarheen nou? Migration and settlement in the Cape Metropolitan Area (CMA). Occasional Paper No. 6. Department of Housing, Cape Metropolitan Council & Department of Sociology, University of Stellenbosch, August 1999.

Crouzel, I. 2000. La 'Renaissance Africaine': Un discours Sud-Africain? *Politique Africaine*, 77: 171–182.

Crush, J. 1995. *Power of development*. London & New York: Routledge.

Danioué, RT. 2004. Espace urbain, migrations internes et identités en Afrique subsaharienne: Logiques spatiales et logiques sociales a Lomé. Unpublished paper.

Data Desk. 1999. *Socio economic profile of inhabitants of Thembalethu*. Department of Sociology, University of Stellenbosch.

Davenport, T.R.H. 1971. *The beginnings of urban segregation in South Africa*. Grahamstown: Institute of Social and Economic Research (ISER).

Davenport, T.R.H. 1987. *South Africa: A modern history*. Johannesburg: Macmillan.

Davis, M. 1996. Fortress LA. In R.T. LeGates & F. Stout (eds.), *The city reader* (pp. 158–163) London: Routledge.

De Haan, L. 1993. *La région des savanes au Togo: L'etat, les paysans et l'intégration régionale (1885–1985)*. Paris: Karthala.

Delport, E. 1994. Domestic workers at the end of the tunnel. In M. Lessing, (ed.), *South African women today*. Cape Town: Maskew Miller Longman.

De Menton, J. 1993. *A la recontre du Togo*. Paris: Harmattan.

Denzin, N.K. 1989. *The research act: A theoretical introduction to sociological methods*. Englewood Cliffs, NJ: Prentice Hall.

Denzin, N.K. & Lincoln, Y.S. 1994. Introduction: Entering the field of qualitative research. In N.K. Denzin & Y.S. Lincoln (eds.), *Handbook of qualitative research* (pp. 1–17). Thousand Oaks, CA: Sage.

Deprez, K. & Du Plessis, T. (eds.). 2000. *Multilingualism and government: Belgium, Luxembourg, Switzerland, former Yugoslavia, South Africa*. Pretoria: Van Schaik.

De Satge, R. 1997. *Upgrading informal settlements: An assessment of training and support needs in KwaZulu-Natal and Gauteng Provinces*. Developmental Services: Report commissioned by the Department of Land Affairs, February 1997.

De Soto, H. 2000. *The mystery of capital: Why capitalism triumphs in the west and fails everywhere else*. London: Black Swan.

Destremau, B. & Lautier, B. 2002. Femmes en domesticité: Les domestiques du Sud, au Nord et au Sud. *Revue Tiers Monde*, 170(April–June): 249–264.

Development Action Group. 1993. Towards a concept plan for the development of Marconi Beam, August 1993.

Development Action Group. 1994a. Marconi Beam Affordable Housing Project: Project description and budget, April 1994, draft, no pagination.

Development Action Group. 1994b. Marconi Beam Affordable Housing Project: Project description and budget, April 1994.

Development Action Group. 2003. *Rainbow Housing Co-operative socio-economic survey report*. Cape Town: DAG.

De Wet, C.J. 1986. An analysis of the social and economic consequences of residential relocation arising out of the implementation of an agricultural development scheme in a rural Ciskei village. Unpublished doctoral dissertation, Rhodes University.

De Wet, C. J. & McAllister. P.A. 1984. Rural communities in transition: A study of the socio-economic and agricultural implications of agricultural betterment and development. Development Studies Working Paper 16. Institute of Social and Economic Research (ISER), Rhodes University, Grahamstown.

Djarangar Djita, I. 2003. Les languages Africaines dans les écoles d'Afrique: Est-ce bien raisonnable? *iBoogha* 7(Novembre): 83–92.

Dolbeau, J.M. 2000. Christianisme et changement social en Afrique du Sud: Les cas de l'Eglise Reformée Hollandaise (NGK) et de l'Eglise Chrétienne de Sion (ZCC). In V. Faure (ed.), *Dynamiques religieuses en Afrique Australe*. Paris: Karthala.

Donaldson, S.E. & Van der Merwe, I.J. 2000. Urban restructuring during transition: A model for South African urban development in the 21st century. *Africa Insight* (May): 46–57.

Dovi Kuevi, A. 1996. *Lomé, capitale politique et économique: De la nécessité de préserver son patrimoine culturel*. Mémoire pour le Bureau Régional pour l'Afrique du Programme de Gestion Urbaine, Accra.

Dovi, Q. 1998. Quelques aspects de la population de Lomé dans sa dynamique de peuplement. In N. Gayibor, Y. Marguerat & K. Nyassogbo (eds.), *Le centenaire de Lomé, capitale du Togo (1897–1997)*. Lomé: Presses de l'Université du Benin.

Driessen, H. & Otto, T. 2000. Protean perplexities: An introduction. In H. Driessen & T. Otto (eds.), *Perplexities of identification: Anthropological studies in cultural differentiation and the use of resources* (pp. 9–26). Aarhus: Aarhus UP.

Drinkwater, M. J. 1989. Technical development and peasant impoverishment: Land use policy in Zimbabwe's Midland Province. *Journal of Southern African Siudies*, 15(1989): 287–305.

DuBois, M. 1991. Governance of the Third World: A Foucauldian perspective on power relations in development. *Alternatives*, 16(1991): 1–30.

Du Plesssis, T. 2000. South Africa: From two to eleven languages. In K. Deprez & T. Du Plesssis (eds.), *Multilingualism and government in Belgium, Luxembourg, former Yugoslavia, South Africa*. Pretoria: Van Schaik.

Durrheim, K. & Dixon, J. 2001. The role of place and metaphor in racial exclusion: South Africa's beaches as sites of shifting racialization. *Ethnic and Racial Studies* 24(3): 433–450.

Edzodzomo-Ela, M. 1993. *De la démocratie au Gabon : Les fondements d'un renouveau national.* Paris: Karthala.

Elias, N. 1939. *La société des individus.* Paris: Fayard.

Escobar, A. 1985. Discourse and power in development: Michel Foucault and the relevance of his work to the Third World. *Alternatives*, 103(1984-85): 377-400.

Escobar, A. 1988. Power and visibility: The invention and management of development in the third world. *Cultural Anthropology*, 3(40): 424-443.

Escobar, A. 1991. Anthropology and the development encounter: The making and marketing of development anthropology. *American Ethnologist*, 18(4): 658-682.

Escobar, A. 1995. *Encountering development: The making and unmaking of the Third World.* Princeton, NJ: Princeton University Press.

Etoughe, D. & Ngadi, B. (eds.). 2003. *Refonder l'etat au Gabon: Contributions au débat.* Paris: L'Harmattan.

Eva, G. 2002. Evaluation of a vision for Cape Town by stakeholder groups. Occasional paper No. 13, Department of Sociology, Stellenbosch University.

Ferguson, J. 1990. The anti politics machine: 'Development', depoliticization and bureaucratic state power in Lesotho. Cambridge: Cambridge University Press & Cape Town: David Philip.

Fielding, N. 1993. Qualitative interviewing. In N. Gilbert (ed.), *Researching social life* (pp. 135-153). London: Sage.

Fine, M. 1994. Working the hyphens: Reinventing self and other in qualitative research. In N.K. Denzin & Y.S. Lincoln (eds.), *Handbook of qualitative research* (pp. 70-82). Thousand Oaks, CA: Sage.

Fine, M. & Weis, L. 1998. Writing the 'wrongs' of fieldwork: Confronting our own research/ writing dilemmas in urban ethnographies. In G. Shacklock & J. Smyth (eds.), *Being reflexive in critical educational and social research* (pp. 13-35). London: Falmer Press.

Fontana, A. & Frey, J.H. 1994. Interviewing: The art of science. In N.K. Denzin & Y.S. Lincoln. (eds.), *Handbook of qualitative research* (pp. 361-376). Thousand Oaks, CA: Sage.

François, Y. 1993. *Le Togo.* Paris: Karthala.

Friguglietti, R.S. 1989. Domestic workers' dependency vs. self-assertiveness in the workplace. Unpublished document, University of Pretoria.

Fyle, C.N. 2000. Language and literacy in West Africa. *International Journal of the Sociology of Language* 141: 61-73.

Gans, H.J. 1996. Levittown and America. In R.T. LeGates & F. Stout (eds.) *The city reader* (pp. 63-68). London: Routledge.

Gardinier, D.E. 1994. *Historical dictionary of Gabon.* 2nd edition. Lanham, MD & London: The Scarecrow Press.

Gaskell, G. 2000. Individual and group interviewing. In M.W. Bauer & G. Gaskell (eds.), *Qualitative researching with text, image and sound: A practical handbook* (pp. 38-56). London: Sage.

Gasson, B. 2000. The urban metabolism of Cape Town, South Africa: Planning imperatives in an ecologically unsustainable metropolis. Paper presented at the Association of European Schools of Planning (AESOP) Congress, Brno, Czech Republic, July 2000.

Gaulme, F. 1998. *Le Gabon et son ombre.* Paris: Karthala.

Gayibor, N., Marguerat, Y., & Nyassogbo, K. 1998. (eds.). *Le centenaire de Lomé, capitale du Togo (1897-1997).* Lomé: Presses de l'Université du Benin.

Gervais-Lambony, P. 1994. *De Lomé á Harare: Le fait citadin. Images et pratiques des villes Africaines.* Paris: Karthala & Nairobi: IFRA.

Gervais-Lambony, P. 1999. Nouvelle Afrique du Sud: Nouveaux territoires, nouvelles identités. *L'Espace Géographique* 28(2): 99–109.

Gervais-Lambony, P. 2002. Les enjeux d'une politique de redéfinition territoriale: La création de l'aire métropolitaine d'Ekurhuleni. *Autre Part*, 21: 27–40.

Gervais-Lambony, P. 2003. *Territoires citadins: 4 Villes Africaines.* Paris: Belin.

Gervais-Lambony, P., Jaglin, S., & Mabin, A. (eds.). 1999. *La question urbaine en Afrique Australe: Perspectives de recherche.* Paris & Johannesburg: Karthala & IFAS.

Gibbs, A. 1997. Focus groups. *Social Research Update* (19): Online at www.soc.surrey.ac.uk/sru/SRU19.html

Giddens, A. 1991. *Modernity and self identity: Self and society in the late modern age.* Cambridge: Polity Press.

Gilroy, P. 2000. *Against race: Imagining political culture beyond the color line.* Cambridge, MA: Harvard University Press.

Ginsburg, R. 2000. Come in dark: Domestic workers and their rooms in apartheid era Johannesburg, South Africa. In S. McMurry and A. Adams, (eds.), *People, powers, places.* Knoxville, TN: University of Tennessee Press.

Glazer, N. 1994. Divided cities, dual cities: The case of New York. In S. Dunn (ed.), *Managing divided cities.* Keele: Ryburn Publishing & Keele University Press.

Goke-Pariola, A. 1993. *The role of language in the struggle for power and legitimacy in Africa.* Lewiston, NY: Mellen.

Goldberg, D.T. 1993. *Racist culture: Philosophy and the politics of meaning.* Oxford: Blackwell.

Goldberg, D.T. & Solomos, J. 2001. General introduction. In D.T. Goldberg & J. Solomos (eds.), *A companion to racial and ethnic studies* (pp. 1–12). Oxford: Blackwell.

Goldin, I. 1984. *The poverty of coloured labour preference: Economics and ideology in the Western Cape.* Cape Town: Southern Africa Labour and Development Research Unit.

Gracq, J. 1990. *La forme d'une ville.* Paris: José Corti.

Grillo, R.D. 2000. Plural cities in comparative perspective. *Ethnic and Racial Studies* 23(6): 957–981.

Guillaume, P. 2001. *Johannesburg: Géographies de l'exclusion.* Johannesburg & Paris: IFAS & Karthala.

Hall, P. & Pfeiffer, U. 2000. *Urban future 21: A global agenda for twenty-first century cities.* London: E & F.N. Spon.

Hall, S. 1996. Introduction: Who needs identity? In S. Hall & P. du Gay (eds.), *Questions of cultural identity* (pp. 1–17). London: Sage.

Harré, R. 1998. When the knower is also the known. In T. May & M. Williams (eds.), *Knowing the social world* (pp. 37–49). Buckingham: Open University Press.

Harries, P. 1989. Exclusion, classification and internal colonialism: The emergence of ethnicity among the Tsonga-speakers of South Africa. In L. Vail (ed.), *The creation of tribalism in Southern Africa.* London: James Currey.

Harries, P. 1994. *Work, culture, and identity: Migrant labourers in Mozambique and South Africa c. 1860–1910.* Johannesburg: Witwatersrand University Press.

Harrison, P., Todes, A., & Watson, V. 1997. Transforming South Africa's cities: Prospects for the economic development of urban townships. *Development Southern Africa* 14(1): 43–60.

Hendricks, C & Whiteman, K. 2004. *South Africa in Africa: The post-apartheid decade.* Report on a seminar organised by the Centre for Conflict Resolution, the Centre for Policy Studies, and the African Centre for Development and Strategic Studies, Stellenbosch, 29 July–1 August 2004.

Hindson. D. 1987. *Pass controls and the urban African proletariat in South Africa.* Johannesburg: Ravan Press.

232 REFERENCES

Hindson, D. & McCarthy, J. 1994. *Here to stay: Informal settlements in KwaZulu-Natal*. Durban: Indicator Press.

Holston, J. (ed.). 1998. *Cities and citizenship*. Durham, NC & London: Duke University Press.

Horrell, M. 1978. *Laws affecting race relations in South Africa*. Johannesburg: South African Institute of Race Relations.

Houssay-Holzschuch, M. 1999. *Le Cap, ville Sud-Africaine: Ville blanche, vies noires*. Paris: L'Harmattan.

Huchzermeyer, M. 2003. Addressing segregation through housing policy and finance. In P. Harrison, M. Huchzermeyer, & M. Mayekiso (eds.), *Confronting fragmentation: Housing and urban development in a democratising society*. Cape Town: UCT Press: 211–227.

Hughes, J. & Sharrock, W. 1997. *The philosophy of social research*. London: Longman.

Hyslop, J. 2000. Why did apartheid's supporters capitulate? 'Whiteness', class and consumption in urban South Africa, 1985–1995. *Society in Transition* 31(1):36–44.

Idiata, D.F. 2002. *Il était une fois les langues Gabonaises*. Libreville: Editions Raponda-Walker.

Inama, K. 1994. *Sur les sentiers de la democratie Gabonaise*. Libreville: Editions de L'Ogooue.

Isserow, M. 2001. Crime in South Africa's metropolitan areas, 2001. Centre for the Study of Violence and Reconciliation. Online at www.csvr.org.za/papers/papstats.htm

Jacquemin, M. 2002. Travail domestique et travail des enfants, le cas d'Abidjan (Côte d'Ivoire). *Revue Tiers Monde* 170(April – June 2002): 307–26.

Janssens, M. 1998. Lomé, 100 ans de croissance démographique. In N. Gayibor, Y. Marguerat & K. Nyassogbo (eds.) *Le centenaire de Lomé, capitale du Togo (1897–1997)*. Lomé: Presses de l'Université du Benin.

Jensen, S. & Turner, S. 1996. *A place called Heideveld: Identities and strategies among the coloureds in Cape Town, South Africa*. Research report No.112, Department of Geography and International Development Studies, Roskilde University, Denmark.

Joubert, E. 1980. *The long journey of Poppie Nongena*. Johannesburg: Jonathan Ball.

Jooma. A. 1991. *Migrancy: After influx control*. Braamfontein: South African Institute of Race Relations.

Kamwangamalu, N.M. 2001. Ethnicity and language crossing in post-apartheid South Africa. *International Journal of the Sociology of Language*, 152: 75–95.

Kehler, J. 2002. *Domestic workers are workers too: A resource book on the rights of domestic workers in South Africa*. National Association of Democratic Lawyers, Human Rights Research and Advocacy Project, Vlaeberg.

Kenyon, H. 1991. Domestic workers: An invisible service. Unpublished honours dissertation, University of Cape Town.

Kram, K.E. 1988. On the researcher's group memberships. In D.N. Berg & K.K. Smith (eds.), *The self in social inquiry: Researching methods* (pp. 247–265). Newbury Park, CA: Sage.

Kriel, M. 2003. Approaches to multilingualism in language planning and identity politics: A critique. *Society in Transition* 34(1): 159–177.

Kwenzi Mikala, J. 1998. Parlers du Gabon: Classification du 11-12-97. In Raponda-Walker, *Les languages du Gabon*. Libreville: Réédition des Editions Raponda-Walker.

Lafage, S. n.d. Le Français en Afrique noire à l'aube de l'an 2000: Éléments de problématique. Online at http://ancilla.unice.fr/~brunet/pub/lafage.htlm

Laitin, D.D. 1986. *Hegemony and culture*. Chicago: University of Chicago Press.

Laitin, D.D. 1992 *Language repertoires and state construction in Africa*. Cambridge: Cambridge University Press.

Laitin, D.D. 1998. Nationalism and language: A post-Soviet perspective. In J.A. Hall (ed.), *The state of the nation: Ernest Gellner and the theory of nationalism*. Cambridge: Cambridge University Press.

Laitin, D.D. 2000. What is a language community? *American Journal of Political Science* 44(1): 142–155.

Lebikaza, K.K. 1997. Les langues des minorités au Togo: Une étude sociolinguistique. *Annales de l'Université du Bénin, Série Lettres* XVII: 149–164.

Lebikaza, K.K. 2003. La politique des langues au Togo au temps de Westermann et aujourd'hui. In A.P. Oloukpona-Yinnon & J. Riesz (eds.), *Plumes Allemandes: Biographies et autobiographies Africaines*. Lomé: Presses de l'Université de Lomé.

Lebikaza, K.K. Forthcoming. Une politique des langues pour le développement et la paix dans un pays multilingue sans lingua franca. *Traduit de l'Allemand.*

Le Corbusier, C. 1929. *The city of tomorrow and its planning.* London: John Rodker.

Léger, J-M. 1987. *La Francophonie: Grand dessein, grande ambiguïté.* Louiseville, Canada: Nathan.

Leildé, A. 2006. Studying identity formation in the context of Cape Town. Paper presented at GDRI seminar, 22 September 2006.

Lemon, A 1976. *Apartheid: A geography of separation.* Farnborough, UK: Saxon House.

Lemon, A. 1991. The apartheid city. In A. Lemon (ed.), *Homes apart: South Africa's segregated cities* (pp.1–25). Cape Town: David Philip.

Lepper, G. 2000. *Categories in text and talk: A practical introduction to categorization analysis.* London: Sage.

Le Roux, T. 1995. *We have families too: Live-in domestic workers talk about their lives.* Department of Sociology, University of Pretoria & Human Sciences Research Council.

Levi-Straus, C. 1973. *Tristes tropiques* (Translated from the French by J. & D. Weightman). London: Jonathan Cape.

Lévy, J. 1994. *L'espace légitime: Sur la dimension géographique de la fonction politique.* Paris: FNSP.

Levy, J. 1999. *Le tournant géographique: Penser l'espace pour lire le monde.* Paris: Belin.

Limbrick, J. 1993. *Extending the provisions of the Workmen's Compensation Act and the Unemployment Insurance Act to domestic workers.* (John Limbrick research report). Pretoria: Department of Manpower.

Lohnert, B., Oldfield, S., & Parnell, S. 1998. Post-apartheid social polarisations: The creation of sub-urban identities in Cape Town. *South African Geographical Journal* 80(2): 86–92.

Macun, I. & Posel, D. 1998. Focus groups: A South African experience and a methodological reflection. *African Sociological Review* 2(1):114–135.

Mabin, A. 2001a. Contested urban futures: Report on a global gathering in Johannesburg, 2000. *International Journal of Urban and Regional Research* 25(1):180–184.

Mabin, A. 2001b. Suburbs and segregation in the urbanising cities of the South: A challenge for metropolitan governance in the early twenty-first century. Paper presented at the Lincoln Institute of Land Policy, Cambridge, MA.

Mainet-Valleix, H. 2002. *Durban, les Indiens, leurs territoires, leur identité.* Paris: Karthala.

Mamdani, M. 1998. Is African Studies to be turned into a new home for Bantu Education at UCT? Unpublished transcription of remarks by Professor Mahmood Mamdani at a seminar at the University of Cape Town, 22 April 1998.

Mandaza, I. 2001. Southern African identity: A critical assessment. In S. Bekker, M. Dodds, & M. Khosa (eds.), *Shifting African identities*. Pretoria: Human Sciences Research Council.

Mandivenga, E.C. 2000. The Cape Muslims and the Indian Muslims of South Africa: A comparative analysis. *Journal of Muslim Minority Affairs* 20(2): 347–352.

Mare, G. 1992. *Brothers born of warrior blood: Politics and ethnicity in South Africa.* Johannesburg: Ravan Press.

Marguerat, Y. 1981. *Lomé et ses quartiers.* Lomé: Orstom.

Marguerat, Y. 1985. *L'armature urbaine du Togo*. Paris: Editions de l'Orstom, Institut Français de recherche scientifique pour le développement en coopération.

Marguerat, Y. 1992. *Lomé: Les étapes de la croissance. Une brève histoire de la capitale du Togo*. Lomé & Paris: Editions Halo et Karthala.

Marguerat, Y. 1998. La répartition spatiale de l'emploi moderne à Lomé. In N. Gayibor, Y. Marguerat, & K. Nyassogbo (eds.), *Le centenaire de Lomé, capitale du Togo (1897–1997)*, Lomé: Presses de l'Université du Benin.

Marguerat, Y. 1999. *Dynamique urbaine, jeunesse et histoire au Togo: Articles et documents (1984–1993)*. 2nd edition. Lomé: Presses de l'Université du Bénin.

Marivate, C. 2000. The mission and activities of the Pan South African Language Board. In K. Deprez & T. du Plessis (eds.), *Multilingualism and government* (pp. 130–137). Pretoria: Van Schaik.

MarkData-PANSALB. 2000. *Language and language interaction in South Africa: Brief descriptive overview of the findings of a national survey undertaken on behalf of the Pan South African Language Board*. Pretoria: PANSALB.

Marks, R. & Bezzoli, M. 2001. Palaces of desire: Century City, Cape Town and the ambiguities of development. *Urban Forum* 12(1): 27–47.

Martin, D-C. 1994. Identités et politique: Récit, mythe et idéologie. In D-C. Martin (ed.), *Cartes d'identité: Comment dit-on 'nous' en politique?* Paris: Presses de la FNSP.

Martin, D-C. 1995. The choices of identity. *Social Identities* 1(1): 5–20.

Martin, D-C. 1998. Le poids du nom, culture populaire et constructions identitaires chez les métis du Cap. *Critique Internationale*, 1(Automne): 73–100.

Martin, D-C. 1999. Identity, culture, pride and conflict. In S. Bekker & R. Prinsloo (eds.), *Identity? Theory, politics, history* (Vol. 1). Pretoria: Human Sciences Research Council.

Martin, D-C. 2000. The burden of the name: Classifications and constructions of identity. The case of the 'Coloureds' in Cape Town (South Africa). *African Philosophy* 13(2): 99–124.

Martin, D-C. 1999. Identity, culture, pride and conflict. In S. Bekker & R. Prinsloo (eds.), *Identity? Theory, politics, history* (Vol. 1). Pretoria: Human Sciences Research Council.

Masekela, H. 1993. *Hope*. (Background to track no 12, CDCOL 8215). Malibu, CA: Triloka Records.

Massey, D., Allen, J., & Pile, S. 1999. Introduction. In D. Massey, J. Allan, and S. Pile (eds.), *City worlds*. London: Routledge.

May, T. 2002. Introduction: Transformation in principles and practice. In T. May (ed.), *Qualitative research in action* (pp. 1–14). London: Sage.

Mbeki, T. 2003. Quoted in M. Makhana, The 'African story' is not the only one the rulers want to hear. *Mail and Guardian* 17–24 April 2003.

Mbembe, A. 1992. Provisional notes on the postcolony. *Africa* 62(1): 3–37.

Mbembe, A. 2002a. African modes of self-writing. *Public Culture* 14(1): 239–273.

Mbembe, A. 2002b. The power of the false. *Public Culture* 14(3): 629–641.

McAllister, P. 1999. Can we measure ethnicity? In S. Bekker & R. Prinsloo (eds.), *Identity? Theory, politics, history*. Pretoria: Human Sciences Research Council.

McGowan P. 2004 Comments on the foreign policies of Gabon and Togo. In S. Bekker & A. Leildé (eds.), The African continent: New perceptions and new policies. Occasional paper No.15. Department of Sociology and Social Anthropology, University of Stellenbosch.

Meillassoux, C. & Messiant, C. (eds.). 1991. *Génie social et manipulations culturelles en Afrique du Sud*. Paris: Arcantère.

Meintjies, H. 2000. Poverty, possessions and 'proper living': Constructing and contesting propriety in Soweto and Lusaka City. Unpublished master's thesis, University of Cape Town.

Michael, M. 1996. *Constructing identities*. London: Sage.

Mitchell, T. 1988. *Colonizing Egypt*. Cambridge: Cambridge University Press.

Mkhulisi, N. 2000. The National Language Service and the language policy. In K. Deprez & T. du Plessis (eds.), *Multilingualism and government* (pp. 121–129). Pretoria: Van Schaik.

Mollenkopf, J.H. & Castells, M. (eds.). 1991. *Dual city: Restructuring New York*. New York: Russell Sage Foundation.

Moodie, D.T. & Ndatshe, V. 1999. *Going for gold: Men, mines and migration*. Johannesburg: Witwatersrand University Press.

Moodley, K. 2000. African renaissance and language policies in comparative perspective. *Politikon*, 27(1): 103–115.

Morange, M. 2006. *La question du logement à Mandela-City (ex Port Elizabeth)*. Paris: IFAS-Karthala.

Morgan, D.L. 1997. *Focus groups as qualitative research*. Thousand Oaks, CA: Sage.

Morris, A. 1996. *Bleakness and light: City transition in Hillbrow, Johannesburg*. Johannesburg: Witwatersrand University Press.

Moscovici, S. 1988. Notes towards a description of social representations. *European Journal of Social Psychology* 18: 211–250.

Moussirou-Mouyama, A. 1999. *France Afrique et parfait silence: Essai sur les enjeux Africains de la Francophonie*. Libreville: Les Editions du Silence.

Moyo, T. 2002. Mother tongues versus an ex-colonial language as media of instruction and the promotion of multilingualism: The South African experience. *South African Journal of African Languages* 22(2): 149–160.

Mufwene, S.S. 2002. Colonization, globalization, and the future of languages in the twenty-first century. *International Journal on Multicultural Societies* 4(2): 162–193.

Murphy, P. & Watson, S. 1997. *Surface city: Sydney at the millennium*. Sydney: Pluto Press.

Murunga, G.R. 2004. Mbembe's African modes of self-writing and the critics in public culture. *Codesria Bulletin* (1/2): 27–32.

Naledi (National Labour and Economic Development Institute). 1996. An organisational challenge: The unionisation of domestic workers. Policy memo, December. Johannesburg: Naledi.

Nair-Venugopal, S. 2001. The sociolinguistics of choice in Malaysian business settings. *International Journal of the Sociology of Language*. 152: 21–52.

Nasi, R. 2001. Biodiversity planning support programme. Integration of biodiversity into national forest programmes: The case of Gabon. Paper prepared for an international workshop on 'Integration of Biodiversity in National Forestry Planning Programmes', CIFOR Headquarters, Bogor, Indonesia, 13–16 August 2001.

Ndong Mba, J-C. 2003. Activités économiques et environnement urbain au Gabon. *iBoogha* 7(Novembre): 27–47.

Ndong Mba, J-C. 2004. Libreville, Owendo. *Atlas de l'Afrique. Gabon*. Paris: Les Editions J.A.

Njoh, A.J. 2004. The experience and legacy of French colonial urban planning in sub-Saharan Africa. *Planning Perspectives* 19(4): 435–454. London: Routledge.

Nyamnjoh, F.B. 1997. Africa and the information superhighway: The need for mitigated euphoria. Paper presented at the WACC-UNESCO workshop on 'Communication and the Globalisation of Poverty', Yaounde, Cameroon.

Nyamnjoh, F.B. Forthcoming. 'For many are called but few are chosen': Globalisation and popular disenchantment in Africa.

Nyamnjoh, F.B. & Page, B. 2002. Whiteman Kontri and the enduring allure of modernity among Cameroonian youth. *African Affairs* 101: 607–634.

Nyassogbo, G.K. 1998. Qu'est-ce qu'une capitale? Essai de définition. In N. Gayibor, Y. Marguerat, & K. Nyassogbo (eds.), *Le centenaire de Lomé, capitale du Togo (1897–1997)*. Lomé: Presses de l'Université du Benin.

Nyassogbo, K. 1994. Comment une capitale devient macrocephale en Afrique subsaharienne. Le cas de Lomé au Togo (Afrique de l'Ouest). *Annales de l'Université du Benin* XIV: 3–19.

Nze-Nguema, F-P. 1997. *La Francophonie entre fable et séduction: Pour une sociologie de l'interculturalité*. Libreville: CERGEP/Les Editions Udégiennes.

Nze-Nguema, F-P. 1998. *L'etat au Gabon de 1929 á 1990: Le partage institutionnel du pouvoir*. Paris: L'Harmattan.

Otayek, R. 2000. *Identité et démocratie dans un monde global*. Paris: Presse de la Fondation Nationale des Sciences Politiques.

Owanga Biye, G. 2003. Disparités spatiales et démographiques en pays sous peuplé. *iBoogha* 7(Novembre): 49–71.

Pambou, J-A. 2003. Transposition didactique et prépositions en Français langue seconde au Gabon. *iBoogha* 7(Novembre): 95–110.

PANSALB (Pan South African Board of Languages). 2000. *Guidelines for language planning and policy development*. Pretoria. PANSALB.

Parker, I. 2002. Theoretical discourse, subjectivity and critical psychology. In I. Parker (ed.), *Critical discursive psychology* (pp. 1–18). Houndmills: Palgrave.

Parnell, S. & Mabin, A. 1995. Rethinking urban South Africa. *Journal of Southern African Studies* 21(1): 39–61.

Parnell, S.M. & Pirie, G.H. 1991. Johannesburg. In A. Lemon (ed.), *Homes apart: South Africa's segregated cities* (pp. 129–145). Cape Town: David Philip.

Pienaar, H. 1994. Economic study: Johannesburg/Central Wits. Unpublished memo. Johannesburg City Council Urban Strategies Division.

Pieterse, E. 1997. From divided to integrated city? Critical overview of the emerging metropolitan governance system in Cape Town. *Urban Forum* 8(1): 3–37.

Pottie, D. 2003. Housing the nation: The politics of low cost housing in South Africa since 1994. *Politeia* 22 (1): 119–143.

Pottier, J. 2003. Fevered imaginings: 'The Congo' in popular culture, globalisation, conflict and diplomacy. New Social Forms Seminar Series, Department of Sociology, Stellenbosch University, 29 July 2003.

Prah, K.K. 1995. *Mother tongue for scientific and technological development in Africa*. Bonn: German Foundation for International Development.

Prah, K.K. 2002. African renaissance, African culture and language. In A. Osmanovic (ed.), *Transforming South Africa* (pp. 207–242). Hamburg: Hamburg African Studies.

Prinsloo, R.C. & de la Rey, C. 1999. Processes of reshaping, reclaiming and renegotiating identity in South Africa. In S. Bekker & R. Prinsloo (eds.), *Identity? Theory, politics, history* (Vol. I). Pretoria: Human Sciences Research Council.

Punch, M. 1994. Politics and ethics in qualitative research. In N.K. Denzin & Y.S. Lincoln (eds.), *Handbook of qualitative research* (pp. 83–97). Thousand Oaks, CA: Sage.

Radebe, N. 1995. Domestic workers in Kenilworth: Study of the lives of domestic workers who live and work in the Kenilworth area. Unpublished master's thesis, University of Cape Town.

Raffestin, C. 1980. *Pour une géographie du pouvoir*. Genève: Litec.

Ragin, C.C. 1994. *Constructing social research: The unity and diversity of method*. Thousand Oaks, CA: Pine Forge.

Rahman, T. 2001. Language learning and power: A theoretical approach. *International Journal of the Sociology of Language*, 152: 75–95.

Ramphele, M. 1993. *A bed called home: Life in the migrant labour hostels of Cape Town*. Cape Town. David Philip.

Raponda-Walker, A. 1998. *Les langues du Gabon*. Libreville: Editions Raponda-Walker.

Republic of South Africa. 1997. *Urban development framework*. Department of Housing, Pretoria.

Republic of South Africa. 2001. *Report on a survey of language infrastructure in national government departments and provinces*. Pretoria: Department of Arts, Culture, Science and Technology.

Republic of South Africa. 2004a. *Department of Provincial and Local Government: Local government fact book – 2003/2004*. Pretoria: Department of Provincial and Local Government.

Republic of South Africa. 2004b. *Ikapa elihlumayo: A framework for the development of the Western Cape Province, 2004–2007*. Department of the Premier, Western Cape Provincial Government.

Republic of South Africa. 2006. *A nation in the making: A discussion document on macro-social trends in South Africa*. Policy Coordinator and Advisory Services, Office of the South African Presidency. Pretoria: Government Printer.

RHC (Rainbow Housing Co-operative). 2003a. *Statute of RHC Limited (HCL)*. (Statute No. 2721). Cape Town: RHC & City of Cape Town.

RHC. 2003b. *Feasibility Report*. Cape Town: RHC & Development Action Group.

Riessman, C.K. 1993. *Narrative analysis*. Newbury Park, CA: Sage.

Robins, S. 1994. Contesting the social geometry of state power: A case study of land-use planning in Matabeleland, Zimbabwe. *Social Dynamics* 20(1): 32–55; 91–118.

Robins, S. 1999. Spicing up the multicultural (post-)apartheid city. *Kronos. Journal of Cape History* 25 (Pre-Millenium Issue): 280–293.

Robins, S. 2001. 'A house is much more than brick and mortar': Housing citizens in the Cape of Storms. Paper presented at conference on 'Interrogating the New Political Culture in Southern Africa', Harare Sheraton Hotel, Zimbabwe, 13–15 June 2001.

Robins, S. 2002. At the limits of spatial governmentality: A message from the tip of Africa. *Third World Quarterly* 23(4).

Robins, S. 2004. 'The (third) world is a ghetto?' Looking for a third space between 'postmodern' cosmopolitanism and cultural nationalism. *CODESRIA Bulletin* (1/2): 18–26.

Robinson, C.D.W. 1997. Language policy from the bottom up? Reclaiming language use in Africa. In B. Synak & T. Wicherkiewicz (eds.), *Language minorities and minority languages in the changing Europe: Proceedings of the 6th International Conference on Minority Languages*. Gdansk: Wydawnictwo Uniwersytetu Gdanskiego.

Robinson, C.D.W. 1999. Thread, web and tapestry-making: Processes of development and language. *Compare* 29(1): 23–39.

Robinson, C.D.W. & Varley, F. 1998. Language diversity and accountability in the South: Perspectives and dilemmas. *Journal of Sociolinguistics* 2(2): 189–203.

Robinson, J. 1996. *The power of apartheid*. Oxford. Butterworth/Heinemann.

Robinson, J. 1997. The geopolitics of South African cities. States, citizens, territory. *Political Geography* 16(5): 365–386.

Rogerson, C.M. 1996. Image enhancement of local economic development in Johannesburg. *Urban Forum* 7: 139–58.

Romaine, S. 2002. The impact of language policy on endangered languages. *International Journal on Multicultural Societies*, 4(2): 194–202.

Roncayolo, M. 2002. *Lectures de villes: Formes et temps*. Marseille: Parenthèses.

Roudie, P. 1978. Aspect du développement de l'économie Togolaise. *Les cahiers d'outre-mer: Revue de géographie* 31: 359–374.

Russell, D.E.H. 1997. *Behind closed doors in white South Africa: Incest survivors tell their stories.* London: Macmillan.

SADSAWU (South African Domestic Service and Allied Workers Union). 2002a. *Minimum wage submission.* SADSAWU.

SADSAWU. 2002b. *Summarised report on the activities of SADSAWU, January – April 2002,* 2002. SADSAWU.

Saff, G. 1998. *Changing Cape Town: Urban dynamics, policy, and planning during the political transition in South Africa.* Lanham, MD: University Press of America.

Salo, E. 2004. Negotiating gender and personhood in the new South Africa: Adolescent women and gangsters in Manenberg township on the Cape Flats. Paper presented at the New Social Formations seminar series, Department of Sociology, Stellenbosch University, 3 September 2004.

Sandercock, L. (ed.). 1998. *Making the invisible visible: A multicultural planning history.* Berkeley, CA: University of California Press.

Sassen, S. 1994. Ethnicity and space in the global city: A new frontier. In S. Dunn (ed.), *Managing divided cities.* Keele: Ryburn Publishing & Keele University Press.

Schutte, G. 1991. Racial oppression and social research: Field work under racial conflict in South Africa. *Qualitative Sociology* 14(2): 127–146.

Schutte G. 1995. *What racists believe: Race relations in South Africa and the United States.* Thousand Oaks, CA: Sage.

Scott, J. 1998. *Seeing like a state: How certain schemes to improve the human condition have failed.* New Haven, CT: Yale University Press.

Seekings, J. 2003. Are South Africa's cities changing? Indications from the mid-1990s. *International Journal of Urban and Regional Research* 27(1):197–202.

Seepe, S. (ed.). 2004. *Towards an African identity in institutions of higher learning.* Pretoria: Vista University & Skotaville Media.

Seidman, I. 1998. *Interviewing as qualitative research: A guide for researchers in education and the social sciences.* New York: Teachers College.

Sewpaul, V. 2004. For a non-essentialist position: Multiple and shifting identities. *Journal of African Scholarship* 1(1): Online at www.ingedej.ukzn.ac.za

Sharp, J. 1997. 'Non-racialism' and its discontents: A post-apartheid paradox. Paper presented at conference on 'Identity? Theory, Politics, History', HSRC, Pretoria. 1–4 April 1997.

Sharp, J. & Boonzaier, E. 1995. 'Sieners in die suburbs'? Exploring new directions for South African anthropology. *South African Journal of Ethnology* 18(2): 64–70.

Shotter, J. 1993a. *Conversational realities: Constructing life through language.* London: Sage.

Shotter, J. 1993b. *Cultural politics of everyday life: Social constructionism and knowing of the third kind.* Buckingham: Open University Press.

Sichone, O. 2004. Africanization: An alternative perspective on African ness in global identity politics. Paper presented at the New Social Formations seminar series, Department of Sociology, Stellenbosch University.

Silverman, D. 1993. *Interpreting qualitative data: Methods for analysing talk, text and interaction.* London: Sage.

Sindjoun, L. 1999. La France et l'Afrique du Sud dans l'Afrique postcoloniale: Un fauteuil pour deux ? In *L'Afrique politique 1999* (pp. 35–48). Paris: Karthala.

Sindjoun, L. 2002. *Sociologie des relations internationales Africaines.* Paris: Karthala.

Smyth, J. & Shacklock, G. 1998. Behind the 'cleansing' of socially critical research accounts. In G. Shacklock & J. Smyth (eds.), *Being reflexive in critical educational and social research* (pp. 1–12). London: Falmer Press.

Soja, E.W. 2000. *Postmetropolis: Critical studies of cities and regions.* Oxford: Blackwell.

South African Cities Network. 2004. *State of the cities report.*

Sow, A.I. (ed.). 1977. *Langues et politiques de langues en Afrique Noire: L'expérience de l'Unesco.* Abbeville: Nubia/Unesco.

Spiegel, A., Watson, V., & Wilkinson, P. 1996. Domestic diversity and fluidity among some African households in Greater Cape Town. *Social Dynamics*, 22(1), 7–30.

Spiegel, A., Watson, V., & Wilkinson, P. 1999. Speaking truth to power: Some problems using ethnographic methods to influence the formulation of housing policy in South Africa. In A. Cheater (ed.), *The anthropology of power: Empowerment and disempowerment in changing structures* (pp. 175–190). London & New York, Routledge.

Statistics South Africa. 2001. *Labour force survey, February 2001.* Pretoria: SSA.

Statistics South Africa. 2002. *Labour force survey, February 2002.* Pretoria: SSA.

Statistics South Africa. 2002. *Labour force survey, March 2001.* Pretoria: SSA.

Statistics South Africa. 2003. *Census 2001: Census in brief.* Pretoria: Statistics South Africa.

Steinberg, J. 2004. *The number: One man's search for identity in the Cape underworld and prison gangs.* Johannesburg & Cape Town: Jonathan Ball.

Steytler, N. (ed.). 2005. *The place and role of local government in federal systems.* Johannesburg: KAS.

Suarez, D. 2002. The paradox of linguistic hegemony and the maintenance of Spanish as heritage language in the United States. *Journal of Multilingual and Multicultural Development*, 23(6): 512–530.

Swilling, M., Humphries, R., & Shubane, K. (eds.). 1991. *The apartheid city in transition.* Cape Town: Oxford University Press.

Takassi, I. 1983. *Inventaire linguistique du Togo.* Agence de Coopération Culturelle et Technique et Institut de Linguistique Appliquée, Université d'Abidjan.

Taylor, P.J. 2004. *World city network: A global urban analysis.* London: Routledge.

Ten Have, P. 1999. *Doing conversation analysis: A practical guide.* London: Sage.

Themba, C. 1985. *The world of Can Themba.* Johannesburg: Ravan Press.

Thompson, L. 2001. *A history of South Africa.* New Haven, CT: Yale Nota Bene.

Thornborrow, J. 1999. Language and identity. In L. Thomas & S. Waireng, *Language, society and power.* London & New York: Routledge.

Todorov, T. 1996. La coexistence des cultures. In B. Badie & M. Sadoun (eds.), *L'autre: Etudes réunies pour Alfred Grosser.* Paris: Presses de Sciences Po.

Tollefson J.W. 1991 *Planning language, planning inequality: Language policy in the community.* London: Longman.

Tomlinson, R. 1990. *Urbanization in post-apartheid South Africa.* London: Unwin Hyman.

Tomlinson, R., Hunter, R., Jonker, M., Rogerson, C., & Rogerson, J. 1995. *Johannesburg inner city strategic development framework: Economic analysis.* Planning Department, Greater Johannesburg Transitional Metropolitan Council.

Toulabor, C. 1986. *Le Togo sous Eyadéma.* Paris: Karthala.

Tuan, Y.F. 1977. *Space and place: The perspective of experience.* Minneapolis: University of Minnesota Press.

Turok, I. 2000. Persistent polarisation post-apartheid? Progress towards urban integration in Cape Town. Discussion paper UCAP 1, Urban Change and Policy Research Group, Department of Urban Studies, University of Glasgow.

Turok, I. & Watson, V. 2001 Divergent development in South African cities: Strategic challenges facing Cape Town. *Urban Forum* 12(2): 119–138.

240 References

Van der Berg, S. & Acheterbosch, T. 2001. *School education in the Western Cape: Matching supply to demand.* (Research report to the Western Cape Department of Education).

Van der Merwe, I.J. 1993. The South African city in relation to international city form. *Development Southern Africa* 10: 481–96.

Van der Merwe, I.J. 2004. The global cities of sub-Saharan Africa: Fact or fiction? *Urban Forum* 15: 36–47.

Van Onsenlen, C. 1982. *Studies in the social and economic history of the Witwatersrand 1886–1914* (Vol. 1: New Babylon; Vol. 2: New Nineveh). New York: Longman.

Vidal, D. 2002. Le bel avenir de la mulata: La bonne, sa patronne et son patron. *Cahiers du Brésil Contemporain* 2002(49/50): 153–166.

Von Lieres, B. 1999. Review article: New perspectives on citizenship in Africa. *Journal of Southern African Studies*, 25(1): 139–148.

Vuarin, R. 1997. Un siècle d'individu, de communauté et d'etat. In A. Marie (ed.), *L'Afrique des individus*. Paris: Karthala.

Watson, S. 1996. Spaces of the 'other': Planning for cultural diversity in Western Sydney. In K. Darien-Smith, L. Gunner, & S. Nuttall (eds.), *Text, theory, space: Land, literature and history in South Africa and Australia* (pp. 203–218). London and New York: Routledge.

Watson, V. 1998. Planning under political transition: Lessons from Cape Town's metropolitan planning forum. *International Planning Studies* 3(3): 335–350.

Watson, V. 2002. *Change and continuity in spatial planning: Metropolitan planning in Cape Town under political transition.* London: Routledge.

Watson, V. 2003. Conflicting rationalities: Implications for planning theory and ethics. *Planning Theory and Practice* 4(4): 395–407.

Weber, L.R. & Carter, A.I. 2003. *The social construction of trust.* New York: Kluwer.

Webb, V. 2002. *Language in South Africa: The role of language in national transformation, reconstruction and development.* Philadelphia, PA: John Benjamins.

Weiss, R.S. 1994. *Learning from strangers: The art and method of qualitative interview studies.* New York: Free Press.

Werbner, R. 1996. Multiple identities, plural arenas. In R. Werbner & T. Ranger (eds.), *Postcolonial identities in Africa.* London & New Jersey: Zed Books.

Werbner, R. & Ranger, T. (eds.). 1996. *Postcolonial identities in Africa.* London & New Jersey: Zed Books.

Whiteman, K. 1993. Francophonie et Anglophonie: Regards portés sur l'autre' en Afrique. In D.C. Bach & A.A. Kirk-Greene (eds.), *Etats et sociétés en Afrique Francophone.* Paris: Economica.

Whitlow, R. & Brooker, C. 1995. The historical context of urban hydrology in Johannesburg, Part I: Johannesburg, 1900–1990. *Journal of the South African Institute of Civil Engineering* 27: 7–12.

Wilkinson, P. 2000. City profile: Cape Town. *Cities* 17(3): 195–205.

Williams, J.J. 2000. South Africa: Urban transformation. *Cities* 17(3): 167–183.

Wilson, M. & Mafeje, A. 1963. *Langa: A study of social groups in an African township.* London: Oxford University Press.

Wright, S. 2001. Language and power: Background to the debate on linguistic rights. *International Journal on Multicultural Societies* 3(1): 44–45.

Yose, C.N. 1999. From shacks to houses: A study of space usage in a Western Cape shantytown. Unpublished master's dissertation, University of Cape Town.

Young, C. 1993. The dialectics of cultural pluralism: Concept and reality. In C. Young (ed.), *The rising tide of cultural pluralism: The nation state at bay?* Madison, WI: The University of Wisconsin Press.

Young, C. 1994. Ethnic diversity and public policy: An overview. Occasional paper No. 8, United Nations Research Institute for Social Development.

Zegeye, A. (ed.). 2001. Social identities in the new South Africa. *After apartheid* (Vol. 1). Cape Town: Kwela Books.

Zeleza, P.T. Forthcoming. *Rethinking Africa's globalisation: The intellectual challenges.* Trenton, NJ: Africa World Press.

Zoo, C. & Moussirou-Mouyama, A. 2001. La répartition des communautés linguistiques dans l'espace urbain de Libreville. *Plurilinguismes* 18(5): 183–204.

List of contributors

Simon Bekker, Professor of Sociology, University of Stellenbosch

Claire Bénit, Assistant Professor in Geography, University of Aix-Marseille

Arlene Davids, Doctoral student, Department of Geography and Environmental Studies, University of Stellenbosch

Philippe Gervais-Lambony, Professor of Geography, University of Paris (Nanterre)

Anne Leildé, Doctoral student, Department of Sociology and Social Anthropology, University of Stellenbosch

Robert Mongwe, Doctoral fellow, Department of Social Anthropology, University of Bergen

Marianne Morange, Assistant Professor in Geography, University of Paris 13

Hugues Steve Ndinga-Koumba-Binza, Doctoral student, Centre for Language and Speech Technology, University of Stellenbosch

Charles Puttergill, Lecturer in Sociology, University of Pretoria

Steven Robins, Professor of Anthropology, University of Stellenbosch

Izak van der Merwe, Research Fellow, Department of Geography and Environmental Studies, University of Stellenbosch

Index

Page numbers in italics indicate figures and tables.

www.ingramcontent.com/pod-product-compliance
Lightning Source LLC
Chambersburg PA
CBHW021859020426
42334CB00013B/394